WRITE GREAT FICTION

Plot & Structure

[TECHNIQUES AND EXERCISES FOR CRAFTING A PLOT THAT GRIPS READERS FROM START TO FINISH]

BY JAMES SCOTT BELL

WRITER'S DIGEST BOOKS

Writer's Digest Books
Cincinnati, Ohio
www.writersdigest.com

[COPYRIGHT]

Visit our Web site at www.writersdigest.com for information on more resources for writers.

To receive a free weekly e-mail newsletter delivering tips and updates about writing and about Writer's Digest products, register directly at our Web site at http://newsletters.fwpublications.com.

10 09 08 07 06   7 6 5 4

Library of Congress Cataloging-in-Publication Data

Bell, James Scott.
  Write great fiction: plot & structure: techniques and exercises for crafting a plot that grips readers from start to finish / by James Scott Bell.
      p. cm.
  Includes index.
  ISBN-13: 978-1-58297-294-7 (alk. paper)
  ISBN-10: 1-58297-294-X (alk. paper)
  1. Plots (drama, novel, etc.).   2. Fiction—Authorship.   I. Title
PN3378.B45 2004   2004053032
808.3'94—dc22   CIP

Edited by Kelly Nickell
Designed by Stanard Design Partners
Cover by Nick Gliebe/Design Matters
Cover illustration © Getty Images
Interior illustrations © Getty Images
Production coordinated by Robin Richie and Logan Cummins

F+W PUBLICATIONS, INC.

[ABOUT THE AUTHOR]

James Scott Bell is the best-selling author of *Breach of Promise*, *Deadlock*, *A Greater Glory*, and several other thrillers. He is a winner of the Christy Award for Excellence in inspirational fiction, and is currently a fiction columnist for *Writer's Digest* magazine. A former trial lawyer, Jim now writes and speaks full time. His Web site is www.jamesscottbell.com.

[DEDICATION]

To my wife, Cindy, who is my inspiration, editor-in-chief, and best friend. Thanks for helping make my dreams come true.

And to my children, Nate and Allegra, who make me proud.

[ACKNOWLEDGMENTS]

I must thank all of the generous and thoughtful writers who have given us, in books and articles, their collective wisdom on the art of fiction. When I finally figured out that the craft was something that could be taught, I dove into a massive reading program and found a body of advice that gave me hope I could someday learn to write.

While I can't possibly thank all of those who have helped me, I want to give credit to at least the following books that I continue to turn to:

Bickham, Jack, *Writing and Selling Your Novel*
Bishop, Leonard, *Dare to be a Great Writer*
Block, Lawrence, *Writing the Novel*
Browne, Renni & King, Dave, *Self-Editing for Fiction Writers*
Bradbury, Ray, *Zen in the Art of Writing*
Cleaver, Jerry, *Immediate Fiction*
Conrad, Barnaby, *Complete Guide to Writing Fiction*
Egri, Lajos, *The Art of Creative Writing*
Frey, James N., *How to Write a Damn Good Novel I & II*
Hall, Oakley, *The Art & Craft of Novel Writing*
Kernen, Robert, *Building Better Plots*
King, Stephen, *On Writing*
Koontz, Dean, *How to Write Best-Selling Fiction*
Maass, Donald, *Writing the Breakout Novel*
Morrell, David, *Lessons From a Lifetime of Writing*
Stein, Sol, *Stein on Writing*
Swain, Dwight, *Techniques of the Selling Writer*
Whitney, Phyllis, *Guide to Fiction Writing*

Thanks also to some writer friends who looked at early portions of this work: Angela Hunt, Randall Ingermanson, and Janelle Schneider. And special thanks to my editor on this project, Kelly Nickell, and to all the folks I work with at *Writer's Digest* magazine, who *know* that writing can be taught and prove it every day.

table of contents

introduction

[PUTTING THE BIG LIE TO SLEEP]

I wasted ten years of prime writing life because of the Big Lie.

In my twenties, I gave up the dream of becoming a writer because I had been told that writing could not be taught. Writers are born, people said. You either have what it takes or you don't, and if you don't you'll never get it.

My first writing efforts didn't have it. I thought I was doomed. Outside of my high school English teacher, Mrs. Marjorie Bruce, I didn't get any encouragement at all.

In college, I took a writing course taught by Raymond Carver. I looked at the stuff he wrote; I looked at my stuff.

It wasn't the same.

Because writing can't be taught.

I started to believe it. I figured I didn't have it and never would.

So I did other stuff. Like go to law school. Like join a law firm. Like give up my dream.

But the itch to write would not go away.

At age thirty-four, I read an interview with a lawyer who'd had a novel published. And what he said hit me in my lengthy briefs. He said he'd had an accident and was almost killed. In the hospital, given a second chance at life, he decided the one thing he wanted was to be a writer. And he would write and write, even if he never got published because that was what he wanted.

Well, I wanted it, too.

But the Big Lie was still there, hovering around my brain, mocking me.

Especially when I began to study the craft of writing.

I went out and bought my first book on fiction writing. It was Lawrence Block's *Writing the Novel.* I also bought Syd Field's book on screenwriting because anyone living in Los Angeles who has opposable thumbs is required to write a screenplay.

And I discovered the most incredible thing. The Big Lie was a *lie*. A person *could* learn how to write because I was learning.

HOW I BECAME A HAPPY PLOTTER

While in the throes of the Big Lie, the most frustrating thing to me was *Plot*. Because what I wrote didn't have it.

I would read short stories and novels, and wonder how the writers did it. How did they get all this great story material? The Big Lie said they had it in their heads, naturally, and it just flowed out on the page as they went along.

I tried it. I tried to let plot flow. But what came out on the page was dreadful. No plot! No story! Zip!

But when I began to learn about the craft, I saw that plotting had elements I could learn. And I found out about structure: when plot elements were put in a certain order, a stronger story resulted.

I can still remember the day it came together for me. It was an epiphany. All of a sudden, something clicked in my head. The pieces started to fit. The Jell-O hardened.

About a year later, I had a screenplay optioned. Then another.

Then I wrote a novel. It was published.

Then I got a five-book fiction contract. I wrote those books, and they were published, too.

Suddenly, I took a deep breath and looked behind me. Somehow, some way, I had learned how to write after all.

The Big Lie was exposed.

I was so ticked off about the Big Lie that I started teaching others what I'd learned about the craft of writing. I wanted new writers to know that they weren't doomed to stay where they were. They could learn craft, as I did. I never taught fancy theory, just nuts and bolts. Things that worked for me, that new writers could understand and use *right now*.

And then a funny thing happened. Some of my students started selling *their* books.

I still find this the most satisfying part of the whole deal.

And this is what I hope you will learn. Let's replace the Big Lie with the Truth. The Truth is that craft can be taught and that you, with diligence and practice and patience, can improve your writing. This is one book that's going to be as practical on that score as I can make it.

WHAT IT TAKES TO LEARN PLOT

My high school basketball coach was a strict disciplinarian. If it had been up to me, I would have spent my practice time shooting jump shots. But Coach made us do fundamental drills—dribbling, passing, cutting, setting picks. And, of course, the dreaded wind sprints when we messed up.

We all hated the drudgery, but come game time, we knew we were better players for it. And all of his teams overachieved.

If you want to break through with this thing called craft, you'll need to be your own disciplinarian. Here are some things you can do to become your own plotting coach. Tweak them to fit your preferences, but use them. You'll like the results.

Otherwise, I may have to make you do wind sprints.

[1] Get motivated. I remember the exact date I decided I was going to be a writer. I jotted this in my journal: "Today I resolve to take writing seriously, to keep going and never stop, to learn everything I can and make it as a writer."

Remember, this was after I was steeped in the Big Lie. So what I wrote was a declaration of independence of sorts.

Why don't you do the same? Write a statement of purpose, one that gets you excited, and print it. Put it on your wall where you can see it every day.

The next thing I did was buy a black coffee mug with *Writer* written in gold across it. I would look at that cup every day to remind me of my commitment. In fact, on days when the writing drags, I'll look at it again. It gives me a fresh jolt of enthusiasm.

Come up with your own item of visual motivation. It might be inspirational words taped to your computer, a photograph of an admired writer (on my wall I have a shot of Stephen King, feet up on his writing desk and dog under his chair, revising a manuscript), or your own rendering of your first novel's cover (be lavish in the critical praise on the back!).

I was also motivated early on by going to bookstores and browsing in the bestseller section. I'd look at the authors' pictures and bios, I'd read their openings (and think *I can do this!*), and I'd imagine what my face would look like on the back of a dust jacket (nicely retouched, of course).

Then—and this is crucial—I'd race back to my office and start writing.

Find some ritual that gets your juices flowing, and don't waste it. Turn it into words on the page.

[2] **Try stuff.** Just reading a book on plotting is not going to make you a better writer. You have to try out what you learn, see if you get it, and try some more. You test the principles in the fire of the blank page.

As you read this book, take time to digest and then apply what you learn about plot and structure to your own writing.

I love books on writing. I have shelves full of them. I've read every one with a yellow highlighter. Then I've reread almost all of them with a red, felt-tip pen, marking things I missed the first time.

Then I've gone through most of them a third time, writing out new insights on a yellow legal pad.

Then I've taken my notes and typed them up.

What I'm doing is digesting the material as deeply as I possibly can. I want it to be part of me. I want it there when I write my next novel.

So please be on the lookout for new techniques in the craft of fiction writing, and try them out yourself. This is how you learn and grow.

[3] **Stay loose.** Writing is never any good when it is done in the grip of anxiety. A tense brain freezes creativity. If you try to make writing too much of a military exercise, if you go at it with a clenched jaw and fevered brow, you'll be working against yourself. The guidelines in this book will give you material to work with and techniques that can help you. Your job is to write, as Brenda Ueland puts it, "freely and rollickingly."

[4] **"First get it written, then get it right."** I can't remember who said them, but these are words of wisdom. Don't spend too much time worrying and fretting and tinkering with your first draft. The guidelines in this book will help you not only in the planning of your plot and the writing of it, but most of all when you get to the revision stage. Your job with that first draft is to pour yourself onto the page. In *Zen in the Art of Writing: Essays on Creativity*, Ray Bradbury says, "Let the world burn through you. Throw the prism light, white hot, on paper."

[5] **Set a quota.** Writing is how you learn to write. Writing daily, as a discipline, is the best way to learn.

Most successful fiction writers make a word goal and stick to it. A time goal can easily be squandered as you sit and agonize over sentences or paragraphs. Sure you were at your writing desk for three hours, but what did you produce? Write a certain number of words instead.

I have a spreadsheet that logs my words. I record the number of words I write on my projects. The spreadsheet automatically tallies my daily and weekly production.

I review this log each week. If I'm not making my quota, I give myself a talking to and get back on track.

But be kind to yourself. If you don't make your quota one day or one week, forget about it. Get to work on your new week.

The daily writing of words, once it becomes a habit, will be the most fruitful discipline of your writing life. You'll be amazed at how productive you'll become, and how much you'll learn about the craft.

But if you're one of those writers who thinks he needs inspiration to write, then I ask you to please follow the advice of Peter DeVries: "I only write when I'm inspired, and I make sure I'm inspired every morning at 9 a.m."

[6] Don't give up. The main difference between successful writers and unsuccessful writers is persistence. There are legions of published novelists who went years and years without acceptance. They continued to write because that's what they were inside, writers. That's what you are. That's why you're reading this book. Whenever I hear from students I've taught at writers' conferences, I always end my communication with them with two words: Keep writing.

In the end, that's the best advice there is.

Are you ready now? Are you convinced of the Truth? Do you dream of writing novels with plots that keep readers up at night? Then come along. I'm going to do my very best to show you how.

chapter 1

[WHAT'S A PLOT, ANYWAY?]

plot / 'plät / n.: 1. A small piece of ground, generally used for burying dead people, including writers. 2. A plan, as for designing a building or novel.

Plot happens.

You might be one of those writers who likes to have the story all worked out in your mind before you write your novel. You preplan, plan, and revise the plan before writing. Maybe you have index cards all over your wall or you store your scenes in your computer.

Or you might be one of those seat-of-the-pants writers who loves to plop down each day at the computer or over a pad of paper and just write, letting the story flow without planning, anxious to see what your wild writer's mind comes up with.

You could also be a 'tweener who does a bit of planning but still seeks some surprise and spontaneity in the daily output of words.

No matter what kind of novelist you are, there's one thing you will have when you've completed your manuscript—a plot.

It might be a lousy plot, a disjointed plot, a mess, or a masterpiece. But the plot will be there, staring you in the face.

The only question at that point will be, "Does it work?"

By "work" I mean *connect with readers.* That's the function of plot after all. The reading experience is supposed to transport people, move them through the power of story. Plot is the power grid that makes it happen.

You may be one of those writers who doesn't care if your novel connects with readers. You write what you want, the way you want it, and that's that. Writing is its own reward. If someone happens to like it, fine. But you don't want to be bothered with bourgeois concepts like plot.

Fine. No one's forcing you to connect with readers. But if you want readers, if you dream of writing novels that get published and sell, then you have to give plotting its due. Because that's what agents, publishers, and readers think about when they open books. Consciously or not, they are asking questions:

- What's this story about?
- Is anything happening?
- Why should I keep reading?
- Why should I care?

These are all plot questions, and if you want to make it as a writer of novel-length fiction, you must learn how to answer them satisfactorily, wonderfully, surprisingly.

That's what this book is about.

"What about character?" you might ask. "Can't I just write about a fascinating character and see what happens?"

Yes. The *what happens* is your plot. And, as with any plot, it can turn out flabby and incoherent even with great characters. This book will help you avoid that outcome.

How about a stream-of-consciousness novel? One that's all about the language, and can't be limited by such mundane matters as plotting?

It's a stretch to call such a thing a novel. Fiction, yes. I'll even accept *experimental novel*. It might be fascinating in its own right, but is it really a story? I suppose that's an academic debate.

But if you're interested in selling your books, plot is something you need to wrestle with.

And wrestling makes you stronger. Even if you ultimately decide, as a writer, that you want to forget about plotting conventions, the effort to understand them will serve you well. You'll become a better novelist.

VIEWS ON PLOT

Some writers, critics, and other assorted literati sniff at plotting as a tool of craft. A synonym for plotting, in this mindset, is *slumming*, something decent people just don't do.

Author Jean Hanff Korelitz sums up this thinking. She wrote about her experience as a young editorial assistant in New York trying to be a novelist. She and her contemporaries were snobs about literary prose, she says, elevating wordsmithery above such mundane matters as telling a good story.

But then Ms. Korelitz ended up writing a legal thriller, and discovered—

gasp—that she liked it! Her mind was changed, as you'll see below in this excerpt from "Story Love," which appeared on Salon.com:

> When you get right down to it, there's something uniquely satisfying in being gripped by a great plot, in begrudging whatever real-world obligations might prevent you from finding out what happens next. And it is especially satisfying to surrender to an author who is utterly in command of a thrilling and original story, an author capable of playing us like fish, of letting us get worried, then riled up, then complacent and then finally blowing us away when the final shocks are delivered.

Ms. Korelitz ultimately concluded that, while glorious prose is a fine thing, "without an enthralling story, it's just so much verbal tapioca."

Now, if verbal tapioca is your thing, we have a First Amendment that guarantees your right to produce it.

But if you want readers, you must consider plot, whether you sniff at it or not.

THE POWER OF STORY

Plot and structure both serve the larger enterprise—story. In the end, that's what this whole novel thing is about. Telling a story in a way that transports the reader. Let's talk a little about that.

If a reader picks up a book and remains in his own world, there was no point in picking up the book in the first place. What the reader seeks is *an experience that is other*. Other than what he normally sees each day.

Story is how he gets there. A good story transports the reader to a new place via experience. Not through arguments or facts, but through the illusion that life is taking place on the page. Not his life. Someone else's. Your characters' lives.

Author James N. Frey calls this the *fictive dream*, and that's accurate. When we dream, we experience that as reality.

I still get those *late-for-an-important-event* dreams. When I was in school, it was usually a test. Lately, it's been a speaking engagement or a meeting with some important person relating to my work.

I'm late, and I realize it with about two minutes left, though I'm miles away and can move only in slow motion. And everything I do seems to create a further obstacle.

You see what's happening? Conflict. Story. Experience.

I'll leave it to the professionals to determine what this indicates about my psyche. But as writers, we need to understand that story is how readers dream. They demand it.

Plot and structure help them get into the dream and keep them there.

Agent Donald Maass, who has written a superb book called *Writing the Breakout Novel*, is of the opinion that *story* is what sells the book—not advertising, not a huge promotional budget—but story. And he believes the key to long-term success as a novelist is the ability to write book after book that builds up an audience. How? The power of story:

> What causes consumers to get excited about a work of fiction? Reviews? Few
> see them. Awards or nominations? Most folks are oblivious to them. Covers?
> Good ones can cause a consumer to lift a book from its shelf, but covers are
> only wrapping. Classy imprints? When was the last time you purchased a novel
> because of the logo on the spine? Big advances? Does the public know, let
> alone care? Agents with clout? Sad to say, that is not a cause of consumer
> excitement. In reality there is one reason, and one reason only, that readers
> get excited about a novel: great storytelling.

Plot and structure help you reach that mark.

PLOT MADE SIMPLE

In college, I signed up for chess lessons from a fellow who promised I'd be able to compete with master players. He assured me he could teach the basic principles that, if applied, would give me a solid foundation for a good game against anyone. Though I might not win, I'd certainly not look like a fool. From there it would be a matter of applying my talent (if I had any) to study and practice.

He was right. I learned to play a solid game of chess. And while I probably can't go more than fifteen moves with Garry Kasparov—one of the world's greatest chess players—at least he'd know he wasn't playing a chucklehead. By applying the principles I learned, I can play a decent game of chess.

It's the same with plotting the novel. There are a few basics that, if understood and applied, will help you come up with a solid plot every time.

How far you go from there is, like most things, a matter of plain old hard work and practice.

After analyzing hundreds of plots, I've developed a simple set of foundational principles called the LOCK system. LOCK stands for Lead, Objective, Confrontation, and Knockout. We'll talk about each of these in detail later. For now, here's a quick overview. Even if you get nothing else out of this book, a grip on the LOCK system will serve you well your whole writing career.

L Is for Lead

Imagine a guy on a New York City street corner with a *Will Work for Food* sign. Interesting? Not very. We've seen it many times before, and we wouldn't stand and watch him for a minute.

But what if the guy was dressed in a tuxedo, and his sign said *Will Tap Dance for Food*? Hmm, a little more interesting. Maybe he has a yellow pad and the sign says, *Will Write Novel for Food*. I might buy him a hamburger to see what he comes up with.

The point here is that a strong plot starts with an interesting Lead character. In the best plots, that Lead is *compelling*, someone we *have to watch throughout the course of the novel.*

This does *not* mean the Lead has to be entirely sympathetic. This point hit me one day years ago when I was browsing the paperbacks at my local library.

I was looking at the new releases when I saw they'd brought in a new paperback version of *An American Tragedy* by Theodore Dreiser. I'd never read it and didn't know much about Dreiser, though I knew vaguely that his literary reputation has suffered in recent years.

But I also knew the novel was the basis of one of my all-time favorite movies, *A Place in the Sun*, starring Elizabeth Taylor and Montgomery Clift.

So I checked it out, all 814 pages of it, not expecting to actually read the whole thing, but just to skim and see how similar it was to the movie.

Well, I had one of those wondrous reading experiences where I got sucked in. Big time. And as a budding novelist, I asked myself why. The book's style is everything the critics said it was: ponderous, heavy-handed, at times sloppy. On page 156 is the sentence: "Gilbert chilled and bristled." And on page 157: "Gilbert bristled and chilled." I couldn't make that up.

In fact, the *New York Times* once called *An American Tragedy* the "worst written great book ever." But something makes it a great book, even though the Lead character, Clyde Griffiths, is not a nice guy. We first meet Clyde, the son of fundamentalist evangelists, at sixteen, and then watch as he descends to the point that he lets his pregnant lover drown.

Why does it work?

Because Clyde is compelling, though negative. Because Dreiser gets us into his head, there is a "car wreck" dynamic at work here. Just as people slow down to look at wreckage, we can't resist seeing what happens to fully drawn human beings who make an unalterable mess of their lives. A skilled novelist can make us feel that "there but for the grace of God go I."

(*Note to readers:* This book uses the simplest model—one Lead character involved in the main plot—for teaching purposes. Mastering this will enable you to approach increasingly complicated situations later, for example, a multi-viewpoint novel. See chapter eight for more on complex plots.)

O Is for Objective

Back to our *Will Work for Food* guy. What if he tossed down his sign, put a parachute on his back, and started climbing the Empire State Building?

Interest zooms. Why?

This character has an *objective. A want. A desire.*

Objective is the driving force of fiction. It generates forward motion and keeps the Lead from just sitting around.

An objective can take either of two forms: to *get* something or to *get away* from something.

- The Girl Who Loved Tom Gordon is about a girl lost in the woods who desperately wants to get back to civilization.
- In *Jaws*, Brody desperately wants to *get* the shark.
- In *Rose Madder*, Rose wants to *get away* from her psycho husband.
- In *The Firm*, Mitch McDeere wants to *get away* from the Mafia.

Solid plots have one and only one dominant objective for the Lead character. This forms the "story question"—will the Lead realize her objective?

You want readers to worry about the story question, so the objective has to be essential to the well-being of the Lead. If the Lead doesn't get it (or get away from it), her life will take a tremendous hit for the worse.

Here are a few hints on making that objective crucial.

If the objective is related to *staying alive*, that always fits the bill. Most suspense novels have the threat of death hanging over the Lead from the start. Death can also hang over others—Clarice Starling in *The Silence of the Lambs* is driven to stop Buffalo Bill before he kills another innocent victim.

Not all objectives have to involve death, however. The essential thing is that it is crucial to *that Lead's* sense of well-being.

Consider Oscar in Neil Simon's play, *The Odd Couple*. He is a very happy slob. Nothing pleases him more than smoky poker games in his apartment, and he not cleaning up afterward. He takes in his suicidal friend, Felix, out of compassion. But Felix is a clean nut. Eventually, this drives Oscar crazy. If he doesn't get rid of Felix, his happy life as a slob will be ruined! The story works because Simon establishes just how important being sloppy is to Oscar's happiness.

C Is for Confrontation

Now our human fly is halfway up the Empire State Building. We already know he's interesting because he has an objective, and with a little imagination, you can think up a reason why this is crucial to his well-being.

Is there anything we can do to ratchet up the engrossment level? Yes! New York City cops are trying to stop him. They have plans to nab him around floor 65. Worse yet, a mad sniper across Fifth Avenue has him in his sights. Suddenly, things are a lot more interesting.

The reason is *confrontation*. Opposition from characters and outside forces brings your story fully to life. If your Lead moves toward his objective without anything in his way, we deprive readers of what they secretly want: worry. Readers want to fret about the Lead, keeping an intense emotional involvement all the way through the novel.

Some wise old scribe once put it this way: "Get your protagonist up a tree. Throw rocks at him. Then get him down."

Throwing rocks means putting obstacles in your Lead's way. Make things tough on him. Never let him off easy.

K Is for Knockout

I once asked an old sports writer why he thought boxing was so popular. He smacked his fist into his hand. "Pow!" he said, letting his arm fall like a sack of potatoes.

People watch boxing for the knockout, he explained. They'll accept a decision, but they prefer to see one fighter kissing the canvas. What they hate is a draw. That doesn't satisfy anyone.

Readers of commercial fiction want to see a knockout at the end. A literary novel can play with a bit more ambiguity. In either case, the ending must have knockout *power.*

A great ending can leave the reader satisfied, even if the rest of the book is somewhat weak (assuming the reader decides to stick around until the end). But a weak ending will leave the reader with a feeling of disappointment, even if the book up to that point is strong.

So take your Lead through the journey toward her objective, and then send the opposition to the mat.

Our human fly can make it to the top victoriously or fall tragically. He can crawl through a window that is a metaphor for a new life. The range of endings is massive.

Personally, I'd like to see him make it and write a best-selling novel about the experience.

HOW MANY PLOTS ARE THERE?

While there are a number of plot varieties (see chapter twelve for a discussion of patterns in plot), you can boil them all down and fit them into the LOCK system. A Lead with an intense objective, thrust into confrontation, runs through the story until it ends.

Let's see how this stacks up against some popular plots.

How about *Love*? Sure, that's simple. Boy wants girl. Girl denies boy his objective. He battles to win her love. He confronts her resistance by buying her flowers, singing her songs, protecting her from bad guys and all that romantic stuff. He gets her at the end or not. That's one variety of the love plot.

You can substitute the boy's and girl's families as the opposing forces, and you come up with another variety of the love story. See *Romeo and Juliet.*

Take another plot, *Change*. Here, the plot focuses on an inner transformation in the Lead character. The Lead desires to stay as he is. Forces arise that challenge his complacency. He tries to resist the forces. But he is overcome at the end, and he changes. See *A Christmas Carol.*

Objectives can be external or internal. The confrontation can be physical or psychological. But the LOCK system works in all cases.

Your book can be literary or commercial, and you have a huge platter of plot varieties to choose from. But if you keep a compelling Lead battling to achieve his desire, you're going to have a solid story every time. As novelist and writing teacher Barnaby Conrad puts it, "Once you get a character with a problem, a serious problem, 'plotting' is just a fancy name for how he or she tries to get out of the predicament."

WHAT'S THIS ABOUT LITERARY AND COMMERCIAL PLOTS?

The difference between a literary and a commercial plot is a matter of feel and emphasis.

A literary plot often is more leisurely in its pace. Literary fiction is usually more about the inner life of a character than it is about the fast-paced action.

A commercial plot, on the other hand, is mostly about action, things happening to the characters from the outside.

A commercial plot often feels like this:

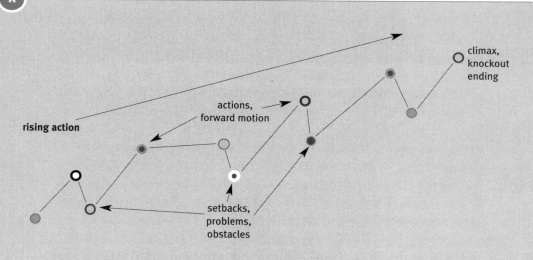

rising action

actions,
forward motion

climax,
knockout
ending

setbacks,
problems,
obstacles

A literary plot often feels like this:

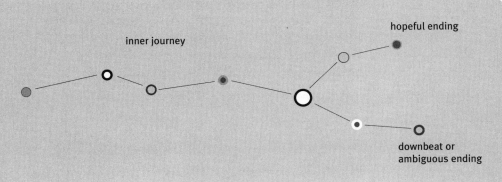

Of course these are overly simplistic diagrams. There can be both literary and commercial elements in a book.

Scott Smith's *A Simple Plan* reads like a literary novel—what happens inside the first-person narrator is primary—while moving ahead like a commercial crime novel.

The strength of Stephen King's commercial plots is in his characterizations. He always seems to be writing about real people, and not merely players for his high-concept concoctions.

Literary fiction is much more comfortable with ambiguities. The endings may be downers or leave the reader wondering. We don't know what's going to happen to Holden at the end of *The Catcher in the Rye*, and that's part of the power of the book.

In commercial fiction, you usually have the good guy winning over the bad guy.

Sometimes literary fiction is called *character driven*, and commercial fiction, *plot driven*. Plot driven usually means heavy on the action and light on character work. Character driven, on the other hand, often implies a slower story with less action and more interior work.

I find this to be an arbitrary and unhelpful distinction. *All* plots are character driven. Without a character facing trouble that is understandable to the reader, you don't have a plot at all. That's why LOCK begins with Lead.

Further, you can have all the action in the world, but if your characters don't ring true, your story will fail.

Instead, I will use the more common markers literary and commercial if only because that's how bookstores and critics and readers often think.

But plots need characters, and characters need plots.

Literary vs. Commercial Fiction: Two Simple Suggestions

Keep these tips in mind as you construct either literary or commercial fiction:

[1] If you write literary fiction, add a good sense of pace and even a commercial element or two. You may find you like these elements. You will probably find your readers do, too.

[2] If you write commercial fiction, deepen your characters. This will make the story much more satisfying to readers.

WON'T THIS LEAD TO FORMULAIC WRITING?

Some writers object to thinking about plot because it may lead to formulaic writing. They miss a critical distinction. Why does something become a formula in the first place? *Because it works!*

Here is a formula for an omelet: Crack a couple of eggs. Scramble them. Heat up a skillet. Butter it. Pour in the eggs. Cook them a bit. Add ingredients. Fold the eggs over the ingredients. Serve.

This is a formula that works. But notice the variables.

Depending on the cook and the experience level, the omelet can be delicious, a disaster, or something in between.

And with the addition of certain spices, the flavor can vary.

It's still an omelet, it's still a formula, but it has a whole range of outcomes.

Same with plotting. There are principles that work. But used alone they don't guarantee an original novel. You still have to add your spices, your skills, your talent.

Knowing why plots work is freeing. Master the principles, and you're at liberty to add all of your personal touches.

Good chefs have their secret spices, ingredients they use to give their creations something extra and unique. For writers, the spices you add to make your plot your own include characters, setting, and dialogue.

Characters

In his book, *The Art of Creative Writing*, Lajos Egri asserts that the key to originality in fiction comes from characters. "Living, vibrating human beings are still the secret and magic formula of great and enduring writing. Read, or better, study the immortals and you will be forced to conclude that their unusual penetration into human character is what has kept their work fresh and alive through the centuries. ..."

Note the word *formula*.

Let's test this.

What is it that sets Dickens apart in our minds? Fagin and Wilkins Micawber; Uriah Heep and Miss Havisham; Peggotty and Barkis. Characters who sparkle in his plots like jewels.

How about a more contemporary example? I mentioned Stephen King. Study his work and you will see that his character development is every bit as original as his plot lines. The two work together. Take a look at the myriad characters in *The Stand*; you will not find a dullard anywhere.

Don't let any of your characters plop into your plot like plain vanilla. Spice them up.

Settings

Can you take us to a place we've never been before? That will enliven any plot. And I don't necessarily mean some place far away from home, although that's an option.

It could mean simply setting your scenes in places that are fresh.

How many times do we have conversations between two potential lovers in a restaurant? Back and forth they go, with the only original element being what they are served by the waiter.

Why not put them in a tree house? Or on the subway stuck in a tunnel? Or underneath the boardwalk by the sea?

Setting also includes the details of life surrounding the Lead character. Tom Clancy created a whole new genre called techno-thriller because he put his hero, Jack Ryan, into a world of complex military hardware. That was new.

Readers love to read about the details of other people's working lives.

Do research. Immerse yourself in some occupation, either by training for it or by interviewing an expert about it.

Whatever you do, don't show characters practicing their chosen professions in the same old predictable way. Dig deeper and find original details.

You can still write about cops and lawyers and truck drivers, but only if you give them updated challenges and settings. Find out what they are and spice up your writing.

Dialogue

Dialogue is a great opportunity to spice up your plots. Don't waste it!

Dialogue helps to create original characters and move the plot along. If it isn't doing either of those things, it probably should be cut.

While the subject of dialogue alone is worthy of another book in this series, here are a few tips for freshening plot through dialogue. First, make sure your characters have unique ways of speaking. No two characters should sound exactly alike. And second, the words they use should tell us something about who they are.

If a character is the *charge-ahead* type, he'll speak that way. His words will be forceful and direct. Sam Spade in Dashiell Hammett's *The Maltese Falcon* is like that. Here he confronts the odd little intruder, Joel Cairo:

> I've got you by the neck, Cairo. You've walked in and tied yourself up, plenty strong enough to suit the police, with last night's killing. Well, now you'll have to play with me or else.

But the dandy Cairo, smelling faintly of gardenia, uses fancier verbiage:

> I made somewhat extensive inquiries about you before taking any action, and was assured that you were far too reasonable to allow other considerations to interfere with profitable business relations.

We know, simply from the words, that these are two very different characters. Think of dialogue as weapons used in the plot. Plot is about confrontation. It's a battle. So verbal weapons are naturally going to be employed by characters who are trying to outmaneuver each other.

There is a whole range of weaponry to choose from—anger, epithets, pouting, name-calling, dodging—virtually anything from the arsenal of human interaction.

John D. MacDonald's *The Executioners* (the basis for the two *Cape Fear* movies) is about a lawyer, Sam Bowden, whose family is stalked by the sadistic rapist Max Cady. Cady's first act is poisoning the family dog, Marilyn. Sam has not been totally up front with his wife, Carol. She challenges him:

> "I'm not a child and I'm not a fool and I resent being ... overprotected."

Her volley is direct, telling him she *resents* the coddling. Sam responds:

> "I should have told you. I'm sorry."

Sam's apology is meant to diminish his wife's anger. But his words ring hollow to her, and she continues to advance:

> "So now this Cady can roam around at will and poison our dog and work his way up to the children. Which do you think he'll start on first? The oldest or the youngest?"
>
> "Carol, honey. Please."
>
> "I'm a hysterical woman? You are so damn right. I am a hysterical woman."

Carol uses sarcasm, Sam tries again to soften her up, and she responds with a bitter observation and a curse word. Sam the lawyer tries another tack:

> "We haven't any proof it was Cady."
>
> She threw a towel into the sink. "Listen to me. *I* have proof it was Cady. I've got that proof. It's not the kind of proof you would like. No evidence. No testimony. Nothing legalistic. I just *know*."

Seeing that this has no effect on her husband, Carol quickly shifts and brings out her heavy artillery:

> "What kind of a man are you? This is your *family*. Marilyn was part of your *family*. Are you going to look up all the precedents and prepare a brief?"

She has attacked both his manhood and his profession. Sam attempts an answer but Carol cuts him off (interruptions are good weapons, too):

> "You don't know how—"
>
> "I don't know anything. This is happening because of something you did a long time ago."
>
> "Something I had to do."
>
> "I'm not saying you shouldn't have. You tell me the man hates you. You don't think he's sane. So *do* something about him!"

Carol wants instant action, and Sam knows he can't provide it. The stress of the situation brings out weaponlike dialogue.

The plot moves ahead with originality and pace because dialogue is used as a weapon.

Words of Wisdom

Alfred Hitchcock once said that a good story *was life, with the dull parts taken out.*

Everything in this book is, in some way, an attempt to follow Hitchcock's Axiom. You would do well to keep it seared into your writer's mind, and let it guide you always.

SCENE SELECTION

The choices you make for scenes, the raw "what happens" material, also contribute to your spice.

But our minds naturally jump to clichés as we decide what to write next.

That's why it's critical to develop the sort of imagination that considers several possibilities before deciding which scene to write.

You can do this just by pausing, writing a quick list of possibilities, and waiting for something to click.

Do this even within the scene you're writing. Maybe you start out thinking that you'll have a cop burst into a house and engage a bad guy in a gunfight, ending with the bad guy dead.

Stop a moment. What if the cop ends up dead? Or there's an innocent bystander in the house? Or a dog? Or there's not really anyone there after all?

Think about it. Choose something fresh.

EXERCISE 1

Set aside ten minutes of undisturbed writing time. For those ten minutes, write a free-form response to the following: When readers read my novels, I want them to feel
_____ at the end. That's because, to me, novels are
_____ .

Write from the gut, quickly.

When you're done, analyze your mini-essay. What does it tell you about the type of plotter you might be? Are you suspicious of plot? Are you more concerned with the "gossamer wings" of literary style? If so, consider how your writing might be doubled in strength if you learn some plotting craft.

EXERCISE 2

Take some of your favorite novels off the shelf and analyze them using the LOCK system. See how each element is at work in the books you love. Use these questions to help you:

- What is it about the Lead character that captures you?
- What is it the Lead is trying to get or get away from?
- When did the story kick into "high gear"?
- What was the main opposition to the Lead's objective?
- How did the ending make you feel? Why did it work?

EXERCISE 3

Write a quick plot for your current idea. Use four lines, one line each for LOCK.

- My Lead is a _____ .
- Her objective is to _____ .
- She is confronted by _____ who oppose(s) her because
  _____ .
- The ending will be a knockout when _____ .

If you have filled in the blanks, you have the skeleton for a solid novel. The rest of this book will help you flesh it out.

EXERCISE 4

Start a collection of your favorite "spices" from the novels you read. Look for:

- Unique settings
- Colorful characters
- Dialogue that zings
- Scenes with tremendous impact

When you come across these things, analyze them. Why do they work? What techniques did the author use?

chapter 2

[STRUCTURE: WHAT HOLDS YOUR PLOT TOGETHER]

> *If you build it, they will come.*
> —OTHERWORLDLY ADVICE FROM *FIELD OF DREAMS*

And if you structure it, they will read.

When my son, Nate, was four, he wrote a novel. It was four pages, each page containing one sentence. Very Hemingway-esque.

Nate spelled the words phonetically. Here is the entire novel, sans the crayon illustrations. The spelling has been updated for modern readers: *Robin Hood went riding. A bad guy came. They fought. He won.*

Now it is true he needed some work on pronouns and subject agreement. But the fact is he wrote a perfectly structured story. Somehow Nate had absorbed the essentials of plot construction—perhaps from Dad's stories at bedtime or the movies he was starting to love on tape and television.

The lessons drawn from this modest example can help us understand the value of structure in a novel. Simply put, structure is what assembles the parts of a story in a way that makes them accessible to readers. It is the orderly arrangement of story material for the benefit of the audience.

Plot is about *elements*, those things that go into the mix of making a good story even better.

Structure is about *timing*—where in the mix those elements go.

When you read a novel that isn't quite grabbing you, the reason is probably structure. Even though it may have good characters, snappy dialogue, and intriguing settings, the story isn't unfolding in the optimum fashion.

Of course, the author may protest that this is *his* way, and how dare anyone dictate what's right and what isn't about his novel!

That's an author's prerogative. But if we are talking about *connection with readers*, we have to talk about structure.

THE THREE-ACT STRUCTURE

Why talk about a three-act structure?

Because it works. It has since Aristotle sat down to figure out what makes drama.

Why does the three-act structure work? Probably because it is in line with how we live our lives. A three-step rhythm is inherent in much that we do.

As the writing teacher Dwight Swain pointed out, we are born, we live, and we die. It feels like three acts. Childhood is relatively short and introduces us to life. That long section in the middle is where we spend most of our time. Then we have a last act that wraps everything up.

Daily life is like that, too. We get up in the morning and get ready to go to work. We work or do whatever we do. Eventually we wrap up the day's business and hit the sack.

We live each day in three acts.

On a micro level, three acts is typical. Say we are confronted with a problem. We react. That's Act I. We spend the greater part of our time figuring out how to solve the problem: Act II. After all of that wrestling, hopefully, we get the insight and answer—the resolution of Act III.

There is something fundamentally sound about the *three* structure. As Buckminster Fuller taught, the triangle is the strongest shape in nature (thus it is the foundation of the geodesic dome he invented).

Similarly, almost all great jokes are built on a structure of three—the setup, the body, and the payoff. It is never just an Irishman and a Frenchman entering a bar; you have to add an Englishman to make the joke work.

In a novel, we must get to know some things in Act I before we can move on in the story. Then the problem is presented, and the Lead spends the greater part of the book wrestling with the problem (Act II). But the book has to end sometime, with the problem solved (Act III).

It has been said in writing classes and books that the three-act structure is dead (or silly or worthless). Don't believe it.

The three-act structure has endured because it works.

If you choose to ignore this structure, you increase the chance of reader frustration. If that's your goal for some artistic reason or other, fine.

But at least understand why structure works—it helps readers get into the story.

Can You *Play* With Structure?

Of course. Once you understand why it works, you are free to use that understanding to fit your artistic purposes. But you will soon come to realize that the further you move from sound structure, the harder it will be to bring your readers along with you. That's okay, too. A little hard work never hurts a novelist, and readers sometimes need to be challenged. So grasp the worth of structure, then write what you will. See chapter eight for more on playing with structure.

Another way to talk about the three acts is simply as the beginning, middle, and end. I like the way one wag put it: beginning, *muddle*, and end.

Here, then, are the things that must happen in the three acts. We will be going into more detail on each act in the next few chapters.

Beginnings

Beginnings are always about the *who* of the story (chapter four goes into greater detail about beginnings). The entry point is a Lead character, and the writer should begin by connecting the reader to the Lead as quickly as possible—*Robin Hood went riding*.

Imagine the courtroom scenes in *To Kill a Mockingbird* coming at the beginning of the book. What connection would there be with Atticus Finch? He'd certainly seem like a competent, caring lawyer, but our caring would not be as deep as it is later on. That's because the beginning gives us glimpses of Atticus as a father, citizen, neighbor, and lawyer. We get to know him better through the eyes of his daughter, before we track him to court.

Beginnings have other tasks to perform. The four most important are:

- Present the story world—tell us something about the setting, the time, and the immediate context.
- Establish the tone the reader will rely upon. Is this to be a sweeping epic or a zany farce? Action packed or dwelling more on character change? Fast moving or leisurely?
- Compel the reader to move on to the middle. Just why should the reader care to continue?
- Introduce the opposition. Who or what wants to stop the Lead?

Middles

The major part of the novel is the confrontation, a series of battles between the Lead and the opposition. *They fought.*

This is also where subplots blossom, adding complexity to the novel and usually reflecting the deeper meaning of the book.

The various plot strands weave in and out of one another, creating a feeling of inevitability while at the same time surprising the reader in various ways. In addition, the middle, which is discussed more in chapter five, should:

- Deepen character relationships.
- Keep us caring about what happens.
- Set up the final battle that will wrap things up at the end.

Ends

The last part of the novel gives us the resolution of the big story. *He won.* The best endings (and we'll look at some examples in chapter six) also:

- Tie up all loose ends. Are there story threads that are left dangling? You must either resolve these in a way that does not distract from the main plot line or go back and snip them out. Readers have long memories.
- Give a feeling of resonance. The best endings leave a sense of something beyond the confines of the book. What does the story *mean* in the larger sense?

What About Mythic Structure?

Ever since *Star Wars* writer-director George Lucas credited Joseph Campbell for the mythic structure of the film, we've had a plethora of books and articles about the value of this template. And it is valuable because it is all about elements lining up—which is what structure means.

Mythic structure, sometimes called "The Hero's Journey" after the title of a book by Campbell, is an order of events. It comes in various forms, but usually follows a pattern similar to this:

- Readers are introduced to the hero's world.
- A "call to adventure" or a disturbance interrupts the hero's world.
- The hero may ignore the call or the disturbance.
- The hero "crosses the threshold" into a dark world.

- A mentor may appear to teach the hero.
- Various encounters occur with forces of darkness.
- The hero has a dark moment within himself that he must overcome in order to continue.
- A talisman aids in battle (e.g., the shield of Athena for Perseus; the sword, Excalibur, for King Arthur).
- The final battle is fought.
- The hero returns to his own world.

Why does this work? Because it perfectly corresponds to the three-act structure:

ACT I
[1] Readers are introduced to the hero's world.
[2] A "call to adventure" or a disturbance interrupts the hero's world.
[3] The hero may ignore the call or the disturbance.
[4] The hero "crosses the threshold" into a dark world.

ACT II
[5] A mentor may appear to teach the hero.
[6] Various encounters occur with forces of darkness.
[7] The hero has a dark moment within himself that he must overcome.
[8] A talisman aids in battle.

ACT III
[9] The final battle is fought.
[10] The hero returns to his own world.

A DISTURBANCE AND TWO DOORWAYS

I find more than a bit of confusion among writers over terms like *plot point*, *inciting incident*, and others commonly used by writing instructors, sometimes in contradictory ways.

I want to stay away from these terms in this book, and instead try to describe what actually should happen at crucial points in the plot. It's all really simple if you don't get hung up on the technical jargon.

I'll refer here to a disturbance and two doorways. If you understand what happens with each, structuring your novel will be a breeze.

The Disturbance

In the beginning of your novel, you start out by introducing a character who lives a certain life. That is his starting point or, in mythic terms, the hero's *ordinary world*. And it's the place he'll stay unless something forces him to change. Unless he does change, we're going to have a pretty boring story because only a threat or a challenge is of interest to readers.

So very early in Act I something has to disturb the status quo. Just think about it from the reader's standpoint—something's got to happen to make us feel there's some threat or challenge happening to the characters. Remember Hitchcock's axiom. If something doesn't happen soon, you've got a *dull part*.

This disturbance does not have to be a major threat, however. It can be anything that disturbs the placid nature of the Lead's ordinary life. Dean Koontz usually begins his novels with such a disturbance. Here's the first line of *The Door to December* (written as Richard Paige):

> As soon as she finished dressing, Laura went to the front door, just in time to see the L.A. Police Department squad car pull to the curb in front of the house.

Now that's a disturbance, something small to begin with, but a disturbance nonetheless. We don't usually feel complacent about a police car pulling up to our home.

The number of possible disturbances is endless. Here are some examples:

- A phone call in the middle of the night
- A letter with some intriguing news
- The boss calling the character into his office
- A child being taken to the hospital
- The car breaking down in a desert town
- The Lead winning the lottery
- The Lead witnessing an accident—or a murder
- A note from the Lead's wife (or husband), who is leaving

From a structural standpoint, the initial disturbance creates reader interest. It is an implicit promise of an interesting story yet to come. But it is not yet the main plot because there is no confrontation. The opponent and Lead are not yet locked in an unavoidable battle.

In Mario Puzo's *The Godfather*, young Michael Corleone is determined to go straight, avoiding his father's way of life. But when the Don is shot and nearly killed, Michael's world is rocked.

Yet Michael is not yet thrust into any confrontation. He can leave New York and start a new life elsewhere. The confrontation doesn't happen, the story doesn't take off, until the Lead passes through the first doorway.

In the George Lucas film *Star Wars*, there is an action prologue. Darth Vader and his troops chase and capture Princess Leia, but not before she dispatches a pod with R2-D2 and C-3PO in it. The droids land on the planet Tatooine and get captured by the Jawas, the junk merchants.

We meet our Lead character, Luke Skywalker, at work in his normal world on Tatooine, where he lives with his aunt and uncle. His uncle buys the two droids. Within five minutes of this, we have a disturbance to Luke's world—the distress hologram from Princess Leia asking for Obi-Wan Kenobi's help.

Eventually, Luke connects with Obi-Wan, who views the hologram and asks Luke to help him answer the call for help. Luke "refuses the call" (in mythic terms) by telling Obi-Wan he can't leave his aunt and uncle.

This is still not the doorway into Act II because Luke can go on with his normal life. But when the Empire forces destroy Luke's home and kill his aunt and uncle, Luke is thrust into the Rebellion. He leaves his planet with Obi-Wan, and his adventure begins.

Doorways

How you get from beginning to middle (Act I to Act II), and from middle to end (Act II to Act III), is a matter of *transitioning*. Rather than calling these *plot points*, I find it helpful to think of these two transitions as "doorways of no return."

That explains the feeling you want to create. A thrusting of the character forward. A sense of inevitability. We are creatures of habit; we search for security. Our characters are the same. So unless there is something to push the Lead into Act II, he will be quite content to stay in Act I! He desires to remain in his ordinary world.

You need to find a way to get him out of the ordinary and into the confrontation. You need something that kicks him through the doorway; otherwise, he'll just keep sitting around the house.

Once through the doorway, the confrontation can take place. The fight goes on throughout Act II, the middle. But you're going to have to end the story sometime. Thus, the second doorway of no return must send the Lead hurtling toward the knockout ending.

These two doorways hold your three acts together, like pins in adjoining railroad cars. If they are weak or nonexistent, your train won't run.

Through Door Number 1

In order to get from beginning to middle—the first doorway—you must create a scene where your Lead is thrust into the main conflict *in a way that keeps him there.*

In a suspense novel, the first doorway might be that point where the Lead happens upon a secret that the opposition wants to keep hidden at all costs. Now there is no way out until one or the other dies. There can be no return to normalcy. Grisham's *The Firm* is an example.

Professional duty can be the doorway. A lawyer taking a case has the duty to see it through. So does a cop with an assignment. Similarly, *moral* duty works for transition. A son lost to a kidnapper obviously leads to a parent's moral duty to find him.

The key question to ask yourself is this: Can my Lead walk away from the plot right now and go on as he has before? If the answer is yes, you haven't gone through the first doorway yet.

Book I of *The Godfather* ends with that transition. Michael shoots the Don's enemy, Sollozzo, and the crooked cop, McCluskey. Now Michael can never go straight again. He's in the conflict up to his eyeballs. He cannot walk away from his choices.

For Nicholas Darrow, the charismatic minister in Susan Howatch's *The Wonder Worker*, the inner stakes are raised when he receives a shock to his upwardly spiraling ministry—his wife and the mother of his two sons leaves him. It's a blow that sends him reeling and forces him to confront his own humanity. He definitely cannot walk away.

[The First Doorway]

Lead's normal world, a place of safety and rest. Problems may happen here, but they don't threaten great change. Lead is content to stay here. Something has to happen to push him through the door.

The outside world, the great unknown, the dark forest. A place where the Lead is going to have to dig deep inside and show courage, learn new things, make new allies, etc.

It's crucial to understand the difference between an initial disturbance (sometimes called an "inciting incident") and the first doorway of no return (sometimes called a "plot point" or "crossing the threshold" in mythic terms).

In the movie *Die Hard*, for example, New York cop John McClane has come to Los Angeles to spend Christmas with his estranged wife, Holly, and their children. He meets up with her at high rise building where she works for a large company. While McClane is washing up in a bathroom, a team of terrorists takes over the building and all the people there. Except McClane, of course. He escapes to an upper floor.

We are now about twenty minutes into the film. This is definitely a disturbance. But it is not yet the transition into Act II.

Why not? Because McClane and the terrorists are not locked in battle yet. They don't know McClane is in the building. He might open a window, climb out, and scurry away for help. Or figure out a way to get a phone call out. While McClane is trying to figure out just what to do, he secretly witnesses the murder of the CEO of the big company.

So McClane gets to an upper floor again and pulls a fire alarm. This is the incident that sets up the conflict of Act II. Now the terrorists know someone is loose in the building. There is no way for McClane to resign from the action. He's through the first doorway, and there's going to be plenty of confrontation to come. This all happens at the one-quarter mark.

Through Door Number 2
To move from the middle to the end—the second doorway of no return—something has to happen that sets up the final confrontation. Usually it is some major clue or piece of information, or a huge setback or crisis, that hurtles the action toward a conclusion—usually with one quarter or less of the novel to go.

In *The Godfather*, the Don's death is a setback to peace among the mafia families. It emboldens the enemies of the Corleone family, forcing Michael to unleash a torrent of death to establish his power once and for all.

These doorways work equally well in literary fiction. Leif Enger's *Peace Like a River* has two perfectly placed transitions. The first occurs when Reuben's older brother, Davy, shoots and kills two people and must flee. This thrusts Reuben into the middle—the quest to find Davy. The second doorway opens when Davy reappears, setting up the final battle within Reuben—should he reveal where Davy is?

Is it possible to write a novel that defies these conventions of structure? Certainly. Just understand that the more structure is ignored, the less chance the novel has to connect with readers.

[The Second Doorway]

Lead is facing a series of confrontations and challenges. It will go on indefinitely unless some crisis, setback, discovery opens the door to a path that leads to the climax.

On this side, the Lead can gather his forces, inner and outer, for the final battle or final choice that will end the story. There's no going back through the door. The story must end.

ORGANIZING STRUCTURAL ELEMENTS

Here is how the structural elements line up in the classic movie *The Wizard of Oz*:

ACT I

In the opening scene, we meet Dorothy, a girl who lives on a farm in Kansas with her aunt and uncle, a dog named Toto, and some goofy farmhands. She dreams of someday going to a place far away, somewhere "over the rainbow."

Next comes the disturbance. Miss Gulch arrives by bicycle, demanding that Toto be turned over to her so she can have him destroyed. Her demand is backed up by the law, so Uncle Henry reluctantly gives Toto to Miss Gulch. Dorothy is devastated.

But Toto escapes from Miss Gulch's basket and runs back to the farm. Dorothy, knowing it could happen again, decides to run away. She meets the Professor, who engineers a little "magic" to induce Dorothy to return home.

She and Toto get back just as the big twister hits. Dorothy gets knocked in the head, and thus enters through the first doorway of no return. The twister picks up the house and lands her and Toto in a Technicolor world called Oz.

ACT II

The "muddle" of *The Wizard of Oz* is all about Dorothy trying to get to the wizard so she can find a way home. Along the way, she encounters plenty of trouble. There's a wicked witch who wants to stop her, some apple-throwing trees, a lion with more bark than bite, and so on. She picks up three allies along the way, including the aforementioned lion. The trouble increases when the quartet finally gets to see the wizard, and he delivers some bad news: Before he'll help Dorothy, she and her allies have to bring him the broomstick of the wicked witch.

So they set out through a dark forest, and then they fall through the second doorway of no return. Dorothy is captured by the flying monkeys and taken away.

ACT III

The final battle has been set up. The three allies—the Scarecrow, the Tin Woodsman, and the Cowardly Lion—must find a way to save Dorothy from the witch. They get inside the castle where things go wrong again, and it looks like they're all going to die at the hands of the witch and her minions. But then the witch goes too far, setting the Scarecrow aflame. Dorothy throws water on him, also dousing the witch. And we all know what happens then!

This is not quite the end. There's a little twist with the wizard that gives an added measure of suspense. But Dorothy winds up at home, and all is well.

WHAT STRUCTURE LOOKS LIKE

The three-act structure comes from drama and is used extensively in film. In this formulation, the first "doorway of no return" usually happens about one-fourth of the way into a film (in other words, within the first thirty minutes of a two-hour movie):

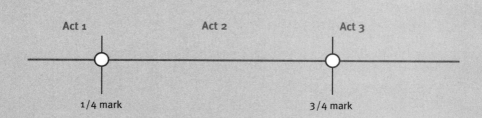

In a novel, however, that first doorway needs to happen earlier, or the book will seem to drag. My rule of thumb is the one-fifth mark, though it can happen sooner.

In addition, the final act may take place more toward the end. So while the three-fourths mark is still a good signpost, you can slide it to the right a little if you so desire.

The three-act structure for a novel should look like this:

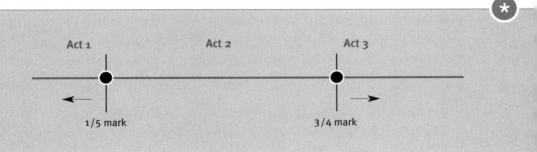

Mastering structure and transitions will make your novels more accessible even if you choose to deviate from a linear unfolding. Add a ripping good story, and your novels may turn out to be unforgettable.

A SUMMARY OF PLOT AND STRUCTURE

These basic plot and structure elements will never fail you.

A plot is about a Lead character who has an *objective*, something crucial to his well-being. The major portion of plot is the *confrontation* with the opposition, a series of battles over the *objective*. This is resolved in a *knockout* ending, an outcome that satisfies the story questions and the readers.

A solid plot unfolds in three acts—a beginning, middle, and end.

In the beginning, we get to know the Lead, his world, the tone of the story to come. We have some sort of disturbance in the beginning to keep away the dull parts.

We move into the middle through a doorway of no return, an incident that thrusts the Lead into conflict with the opposition. We need some sort of adhesive to keep them together, something like professional or moral duty, or a physical location. Death—physical, professional or psychological—is often a real possibility until the conflict is settled. Some setback or crisis, or discovery or clue, pushes the Lead through the second doorway of no return.

Now all the elements are there to get to that final battle or final choice that's going to end the story.

EXERCISE 1

Analyze some novels or movies with a view toward understanding their three-act structure. Specifically note:

- When is there a disturbance to the Lead's ordinary routine? What change happens early on? (If it doesn't, does the book or film seem to drag?)
- At what point is the Lead thrust into the conflict? At what point can he not return to normal?
- When is there a major clue, crisis or setback that makes the climax inevitable?
- If you're bored, ask yourself why. Look to see if the LOCK elements or three-act structure is weak.

EXERCISE 2

Look at the elements of your current plot. Are they lining up in a way that will help readers get into the story? Or are you ignoring structure? If so, why?

EXERCISE 3

Using the structure diagram, map out your current plot. Come up with a disturbance scene and events that make up the two doorways of no return. Write these down in summary form. Tweak them to make them original and involving.

chapter 3

[HOW TO EXPLODE WITH PLOT IDEAS]

> *There is only one type of story in the world—*
> *your story.*
>
> —RAY BRADBURY

In Woody Allen's movie *Annie Hall*, there is a passing conversation between some players at a fancy Hollywood party. One guy says, "Right now it's a notion, but I think I can get money to turn it into a concept … and later turn it into an idea."

As with all satire, the scent of truth lurks underneath. Before your plot exists, it is a notion you have. A spark, which at some point ignites. But it is here where many stories are doomed from the start. Not every idea is of equal value. To find the best plots, you need to come up with *hundreds* of ideas, then choose the best ones to develop.

That's what this chapter is about.

And before you jump into the top twenty ways to get plot ideas, you need to spend some time on the person who is going to turn them into fiction gold—you.

That's where you start in finding plots.

William Saroyan, whose novels have more passion in them than most, was once asked the name of his next book. "I don't have a name and I don't have a plot," he replied. "I have the typewriter and I have white paper and I have me and that should add up to a novel."

That's why Saroyan's work seems so fresh. He was not content with the old advice, *write what you know*. He figured out early that the key to originality was *write who you are*.

Fiction writers, especially those who write to inspire, should follow Saroyan's example. By going deep into your own heart and soul, you will find a wellspring of ideas to write about. Moreover, your writing will come alive, and your stories will have the chance to truly move your readers.

A word of caution, however. To write who you are does *not* mean producing a fictionalized autobiography. All writers have one autobiographical novel inside them, and that's usually a good place to leave it. These days publishers are wary of autobiographical novels because the prospects of turning them into good sellers are practically nil.

The market wants gripping fiction without clichés, standard characters, or tired plots. And the key to satisfying this market, to making your fiction sing with originality, is to write who you are.

TAKE A LOOK INSIDE

All writers should periodically take a good look inside themselves. Before developing your next plot, take some time to answer the following questions. This will create what I call a "personality filter" through which you'll be able to generate original plots full of interesting characters:

- What do you care most about in the world?
- If you were to write your own obituary, how would you want it to read?
- What is your physical appearance? How do you feel about it? How does it affect you?
- What do you fear most?
- What are your major strengths of character?
- What are your major flaws?
- What are you good at? What do you wish you were good at?
- If you could do one thing and know that you would be successful, what would you do?
- What are three events from your childhood that helped shape you into the person you are today?
- What are some of your annoying habits?
- What secret in your life do you hope is never revealed?
- What is your philosophy of life?

Answering these questions opens up a door into your own soul. From that viewpoint, you can better evaluate plot ideas. Does the story you're considering hit a nerve inside you? If not, why write it?

"Know thyself," the sages admonished, and that's still good advice. Especially for writers. By knowing yourself truly and honestly, by writing with passion and intensity, by caring about important issues, you'll find your writing is not only fresh, but a joy. You'll have *you*. And that's enough to start writing.

GOING AFTER IDEAS

Not every idea is worth writing about. Why spend six months, a year—ten years!—hammering out something that editors and agents, not to mention readers, will not care about?

Listen: You haven't got time to waste on mediocre stories.

So what do you do? How do you come up with an idea so good that it *alone* is almost enough to keep readers reading?

In school, I was taught to sit and think and formulate an idea, then set to work.

That's the path to the reaction, "I've seen this before."

You need to do the opposite.

You need to come up with *hundreds* of ideas, toss out the ones that don't grab you, *and then nurture and develop what's left.*

In a moment, I am going to give you twenty ways to come up with hundreds of ideas for your fiction. But first, some rules:

[1] Schedule a regular idea time. Once a week at least.

[2] Get yourself into a relaxed state, in a quiet spot where your imagination can run free.

[3] Give yourself thirty minutes of uninterrupted time.

[4] Select one or more of the exercises below. Read the instructions.

[5] Begin by letting your imagination come up with *anything* it wants to, and record *everything* on paper (or the computer).

[6] The most important rule: Do *not*, I repeat, do *not* censor yourself in any way. Leave your editorial mind out of the loop. Just let the ideas come pouring out in any way, shape, or form they want to. Do not judge anything.

[7] Have fun. Lots of fun. You're even allowed to laugh.

[8] Save all your ideas.

[9] After two or three sessions, it's time to *assess* your ideas. Use the guidelines in "Nurturing Your Ideas" at the end of this chapter.

[10] Repeat the process as often as you want.

And always remember: *The journey of a thousand miles requires plenty of snacks.* So feel free to eat while you do these exercises.

THE TOP TWENTY WAYS TO GET HUNDREDS OF PLOT IDEAS

Here are twenty fast, simple, and fun ways to develop your own unique plot ideas:

1. The What-If Game

This is perhaps the oldest, and still the best, creative game for the novelist. Originality is nothing more than connecting familiar elements in unfamiliar ways. The what-if game gets our minds thinking in such a way as to make those connections.

The what-if game can be played at any stage of the writing process, but it is especially useful for finding ideas. Train your mind to think in terms of what-if, and it will perform marvelous tricks for you.

For example, when you read something interesting, ask yourself, "What if?" Let all sorts of connections burst forth.

For one week do the following:

• Read the newspaper asking "What if?" while encountering each article.
• For every TV show or commercial you watch, ask, "What if?"
• Let your mind roam free.
• Write down your what-if questions on a master list.
• Put the list aside and come back to it a few days later. Take what sounds promising and jot down some more notes about it. Your next story may start here.

2. Titles

Make up a cool title, and then write a book to go with it.

Sound wacky? It isn't. A title can set your imagination zooming, looking for a story.

Titles can come from a variety of sources like poetry, quotations, and the Bible. Go through a book of quotations, like *Bartlett's* and jot down interesting phrases. Make a list of several words randomly drawn from the dictionary and combine them. Story ideas will begin bubbling up around you.

Take first lines from novels and make up a title. Dean Koontz's *Midnight* begins, "Janice Capshaw liked to run at night." What might you do with that? Perhaps something like these: *She Runs by Night. The Night Runner. Runner of Darkness. Night Run.*

Now all you have to do is choose one and write a novel to go with it. It's easy.

3. The List

Early in his career, Ray Bradbury made a list of nouns that flew out of his subconscious. These became fodder for his stories.

Start your own list. Let your mind comb through the mental pictures of your past and quickly write one- or two-word reminders. I did this once, and my own list of more than one hundred items includes:

- The drapes (a memory about a pet puppy who tore my mom's new drapes, so she gave him away the next day. I climbed a tree in protest and refused to come down).
- The hill (that I once accidentally set fire to).
- The fireplace (in front of which we had many a family gathering).
- Cigar smoke (my dad, who loved his stogies).

Each of these is the germ of a possible story or novel. They resonate from my past. I can take one of these items and brainstorm a whole host of possibilities that come straight from the heart. You can do the same.

4. Issues

What issues push your buttons? Robert Ludlum once said, "I think arresting fiction is written out of a sense of outrage." Outrage is a great emotion for a writer. So start an issues list. You might include:

- abortion
- environment
- gun control
- presidential politics
- talk shows
- people who yak on cell phones while driving

The late Edward Abbey based his novels on issues he cared about. For him, writing was a calling as well as a craft, which is one reason his books inspired a wide readership. The writer, Abbey believed, must be a moral voice. "Since we cannot expect truth from our institutions," he wrote, "we must expect it from our writers!"

So one way to write who you are is to find the issues that press your hot buttons, then press them!

If you embody your moral viewpoint in a three-dimensional character who takes vigorous action to vindicate his cause, you'll virtually guarantee a story packed with emotion and dramatic possibilities. Want that in your fiction? Then do this:

- Find an issue that makes your cheeks red. It can be global, like military strategy, or local, like school board policy. It must, however, be something likely to make people mad.
- Choose up sides. What is your moral viewpoint about the issue? Come up with a good argument defending your position.
- Next, *and most important*, come up with a good argument for the other side! Few things are black and white in this world, and even those on the dark side feel justified in what they are doing. Your job as a writer is to see the whole picture, and that means treating your characters—all of them—fairly.
- Now ask yourself, "What kind of person would care *most* about each side of this issue?" Come up with several possibilities for each. Later you can choose the best.

Remember, however, that fiction is not a sermon. Your job is to deliver a gripping story, not a windy lecture.

5. See It

Let your imagination play you a movie:

Sit down first thing in the morning and ask yourself, "What do I *really* want to write about at this moment in time?" List the first three things that come to your mind. This may take the form of issues (crime in the streets, euthanasia, lawyers, religion) or characters (a character who shows guts in the face of danger) or situations (what if somebody got stuck in a blimp over Iraq?). Pick the one that gets your juices flowing the most.

Close your eyes and start the movie. Just sit back and "watch." What do you see? If something is interesting, don't try to control it. Give it a nudge if you want to, but try as much as possible to let the pictures do their own thing. Do this for as long as you want.

Then start writing, with no thought about plot construction, and keep writing for twenty minutes. Write about whatever you remember from the "movie." You can make notes about character, plot ideas, themes, whatever. Just write. Do this every day for five days, adding to your written material each day.

Take a day off, then print a hard copy of your movie journal. Look it over and highlight the parts that turn you on. Go through the nurturing process now and apply the freshness test.

6. Hear It

Music is a shortcut to the heart. Listen to music that moves you. Choose from different styles—classical, movie scores, rock, jazz, whatever lights your fuse—and as you listen, close your eyes and see what pictures, scenes or characters develop.

When you do find something worth writing about (and you will), you can use that piece of music to put you in the mood every time you sit down to write.

7. Character First

Perhaps the best and fastest way to get a story idea is through a character. The process is simple: develop a dynamic character, and see where he leads.

There are a variety of ways to come up with an original character. Here are a few:

- **Visualizing.** Close your eyes and "see" the first person who pops into your mind. Describe this person. Plop him down in a setting, any setting, and see what develops. Later ask yourself, "Why is this character acting this way? What pattern of character is developing here?"
- **Re-Creating Who You Know.** Take a fascinating character from your past. Don't try to copy him. "Re-create" him. Give him a different occupation. Even better, change his sex. *He* becomes *her*. What would your crazy uncle be like if he were really a woman?
- **Obituaries.** Every day the newspapers run obituaries. These are character biographies there for the taking! Adapt them. Take the interesting parts and apply them to a character of your own choosing.

You can alter the age and the sex of the character and see how things play. Let loose.

- **The worst thing.** Once you have your character, ask this question: What is the worst thing that could happen to this person? Your answer may very well be the start of a novel of suspense, a novel the reader just can't put down.

8. Stealing From the Best

If Shakespeare could do it, you can too. Steal your plots. Yes, the Bard of Avon rarely came up with an original story. He took old plots and weaved his own particular magic with them.

Admittedly, that's harder to do today. You can't lift plot and characters wholesale and pretend it's an original story. But you can take the germ of another plot and weave *your* particular magic with it. You can switch key characters and conventions (see "Flipping a Genre" listed next). You can follow the same story movements even as you add your own original developments.

"Originality," says William Noble in *Steal This Plot!*, "is the key to plagiarism." What he means is you cannot lift the exact plot, with the same characters intact. But you may take a pattern (and plot is nothing more than a story's pattern) and use it.

9. Flipping a Genre

All genres have long-standing conventions. We expect certain beats and movements in genre stories. Why not take those expectations and turn them upside down?

It's very easy to take a Western tale, for example, and set it in outer space. *Star Wars* had many Western themes (remember the bar scene?). Likewise, the Sean Connery movie *Outland* is like *High Noon* set on a Jupiter moon. The feel of Dashiell Hammett's *The Thin Man* characters transferred well into the future in Robert A. Heinlein's *The Cat Who Walks Through Walls*.

Even the classic television series *The Wild, Wild West* was simply James Bond in the Old West. A brilliant flipping of a genre that has become part of popular culture.

So play with genres, conventions, expectations. Mix them up. There is an idea there somewhere.

10. Predict a Trend

Novels can be "hot" because of the subject matter alone. If you are able to catch a topical wave before it breaks, you may have a winner.

The trick, of course, is in predicting what will occupy the popular mind. How can you do it?

The best source is specialty magazines. Often you'll get a window into the immediate and long-term future areas of interest to people.

This doesn't need to take a lot of time, either. Go to a newsstand and irritate the manager by scanning magazines like *Scientific American, Popular Mechanics, Wired, Time, Newsweek,* and *U.S. News & World Report.* In addition, *USA Today* often has stories about cutting-edge technologies and issues. Jump on something interesting and ask:

- Who would care about this?
- What would that person do about it next year? In ten years?
- What would happen if all of society embraced this?
- What would happen if all of society rejected this?
- Who would it hurt the most?

11. Noodling the Newspaper

Read newspapers. Scan all the sections. Have your homing device set for sparks that get your mind zooming in original directions.

Read *USA Today.* The paper is written in "arrested attention span" style—lots of little snippets you can scan quickly. One edition will yield at least a dozen possible ideas. Take an item and ask a series of what-if questions to expand on what you find. If an item itself has information you might want later, snip it and toss it in a box.

12. Research

James A. Michener began "writing" a book four or five years in advance. When he "felt something coming on," he would start reading, as many as 150 to 200 books on a subject. He browsed, read, and checked things. He kept it all in his head and then, finally, he began to write. All that material gave him plenty of ideas to draw upon.

Today, the Internet makes research easier than ever. But don't ignore the classic routes. Books are still here, and you can always find people with specialized knowledge to interview. And if the pocketbook permits, travel to a location and drink it in. Rich veins of material abound.

Don't forget experts, either. Find and interview people who lead in their fields. Go to ordinary folks who lived through certain periods or in certain places to get rich detail and factual accuracy.

Here's a quick way to get ideas from research:

- Choose a nonfiction book on some subject you always wanted to know about.
- Skim the book for an overview.
- Jot down plot ideas that come to you.
- Read the book in greater detail.
- Spot more ideas, and flesh out those you already have.

Do this, and soon your heart will connect with some bit of data that fires you up.

13. "What I Really Want to Write About Is …"

Try this exercise first thing in the morning. Your subconscious has been dreamily percolating through the night. It has things to tell you. So grab your cup of Joe and get to a paper or computer screen. Start with, "What I really want to write about is …"

Then write for ten minutes without stopping. Follow the thoughts that come to you, expanding them, going on to others, floating on the streams of your consciousness.

This is not only good for ideas, but also to loosen up your writing muscles. You can use this as a warm-up to your writing day.

14. Obsession

By its nature, an obsession controls the deepest emotions of a character. It pushes the character and prompts her to action. As such, it is a great springboard for ideas.

What sorts of things obsess people? Ego? Looks? Lust? Careers? Enemies? Success?

What is Javert's obsession in *Les Miserables*? Duty. It drives him to fanaticism and finally death.

What is Ahab's obsession? A big, white whale. Without that obsession, we'd have no *Moby Dick*.

Dorian Gray is obsessed with youth.

All of the characters in *The Maltese Falcon* are obsessed with the black bird.

In *Gone With the Wind*, Rhett is obsessed with Scarlett. Scarlett is obsessed with Ashley. Therein lies the tale.

Create a character. Give her an obsession. Watch where she runs.

15. Opening Lines

Dean Koontz wrote *The Voice of the Night* based on an opening line he wrote while just "playing around": "You ever killed anything?" Roy asked.

Only after the line was written did Koontz decide Roy would be a boy of fourteen. He then went on to write two pages of dialogue that opened the book. But it all started with one line that reached out and grabbed him by the throat.

Joseph Heller was famous for using first lines to suggest novels. In desperation one day, needing to start a novel but having no ideas, these opening lines came to Heller: "In the office in which I work, there are four people of whom I am afraid. Each of these four people is afraid of five people."

These two lines immediately suggested what Heller calls "a whole explosion of possibilities and choices." The result was his novel *Something Happened*.

Likewise, Heller's classic *Catch-22* got started when he wrote these lines: "It was love at first sight. The first time he saw the chaplain, *Someone* fell madly in love with him." Only later did Heller replace *Someone* with the character's name, Yossarian, and decide that the chaplain was an army chaplain, as opposed to a prison chaplain. The lines conceived the story.

Writing opening lines is fun. Try it. Your imagination will thank you.

16. Write a Prologue

Page-turning fiction today often begins with an action prologue. It doesn't have to involve the main character either. But something exciting, mysterious, suspenseful, or shocking happens that makes the reader say, "Hey, I better read the rest of the book to find out why this happened."

Gripping openings are fairly easy to write. The trick is putting a book after it. But the ideas you generate with a good prologue may lead to a full story. And writing a prologue of 1,000 to 2,000 words every now and then is great practice for writing page-turning fiction.

17. The Mind Map

The venerable practice of mind mapping is always a promising method of creation. A mind map is simply a web of quick associations, rendered in visual form. The process can be broken down into three phases:

[1] **Ready.** Choose a word or concept to develop. It may be one you have in mind already, or it can be chosen at random. Write the word in the center of a blank sheet of paper and draw a circle around it.

[2] **Fire.** Without much thought, allow your mind to jot down connections and associations. Don't worry about making sense of it at this stage. Just *go*. Allow your associations to spawn other associations. Fill up the paper.

[3] **Aim.** Soon, your pattern-mind will give you what Gabriele Lusser Rico calls a "trial-web shift." This is a new "sense of direction" that comes to you out of the associations you've made. (See Rico's *Writing the Natural Way*, chapter five. This is a superb book on mind mapping for writers.) This shift will provide you with a new sense of direction or focus in terms of your map. You will discern the message that your exploding mind wants to send you. You will have an idea.

For example, my word is *baseball*. Here I go:

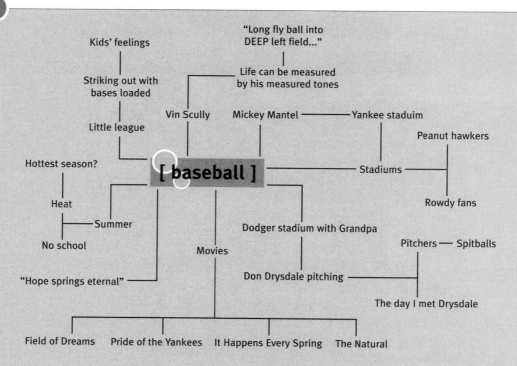

As I pondered this web, it occurred to me that my youth, and the hopes that resided therein, are central. My memories of Dodger Stadium and Little League and Vin Scully on hot summer nights are a rich vein from which I can come up with dozens of possible story ideas.

I think I will.

18. Socko Ending

What is it that makes *Casablanca* more than just a good film? What gives it a lasting resonance that leaves you with a satisfied "Ah"? I believe it is the ending, with that great final line: "Louis, I think this is the start of a beautiful friendship."

A socko ending.

Endings often make or break a story. If the ending is flat, we are unsatisfied, even if what has come before is compelling. Frank Capra said this is what happened with his film, *Meet John Doe*. The story setup was wonderful, but when they got to the ending, Capra and the writers didn't know what to do. The most logical outcome would have been for John Doe to jump from the building and kill himself. But that would have made the film depressing. The choice they finally made, having the common folk rush up to save him, didn't quite ring true. The filmmakers had painted themselves into a corner.

Since endings are so crucial, why not come up with a socko ending first? Try this:

[1] Visualize a climactic scene in the theater of your mind.

[2] Hear music to go with it.

[3] Let the full range of emotions burst forth.

[4] Add characters as you will to heighten conflict.

[5] Play around with variations on this theme until something unforgettable happens.

Then ask:

[6] Who are the characters?

[7] What circumstances brought them here?

[8] How can I trace back the story to its logical starting point?

Many writers feel that having a possible ending in mind is the best available narrative compass. At the very least, this socko ending exercise will give you some strong characters.

19. Occupations

Much of our self-image is tied up with our work—what we do and how well we do it. There is also a culture associated with individual occupations. So there is plenty of material inherent in the kind of work people do.

Try coming up with story ideas based on intriguing work. It will serve you well to keep a list of interesting occupations you come across as you read books, newspapers, and magazines.

One reference I treasure is *Dictionary of Occupational Titles*, published by the U.S. Department of Labor. This huge, two-volume compendium describes thousands of occupations in detail. Here is a sample listing:

> **378.363-010 Armor Reconnaissance Specialist (military serv.)**
> Drives military wheeled or tracked vehicle and observes area to gather information concerning terrain features, enemy strength, and location, serving as member of ground armored reconnaissance unit: Reports information to commander, using secure voice communication procedure. Writes field messages to report combat reconnaissance information. Drives armored, tracked, and wheeled vehicles in support of tactical operations to harass, delay, and destroy enemy troops. Directs gunfire from vehicle to provide covering or flanking fire against enemy attack. Prepares and employs night firing aids to assist in delivering accurate fire. Tests surrounding air to determine presence and identity of chemical agents, using chemical agent detecting equipment, radiac, or radiological monitoring device. Drives vehicle to bridle locations to mark routes and control traffic. Requests and adjusts mortar and artillery fire on targets and reports effectiveness of fire.

The above might suggest a number of stories. What if this character got lost? Drove through a time warp into 1850? Went crazy? What areas of further research are suggested?

20. Desperation

Maybe you're sitting before a blank sheet or screen and there is nothing in your head. Zero. You've exhausted all your possibilities. You are a desperate writer.

Good. Many other great writers have shared your misfortune. And they have found a way out. The answer is *just write anyway*.

Before writing *Ragtime*, E. L. Doctorow was desperate. He explains, "I was so desperate to write something, I was facing the wall of my study in my house in New Rochelle and so I started to write about the wall. That's the kind of day we sometimes have, as writers. Then I wrote about the house that was attached to the wall. It was built in 1906, you see, so I thought about the era and what Broadview Avenue looked like then: trolley cars ran along the avenue down at the bottom of the hill; people wore white clothes in the summer to stay cool. Teddy Roosevelt was President. One thing led to another and that's the way that book began, through desperation to those few images."

Maupassant used to advise, "Get black on white." James Thurber said, "Don't get it right, just get it written."

Are you desperate?

Get black on white. Now!

How NOT to Get Ideas

You now have more than enough idea generators to last your writing lifetime. Here I inject a word of caution. There are certain methods writers have resorted to over the years that you should avoid:

- **Drugs.** By now everyone knows the dangers of drug use. While it may provide the illusion of imagination expansion, there are just too many evils involved to make it worthwhile.
- **Alcohol.** Alcohol and authorship are inextricably linked in literary lore. Many great writers have also been notorious boozers. Untold numbers of aspirants have mistakenly thought there is a logical connection there. There isn't.
- **Stress.** The myth of the struggling writer is another image many young authors hold dear. But nothing suggests that self-inflicted stress creates anything more than anxiety. While that can sometimes lead to deadlines born of desperation, it may also lead to overconcern with economics. This in turn can result in not taking risks and playing it safe, in short, flat writing.

As Gabriel Garcia Marquez said, "I'm very much against the romantic concept of writing which maintains that the act of writing is a sacrifice and that the worse the economic conditions or the emotional state, the better the writing. I think you have to be in a very good emotional and physical state."

Stay healthy, happy, and above all *produce*.

NURTURING YOUR IDEAS

Okay, you've got a bunch of ideas there. (You don't? Get busy!) Now what? Choose your favorite idea and write a *hook*, *line*, and *sinker*.

The hook is the big idea, the reason a reader browsing in the bookstore would look at your cover copy and go, "Wow!" The big idea in *Midnight* by Dean Koontz is the abuse of biotechnology, which affects an entire town. What's the big idea behind your book?

Now comes the line. Write the grabber copy for your idea in one or two sentences. Another of Koontz's novels, *Winter Moon*, was summed up this way: "In Los Angeles, a city street turns into a fiery apocalypse. In a lonely corner of Montana, a mysterious presence invades a forest. As these events converge and career out of control, neither the living nor the dead are safe."

Finally, think hard about a sinker. This is the negative angle, what might possibly sink your idea as a venture. That doesn't mean you get rid of the idea (though you may); you can also strengthen it considerably. Here are the questions you need to ask and answer to your satisfaction before moving on:

[1] **Has this type of story been done before?** (Almost always, the answer will be yes.) If it has, what elements can you add that are unique? Brainstorm a list of possibilities. Keep on brainstorming until you have something no one has seen before.

[2] **Is the setting ordinary?** If so, where else might you set the story? What sort of background has not been done to death?

[3] **Are the characters you're thinking of made of old stock?** If so, how can you make them more interesting? What fresh perspective can you provide? Again, do some free-range brainstorming and don't throw out any ideas until you have generated a long list.

[4] **Is this story "big enough" to grab a substantial number of readers?** If not, what can you do to make it bigger? How might you raise the stakes? Almost always, death (physical or psychological) must be a very real possibility.

[5] **Is there some other element you can add that is fascinating?** Think of the idea from every angle, and how you might add a twist or two that enlivens the whole. Yes, it's more list making. Just do it.

Like cookies and love, story ideas need to be fresh to be truly satisfying. By applying these questions to your story idea, you'll keep yourself from starting down a long path that may turn toward dullsville.

BELL'S PYRAMID

What editors and agents will tell you is that they are looking for a "fresh, original voice" within the cosmos of what has worked before. In other words, they want it both ways: original, yet not so original that the people in the marketing department won't know what to do with it.

So give them both. Give one final pass on your best ideas by putting them into Bell's Pyramid. (Forgive me, but never having had a pyramid bear my name, I went ahead and named this one.)

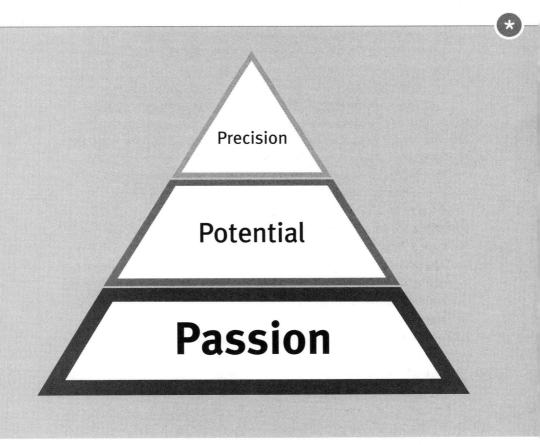

Passion

The base of the pyramid is plot *passion*. You are going to be spending a lot of time with the plots you choose to write. A novel can take months, sometimes years. So you'd better have a passionate desire to take the plunge in order to sustain yourself in the long haul.

Why are so many novels rejected? One reason is they seem "cookie cutter." They follow the crowd because the writer often thinks, "Gee, if I write something like something else that is successful, I can get published."

This is a major mistake. Without a passionate commitment to the plot *as a story you're burning to tell*, your voice will not be original or compelling. You will just end up sounding like the maddening crowd of other wannabes pounding on the doors of opportunity.

Of all the strata of the pyramid, passion is the most important for your writer's soul and, almost always, your ultimate success. While it is fine to do journeyman work for money (if you are learning the craft), I believe we writers must nourish and nurture our individuality. Only then do we rise above the commonplace.

As Brenda Ueland says, "Work with all your intelligence and love. Work freely and rollickingly as though they were talking to a friend who loves you. Mentally (at least three or four times a day) thumb your nose at all the know-it-alls, jeerers, critics, doubters."

You may even, if you wish, thumb your nose at me. Just make sure you're passionate about doing so.

Potential

On the next level, you consider the possible reach of the idea to an audience. For a moment, take off your artist's hat and assume the role of a potential investor. If you were going to put up many dollars to publish this book, do you have a chance to recoup the investment and make a little profit besides?

Be ruthless in your evaluation. Does an eight-hundred-page fictional rendition of a few years of your life hold much interest for a circle wider than your immediate family? It may, but tell your investor-self why.

Are you entranced by the romance of fish gutting? Explain this to your investor-self.

And do a little market research. You ought to subscribe to *Publishers Weekly* and keep up with the business. What is being published? Each issue of *Publishers Weekly* lists "Forecasts," short reviews of upcoming books. Ask yourself what the publisher sees in these plots.

Don't copy. Just be aware that much of the potential of a published work is in the author's original voice and vision.

Note, too, that your assessment of potential need not be with the largest possible audience in mind. Genre writers know they are limiting themselves to a distinct group of potential readers. Even within genres, there are subgroups. Many science fiction writers, for example, are not writing "hard" science fiction, but rather books about deeply held philosophical ideas. They know that such novels appeal to some sci-fi readers and not to others. That's fine. They are motivated by *passion*, which we've already discussed.

Looking at potential, then, is just a tool to help you make a decision. It is not a "rule." As with any tool, use it wisely.

Precision

Finally, be precise in your plot goals. If you are passionate about your idea and reasonably certain about the potential it has to reach readers, trim away anything that is not in line with that potential. If the plot is going to be for a suspense audience, aim it there. Don't anticipate using anything else that will distract from that goal.

THE CASE OF *MIDNIGHT*

I have used Dean Koontz's 1989 thriller, *Midnight*, in my suspense writing class because it was a runaway bestseller (Koontz's first No. 1 hardcover on the *New York Times* list), and it uses many of the techniques discussed. I'll tell you what you need to know about the novel, but if you want the full benefit I suggest you get yourself a copy and read it through at some point.

Since this chapter is about getting ideas, you might ask yourself how Koontz got the idea for *Midnight*. We can only speculate, but here are some distinct possibilities. More than one may have played a part:

- **Predicting a trend.** Koontz often uses the abuse of new technologies in his books. In 1989, he anticipated nanotechnology (tiny, biologically implanted computer chips) and expanded on it brilliantly.
- **Villain.** The villain, Thomas Shadduck, has one of the more bizarre and startling introductions in *Midnight*. He is a supervillain, humanized. The plot could have been written around him. Alfred Hitchcock once said that the strength of a suspense story is equal to the strength of the villain. Perhaps Koontz started with Shadduck and wrote the plot from his machinations.
- **Title.** The word "midnight" conjures up all sorts of images, usually of the

dark and sinister variety. In fact, the novel takes place mostly at night, during a short period of time, and midnight is also the time when something very bad is going to be triggered. All of this may have occurred to Koontz based on the title alone.

- **A great prologue.** Many page-turners begin with a mysterious, shocking, or otherwise gripping prologue. The *Midnight* prologue introduces a character who is jogging at night and who is killed by a mysterious beast at the end of the prologue. We never see her again. But we are left wondering about the cause of her death (as, indeed, are the lead characters). Koontz may have just written this prologue off the top of his head, and only later figured out what to do with it.
- **Stealing a plot.** This is my nominee for most likely device Koontz used to come up with the plot for *Midnight*. Reading it, I was struck that here we had a mixture of two classic plots—the great '50s film *Invasion of the Body Snatchers* and the classic H.G. Wells tale, *The Island of Dr. Moreau*. And, indeed, Koontz cleverly mentions both of these later in the novel. It is as if he is winking at those readers who picked up on the similarities!

So you see, there are any number of ways a master storyteller like Dean Koontz may have come up with the initial idea for his first *New York Times* No. 1 hardcover bestseller. What's stopping you from doing the same?

EXERCISE 1

This week, choose two ways to get ideas. Set aside at least one hour of writing time for each exercise. Do them.

EXERCISE 2

Pick the idea you like the best from the previous exercise, and give this idea a hook, line, and sinker.

EXERCISE 3

Now, apply Bell's Pyramid to your idea. Is there enough passion, potential, and precision to make you want to continue?

EXERCISE 4

Even if you decide not to dedicate a whole novel to this idea, going through the process will help you the next time. But if you like the idea, use the rest of this book to get it into fighting shape.

EXERCISE 5

Resolve to set aside a few hours a month just for getting ideas. Stay alert to the idea possibilities all around you. Jot down notes. Rip out newspaper items. Once a month, go through your ideas and nurture them.

chapter 4

[BEGINNING STRONG]

> *We start to make up our minds about other people*
> *within seven seconds of first meeting them.*
> —ROGER AILES, *YOU ARE THE MESSAGE*

Act I, the beginning portion of the novel, has several tasks to perform:

- Get the reader hooked.
- Establish a bond between the reader and the Lead character.
- Present the story world—tell us something about the setting, the time, and the immediate context.
- Establish the general tone of the novel. Is this to be a sweeping epic or a zany farce? Action packed or dwelling more on character change? Fast moving or leisurely paced?
- Compel the reader to move on to the middle. Just why should the reader care to continue?
- Introduce the opposition. Who or what wants to stop the Lead?

Do these things well, and your plot will have a strong foundation. Your readers will feel they are in the hands of a competent storyteller. And that's not a bad thing to be, is it?

GETTING YOUR READER HOOKED

The first task of your beginning is to hook the reader. Period.

And remember, that first reader is going to be an agent or editor. Tough crowd. These are people who have too many manuscripts to go through each day. They are just itching for a reason to put yours down.

Don't give them that reason.

Then you have the bookstore browser, who might (because the marketing and design departments have done their jobs) open up to the first page to see what's there.

This is the battle you fight. There are nine billion other things the reader can do besides read your book.

First impressions are tough to shake. Make a bad one, and you have to work twice as hard and twice as long to get back to square one. You may not even get the chance.

So it pays—in life and in fiction—to make a great first impression. Here are some ways to grab readers from the start.

Opening Lines

Take a look sometime at the openings of Dean Koontz's novels. Often, they are one-line paragraphs with a named person and some sort of immediate interruption to normality:

> Katharine Sellers was sure that, at any moment, the car would begin to slide along the smooth, icy pavement and she would lose control of it.
> —*Dance With the Devil*, written as "Deanna Dwyer"

> Penny Dawson woke and heard something moving furtively in the dark bedroom.
> —*Darkfall*

> Tuesday was a fine California day, full of sunshine and promise, until Harry Lyon had to shoot someone at lunch.
> —*Dragon Tears*

> In his onyx-walled room in the occupation tower, Hulann—a naoili—had disassociated his overmind from his organic regulating brain.
> —*Beastchild*

What are the successful elements of these opening lines? First, they give the name of a character. This specificity creates the illusion of reality from the get-go. A variation on this is to begin with a pronoun: *She heard something moving in her bedroom.*

What I like about the Koontz approach, however, is that a name gives that extra measure of verisimilitude and makes the "willing suspension of disbelief" that much easier.

The second thing to notice is that something is happening or about to happen to the character. And not just anything—something ominous or dangerous. An interruption to normal life.

Give readers a feeling of motion, of something happening or about to happen. Give them this feeling from the very start.

If you begin with long, descriptive passages (something that was much more acceptable in the past), the feeling you'll create is not one of motion but of stasis.

Don't misunderstand. Descriptions are not out of bounds—*so long as you include text that gives the feeling of motion.*

And only a character can be in motion. So—give us a character as soon as possible. Take a look at this next example from Anne Lamott's *Blue Shoe*:

> The world outside the window was in flames. The leaves on the pistachio trees shone fire-red and orange. Mattie studied the early morning light. She was lying on the side of the bed where her husband should have been sleeping.

Here Lamott starts with description. But she gets a character into it in the third sentence. And then she drops in a line of something amiss—her husband is not there, where he *should have been.*

We have a feeling of motion, that Mattie is in the midst of a troubling situation *and is going to have to do something about it.*

That's what a feeling of motion is. Not necessarily overt action (though that works, too) but the sense that action is or is about to take place.

Unless something disturbing happens to your Lead early on, you risk violating Hitchcock's Axiom: A good story is life with the dull parts taken out.

So stir up the waters.

What happens doesn't have to be huge, like a house blowing up. It can be something as seemingly innocuous as a telephone call in the night or a bit of unsettling news.

For example, we meet Margaret Mitchell's Scarlett O'Hara at the very beginning of *Gone With the Wind* this way:

> Scarlett O'Hara was not beautiful, but men seldom realized it when caught by her charm as the Tarleton twins were.

This is Scarlett and her world at the beginning—she can catch men with her charm. She likes to do so.

> She meant what she said, for she could never long endure any conversation of which she was not the chief subject. But she smiled when she spoke, consciously deepening her dimple and fluttering her bristly black lashes as swiftly as butterflies' wings. The boys were enchanted, as she had intended them to be ...

So far so good. Scarlett is charming the twins, controlling them. Then the conversation turns to the upcoming barbecue at Twelve Oaks. The twins want to tie up Scarlett for the waltzes, and promise to tell her a secret if she'll consent. The secret is that the engagement of Ashley Wilkes and Melanie Hamilton is going to be announced at the party.

> Scarlett's face did not change but her lips went white—like a person who has received a stunning blow without warning and who, in the first moments of shock, does not realize what has happened.

Disturbance! A few pages later, we learn why:

> Ashley to marry Melanie Hamilton!
>   Oh, it couldn't be true! ... No, Ashley couldn't be in love with Melanie, because—oh, she couldn't be mistaken!—because he was in love with her! She, Scarlett, was the one he loved—she knew it!

So the world Scarlett thought she ruled—the world of beaux and marriage—has been riled up.

Consider the opening from Jonathan Harr's brilliant book, *A Civil Action*. This is nonfiction, the true story of a complex case involving several deaths and illnesses caused by two large companies that recklessly poisoned the water supply of a small town. But it reads like the best fiction, and it does so right from the start.

The first sentence reads: "The lawyer Jan Schlichtmann was awakened by the telephone at eight-thirty on a Saturday morning in mid-July."

What this does, from the very start, is give you a Lead character and a phone call that wakes him up. We've all received late night or early morning calls, and they usually portend bad news. So we want to read on and find out why the call was made. We're hooked from the very first sentence.

The opening chapter then goes on to reveal that the call is from a creditor telling Schlichtmann that if he doesn't pay up, his car will be repossessed. Twenty minutes later another call comes from the County Sheriff, who is coming for the car. We learn Schlichtmann is involved in a huge case and is at the end of his financial rope. Things are so bad he could lose everything— his business, his home, his possessions. And we learn that the jury is out, deliberating on this case that will make or break Schlichtmann. We follow the now carless Schlichtmann as he walks down to the courthouse to wait in the corridor while the jury begins another day of deliberations. Our last image is of this lawyer, alone, waiting.

This brilliant opening now allows the author to drop back in time and spend the rest of the book bringing us back to the point where it begins. We want to read because we have a character who is immediately sympathetic and interesting, tied up in the battle of his life. We were there from the very first sentence.

Here are some other ways to grab readers from the start.

Action

James M. Cain's *The Postman Always Rings Twice* begins: "They threw me off the hay truck about noon."

We are, as they say, *in medias res*—in the middle of things.

Another form of immediate action is dialogue. If there is an element of conflict in there, so much the better. I chose this for my opening in *Final Witness*:

> "How old are you?"
>
> "Twenty-four."
>
> "Going into your third year?"
>
> "Yes."
>
> "Second in your class?"
>
> "Temporarily."
>
> "Isn't it true you have a motive to lie?"
>
> "Excuse me?" Rachel Ybarra felt her face start to burn. That question had come from nowhere, like a slap. She sat up a little straighter in the chair.

This cross-examination style plunges us into instant conflict between two characters.

Raw Emotion

The Quiet Game by Greg Iles begins with a father holding his four-year-old daughter in a line at Disney World:

> Annie jerks taut in my arms and points into the crowd.
>
> "Daddy! I saw Mama! Hurry!"
>
> I do not look. I don't ask where. I don't because Annie's mother died seven months ago. I stand motionless in the line, looking just like everyone else except for the hot tears that have begun to sting my eyes.

We bond with the Lead through his deep feeling of a universal emotion.

Look-Back Hook

Still another way to capture attention from the start is with the *look-back hook*. Here is how Stephen King does it:

> The terror, which would not end for another twenty-eight years—if it ever did end—began, so far as I can tell, with a boat made from a sheet of newspaper floating down a gutter swollen with rain.
> —*IT*

> The two things Sarah remembered about that night later were his run of luck at the Wheel of Fortune and the mask. But as time passed, years of it, it was the mask she thought about—when she could bring herself to think about that horrible night at all.
> —*The Dead Zone*

The idea is to immediately suggest there is a not-to-be-missed story about to unfold.

Attitude

When using first-person narration, especially in literary fiction, your can capture attention through voice and attitude as J.D. Salinger does here:

> If you really want to hear about it, the first thing you'll probably want to know is where I was born, and what my lousy childhood was like, and how my parents were occupied and all before they had me, and all that David Copperfield kind of crap, but I don't feel like going into it, if you want to know the truth.
> —*The Catcher in the Rye*

Grab your readers with judicious use of the methods outlined above. You still have a long way to go to keep readers turning the pages, but at least you'll be off to a good start.

Prologues

The use of prologues is a venerable one, used by all sorts of writers in many different ways. But the most effective prologues do one simple thing—entice the reader to move to chapter one.

All of the rules we talk about in this chapter apply to prologues as well, with one primary exception: The prologue does not necessarily *have to* introduce your Lead character. It does, however, eventually have to connect to your main plot.

The primary ways prologues are used are as an action hook, as a frame story, and as a teaser.

Action Prologue

With the *action prologue*, a staple of suspense fiction, we start off with some sort of big scene, many times involving death. This sets up the tone and stakes right away. Chapter one will begin the main plot, and what has just happened will hover over the entire story.

Sometimes the Lead character is involved in the prologue. In *Final Seconds*, by John Lutz and David August, the prologue involves a bomb scare in a New York public school. Harper, the Lead character, is a grizzled veteran of the New York Police Department's bomb squad. He arrives on the scene with his young partner. Tension builds as Harper tries to defuse the bomb. Finally, left holding a bit of explosive, Harper is almost there when … *boom*. And his hand is mostly blown off.

Chapter one opens two-and-a-half years later, with Harper going to see his partner—who was at fault for the accident. Harper is no longer with the NYPD.

Thus we get a prologue of incredible excitement and suspense, and as chapter one begins, we wonder how Harper has handled life after this traumatic experience.

Another example is Harlan Coben's *Tell No One*. The narrator, David Beck, opens by recounting an anniversary trip with his wife Elizabeth to a romantic lakeside, a place of good memories. Eventually they go swimming in the dark lake, make love, and lounge on a raft.

Then Elizabeth steps onto the dock. Beck stays on the raft. He hears a car door slam, and Elizabeth is gone.

Beck swims to the dock, shouting his wife's name.

He hears her scream. As he gets out of the water, he's struck by something and topples back into the lake. He hears her scream again, "but the sound, all sound, gurgled away as I sank under the water."

That's the end of the prologue. Chapter one begins *eight years later*.

More common is the prologue involving characters other than the Lead—characters who may or may not show up in the main plot.

In Dean Koontz's *Midnight*, we are introduced to Janice Capshaw, who, as we know from earlier discussions, likes to run at night. As she jogs through the foreboding darkness, Koontz gives us some of her background, building up identification and even sympathy.

Suspense starts to build as Janice gets the feeling that someone—or something—is following her. How right she is. And at the end of the prologue, she is killed by some mysterious, horrible creatures.

The first chapter begins with Sam Booker, the Lead, arriving in the little town where the killing took place.

Which offers up this rule: If you do not introduce your Lead in the prologue, make sure you do it in chapter one! Readers want to know whom they are supposed to follow.

Note: Koontz labeled this prologue chapter "1" and the real opening chapter, chapter "2." That's a choice you can make if you so desire. What matters is not the tag, but the function.

To use an action prologue, remember:

- Make the action big enough to justify a prologue.
- Keep it relatively short.
- End with trouble—something bad happens or is about to happen.
- Make sure you tie in the prologue with the main plot at some point, or at least explain what happened.

Framing a Story

A prologue can also give us the view of a character about to look back and tell the story. Why do this? In order to set up a feeling that what is about to unfold has consequences that reach into the present and the future.

Stephen King's novella, *The Body*, begins with the narrator looking back to 1960, a "long time ago," when he first saw a dead body. But he indicates that the incident was much deeper than a visual image—it was one of those things that "lie too close to wherever your secret heart is buried. ..."

The Catcher in the Rye is a frame story, though Salinger does not mark it with *Prologue* or *Epilogue*. That comes out purely in the writing.

The narrator, Holden Caulfield, informs us he is going to tell about "this madman stuff that happened to me around last Christmas just before I got pretty run-down and had to come out here and take it easy."

Where is *here*? We don't find out until the last chapter, where we learn Holden is in a sanitarium.

With a frame prologue:

- Establish the kind of feeling and tone you want to hover over the main plot.
- Make it good reading in and of itself, not just dry *telling*. An interesting voice is essential.

- Show us how the events about to unfold are affecting the prologue character *now*.

The Teaser

Though rarely used, the teaser can work on occasion. Mary Higgins Clark has done it more than once.

In the teaser, you present a scene at the beginning that will happen later on in the book. It's like a preview of a coming attraction.

Why do it this way? Because you grab the reader with action. You don't play the scene to full fruition, leaving a mystery. You leave the reader wondering, *How did this character get herself into this predicament?*

When you get to that scene in the novel, you then play it out, and answer the reader's initial question.

Some purists object to the teaser, as it is not adding anything to the plot. It's just using plot material earlier, they say.

To which one answer is, So what? If it functions to grab the reader and create interest, then it is doing its job.

For a teaser, do this:

- Select a highly charged scene from your story.
- You may choose to use the exact same wording, or rework it a bit.
- Stop short of resolution, so you truly tease your readers to move on.

ESTABLISHING A BOND WITH THE READER VIA THE LEAD CHARACTER

Before I started to sell my fiction, I had a major weakness with characters. I would come up with a plot or situation, but I'd stock it with cardboard story people, characters who seemed to be on the page just because I stuck them there.

Then I happened across Lajos Egri's advice about living, vibrating human beings being the secret of great and enduring writing. Egri suggested that if you truly know yourself, deeply and intimately, you will be able to create great, complex, and interesting characters.

That's because we have all experienced, to a greater or lesser degree, every human emotion. By tapping into our emotional memories, we can create an infinite variety of characters.

This is not a book on character creation though there is overlap. Plot doesn't work without characters; the stronger your characters, the better your plot. For your character work, I recommend reading *Creating Dynamic Characters* or *Write Great Fiction: Characters, Emotion & Viewpoint*, both by Nancy Kress. Strong characters draw readers into your plot. This dynamic is called the *bond*.

Ways to Establish the Bond

After conceiving a compelling Lead character, you must go a step further and figure out how to create an emotional bond with the reader. You can accomplish this by mastering four dynamics—identification, sympathy, likability, and inner conflict.

Identification

Since the Lead character provides access to a plot, it follows that the more the reader can identify with the Lead, the greater the intensity of the plot experience. With identification, you create the wondrous feeling that the story, in some way, is happening to *me*.

Identification means, simply, that the Lead is like us. We feel that we could, under the right circumstances, find ourselves in the same position in the plot, with similar reactions.

The Lead appears to us to be a real human being.

What are the marks of a real human being? Look inside yourself. Most likely, you are: (1) trying to make it in the world; (2) a little fearful at times; and (3) not perfect.

In *The Girl Who Loved Tom Gordon*, Stephen King gives us nine-year-old Trisha McFarland, who is walking in the woods with her mother. The trouble begins when Trisha gets lost, and why does she get lost? Because she petulantly stomps away from her mother to relieve herself. It's such a simple, human response that we easily identify with it. That's how King draws us into his Lead character's immediate crisis.

Trisha's not perfect. She has normal human flaws.

Your key question here is: What does your Lead do and think that makes her just like most people? Find those qualities, and readers will begin to warm to the Lead.

This works even with (perhaps most crucially with) the heroic Lead. Take Indiana Jones. In *Raiders of the Lost Ark*, it would have been tempting to leave him as some sort of superman, overcoming all odds without a hitch. But the filmmakers wisely gave him an understandable human flaw: a fear of snakes. This humanizes Jones and makes him more accessible.

Another word for identification is *empathy*.

Sympathy

In contrast to mere empathy, sympathy intensifies the reader's emotional investment in the Lead. In my view, the best plots have a Lead with whom some sympathy is established. Even if the Lead has negative qualities, like Scarlett in *Gone With the Wind*, you can find ways to generate sympathy nonetheless.

There are four simple ways to establish sympathy. Choose wisely. Don't overload them, as it may make the reader feel manipulated.

[1] **Jeopardy.** Put the hero in terrible, imminent trouble and you've got the sympathy factor at work right away. In *Tom Gordon*, Trisha is lost in dangerous woods after she stomps away. That's immediate, physical jeopardy.

Jeopardy can also be *emotional*. Dean Koontz often uses this device. In *Midnight*, FBI agent Sam Booker is close to an emotional abyss. His teenage son hates him, and he is fighting to find reasons to keep on living. He is in emotional jeopardy. Part of the depth of the book comes from his finding reasons to carry on.

[2] **Hardship.** If the Lead has to face some misfortune not of her own making, sympathy abounds. In *The Winner*, David Baldacci gives us a poor, southern woman who grew up without love, education, or good hygiene (even her teeth are bad). So when she takes steps to overcome her state of affairs, we are rooting for her.

Forrest Gump, who suffers from physical and mental challenges as a boy, gains our sympathy from the start.

The key to using hardship is not to allow the character to whine about it. Sure, there can be moments when the character lashes out emotionally due to the hardship, but don't let her stay there. We admire those who take steps to overcome.

[3] **The Underdog.** America loves people who face long odds. John Grisham has used the underdog in many of his books. One of his best, *The Rainmaker*, is the classic David-and-Goliath story switched to the courtroom. We can't help rooting for Rudy Baylor as he battles a huge defense firm.

Rocky Balboa became a permanent part of our culture when Sylvester Stallone brought him to the screen in *Rocky*. The movie was a phenomenon not only because it was about a pug fighter's chance to beat the champ but because it was like Stallone's own story as a struggling actor.

[4] Vulnerability. Readers worry about a Lead who might be crushed at any time. In *Rose Madder*, Stephen King follows a battered wife who, after years in a hellish marriage, finally gets up the courage to run away from her psychopathic cop-husband. But she is so naive about the ways of the world, and her husband so good at tracking people down, we worry about her from the moment she steps out the door.

Likability

A likable Lead, not surprisingly, is someone who does likable things. For example, likeable Leads do favors for people. Or they are witty in conversation. They are supportive and engaging. They are not selfish. They have an expansive view of life. These are people we like to be around. Think about people *you* like, and then incorporate some of those characteristics into your Lead.

A witty character, a character who doesn't take himself too seriously, is likable. So is the character who cares about others without calling attention to himself.

Irwin Fletcher, in the *Fletch* books by Gregory MacDonald, is witty and self-deprecating. So is Elvis Cole, the private investigator creation of Robert Crais.

But note that people who try too hard to be likable often miss the mark. It's a fine line your characters walk, but worth the effort to get it right.

You *can* write about an unlikable Lead *if* you compensate in other areas. Giving the Lead power is one good method. Scarlett O'Hara has a certain power over men. She also demonstrates her power to overcome obstacles as the story progresses.

In *The Godfather*, Michael Corleone is a monster, and a powerful one.

Make the unlikable Lead fascinating in some way, or readers will be turned off.

Inner conflict

Characters who are absolutely sure about what they do, who plunge ahead without fear, are not that interesting. We don't go through life that way. In reality, we have doubts just like everyone else.

Bringing your Lead's doubts to the surface in your plot pulls the reader deeper into the story.

In *How to Write a Damn Good Novel II*, James N. Frey writes that inner conflict "can be thought of as a battle between two 'voices' within the character: one of reason, the other of passion—or of two conflicting passions."

Many times it is fear on one side, telling the Lead not to act. Inner conflict is resolved when the Lead, by listening to the other side—duty, honor, principle, or the like—overcomes doubt and acts accordingly.

Present the Story World

What sort of world does your Lead inhabit? Not merely the setting, though that is important. But what is life like for the Lead?

In *Mystic River*, Dennis Lehane gives us Jimmy Marcus's story world in the first chapter after the prologue:

> After work that night, Jimmy Marcus had a beer with his brother-in-law, Kevin Savage, at the Warren Tap, the two of them sitting at the window and watching some kids play street hockey. There were six kids, and they were fighting in the dark, their faces gone featureless with it. The Warren Tap was tucked away on a side street in the old stockyard district ...

We get a sense of Jimmy's life and routine here. He's an average guy in a working-class location (near the stockyard). The rest of the section gives us more explanation of Jimmy's situation—how he'd been in prison, but now has a wife and three daughters and owns a store. He's a guy just trying to make it in the world.

Sometimes we begin with the Lead practicing his chosen profession. This allows for some explanation, as in Lawrence Block's *Eight Million Ways to Die*:

> She said, "You used to be a policeman."
>
> "A few years back."
>
> "And now you're a private detective."
>
> "Not exactly." The eyes widened. They were very vivid blue, an unusual shade, and I wondered if she were wearing contact lenses. The soft lenses sometimes do curious things to eye color, altering some shades, intensifying others.
>
> "I don't have a license," I explained. "When I decided I didn't want to

carry a badge anymore I didn't figure I wanted to carry a license, either." Or fill out forms or keep records or check with the tax collector. "Anything I do is very unofficial."

"But it's what you do? It's how you make your living?"

"That's right."

Notice this isn't just raw exposition. Block shows us the narrator's close observations, and some of his attitude about "official" things.

Set the Tone

Chapter one of Steve Martini's *The Judge* begins like this:

"You have two choices," he tells me. "Your man testifies, or else."

"Or else what? Thumbscrews?" I say.

He gives me a look as if to say, "If you like."

Armando Acosta would have excelled in another age. Scenes of some dimly lit stone cavern with iron shackles, pinioned to the walls come to mind. Visions of flickering torches, the odor of lard thick in the air, as black-hooded men, hairy and barrel-chested, scurry about with implements of pain, employed at his command. The "Cocoanut" is a man with bad timing. He missed his calling with the passing of the Spanish Inquisition.

We are seated in his chambers behind Department 15 ...

A legal setting and a tough tone from the narrator; a lawyer facing a tough, unfair judge. We know this is going to be a certain kind of book with a distinct voice.

Contrast that to the following excerpt from Tom Robbins's *Another Roadside Attraction*:

The magician's underwear has just been found in a cardboard suitcase floating in a stagnant pond on the outskirts of Miami. However significant that discovery may be—and there is the possibility that it could alter the destiny of each and every one of us—it is not the incident with which to begin this report.

Notice any difference in tone? I think you do. Readers want to settle into a consistent tone. That does not mean a serious novel can't have comic relief, or a comic novel some drama. In fact, that variety is a good thing—it keeps readers engaged.

But the overall impression one gets from a novel should be consistency of tone.

Hook Readers With the First Page

"Don't warm up your engines," Jack M. Bickham counseled in *The 38 Most Common Fiction Writing Mistakes*. "Start your story from the first sentence."

Bickham warns of three beginning motifs that can stall your story on the very first page.

[1] **Excessive description.** If description is what dominates the opening, there is no action, no character in motion. While some brief description of place is necessary, it should be woven briefly into the opening action. If a setting is vital to the story, at least give us a person in the setting to get things rolling.

[2] **Backward looks.** Fiction is forward moving. If you frontload with backstory—those events that happened to the characters before the main plot—it feels like stalling.

[3] **No threat.** "Good fiction," wrote Bickham, "starts with—and deals with—someone's response to threat." Give us that opening bit of disturbance quickly.

COMPEL THE READER TO MOVE ON TO THE MIDDLE

All of this Act I material described above exists to move the reader on to Act II. Why should they care to read on?

Because you have given them the following in Act I:

- A compelling Lead
- Whom they bond with
- And whose world has been disturbed

And when the Lead passes through the first doorway of no return into Act II, we must know who or what the opposition is.

Not that a complete identity has to be established. It is perfectly all right that there is a mysterious opponent out there, someone to be revealed later. But that there *is* an opponent is all important.

Make sure the opponent is as strong as or, preferably, stronger than the Lead. And do not scrimp on the sympathy factor! Give the opponent his due, his justifications. Your novel will be the stronger for it.

Handling Exposition

Nothing will slow down plot faster than an information dump. This is where the author merely tells the reader something he thinks the reader needs to know before moving on with the plot.

It's bad enough when this is done in the narrative portion, but dreadful when it is done in dialogue.

For example, you might run across a paragraph like this:

> John was a doctor from the east. He went to medical school at Johns Hopkins where he was a star student. He completed his residency in New York City when he was 30 years old. He lived with relatives on Long Island while he was an intern. John loved New York.

Now, in certain contexts this might be perfectly fine. Sometimes telling is a short cut, and if it is indeed short, it can work. But take a look at all exposition like the above in your manuscript, and ask yourself if you can be more creative in how you give this information to your readers.

I have a few rules about exposition in the beginnings of books. I have formulated these only because I saw in my own writing the tendency to put in a lot of exposition up front, thinking the reader needed this to understand the story.

Not so. Most of the time I could cut with impunity and not lose the flow of the story; in fact, my novels started to take off from the beginning.

Don't start slowly with useless exposition. Thus, the rules:

Rule 1: Act first, explain later. Begin with a character in motion. Readers will follow a character who is doing something, and won't demand to know everything about the character up front. You then drop in information as necessary, in little bits as you go along.

Rule 2: When you explain, do the iceberg. Don't tell us everything about the character's past history or current situation. Give us the 10 percent above the surface that is necessary to understand what's going on, and leave 90 percent hidden and mysterious below the surface. Later in the story, you can reveal more of that information. Until the right time, however, withhold it.

Rule 3: Set information inside confrontation. Often, the best way to let information come out is within a scene of intense conflict. Using the characters' thoughts or words, you can have crucial information ripped out and thrown in front of the reader.

TWO EXAMPLES OF SUCCESSFUL BEGINNINGS

In the first chapter of *Midnight*, Dean Koontz skillfully weaves in exposition during a tense jog at night:

> **First sentence:** "Janice Capshaw liked to run at night." Follows the rule: Open with a character—named—in motion.
> **Next two sentences:** Author explains something about her running, gives her age and something about her appearance (healthy).
> **Next five sentences:** We learn the time and place (Sunday night, Sept. 21, Moonlight Cove). Description of the place. Mood established (dark, no cars, no other people). Background on the place (quiet little town).
> **Next three sentences:** Mood details in the action (as she runs).
> **Next two sentences:** Background on Janice's likes about night running.
> **Next five sentences:** Deepening details about Janice (why she likes night).
> **Next three sentences:** Action as she runs. More details and mood.
> **Next sentence:** Action as she runs. How she feels.
> **Next seven sentences:** Deepening Janice by describing her past with her late husband.
> **Next two sentences:** First sign of trouble.
> **Next three sentences:** Her reaction to the sign.

And so on throughout. Read this opening chapter. It is a great example of handling exposition.

For the next example, let's widen our scope and look at how *Final Seconds*, by John Lutz and David August, progresses within the first six chapters:

> **Prologue:** New York public school has bomb scare. Harper, a grizzled veteran, and his young partner, arrive. Tension builds as he tries to undo the bomb. Finally, left holding a bit of explosive, Harper is almost there when … boom. His hand is mostly blown off.
> **Chapter one:** Two-and-a-half years later, Harper is going to see his partner (who was sort of at fault for the accident). He's working security for techno-thriller author Rod Buckner. Harper is no longer with the NYPD.
> **Chapter two:** Harper can't talk his old partner into coming back to the NYPD. As he's driving away from this very secure complex, a tremendous explosion is heard. The whole house, along with Buckner and all the others, is blown up.

Chapter three: Harper tries to get information on the investigation into his ex-partner's death, but his old captain isn't giving any. Tension builds here.

Chapter four: We see Harper's home life. Then he gets a message from an old FBI friend to come see him about the case.

Chapter five: Addleman, a profiler who is now a drunk and eccentric, says he has a theory. There is a serial bomber out there, targeting celebrities!

Chapter six: Now a scene with the bomber, the villain, getting stuff from a contact in a remote area. The contact is surly. When the deal is finally made, the contact takes the money. But it is laced with napalm, and a trick detonator. The guy burns up.

We are now on page 64, the plot is set up, and the cat and mouse begins.

SOME GREAT OPENINGS

Let's have a look at some great openings from best-selling novels and see what the writers are doing. We'll begin, once again, with the master, Dean Koontz, and *Sole Survivor*:

> At two-thirty Saturday morning, in Los Angeles, Joe Carpenter woke, clutching a pillow to his chest, calling his lost wife's name in the darkness. The anguished and haunted quality of his own voice had shaken him from sleep. Dreams fell from him not all at once but in trembling veils, as attic dust falls off rafters when a house rolls with an earthquake.

Again, notice that Koontz gives us a specific name and a haunting first line. But then he expands upon that line with two others that are almost poetic in their descriptive power and emotional impact. This is one of the greatest opening paragraphs in any thriller you'll ever read.

From *The Stand* by Stephen King:

> "Sally."
> A mutter.
> "Wake up now, Sally."
> A louder mutter: *lemme alone.*
> He shook her harder.
> "Wake up. You got to wake up!"
> Charlie.

> Charlie's voice. Calling her. For how long?
> Sally swam up out of sleep.

King uses the dialogue starter, which always gives the impression of instant motion. Somebody is saying something, so we've got action (dialogue is a form of action, a physical act to gain a result or reaction). As the dialogue continues, we know only that Charlie is in some distress, and that Sally, swimming out of sleep, is about to find out what it is.

If you're writing a comical novel, there is another possibility for a grabber opening: using the look and sound of the text itself to create an oddball impression. From *Sacred Monster* by Donald E. Westlake:

> "This won't take long, sir."
> Ooooooooooooooooooohoooooooooooooooooooooooooooohoooooooooooooo
> ooooooooooohoooooooooooooooooooooooooohooooooooooooooooooooooooo
> ooooooooooooooooooooooohoooooooooooooooooooooooooooooooooooooooo
> oooo, wow.
> I hurt all over. My *bones* ache. God's giant fists are squeezing my internal organs, twisting and grinding. Why do I *do* it, if it makes me sick?
> "Ready for a few questions, sir?"

Westlake makes sure we are sufficiently intrigued, too, by making us wonder just what it is the narrator does to make himself so sick.

Now let's have a look at some great openings in literary novels. Can we get any more literary than Herman Melville's *Moby Dick*?

> Call me Ishmael. Some years ago—never mind how long precisely—having little or no money in my purse, and nothing particular to interest me on shore, I thought I would sail about a little and see the watery part of the world. It is a way I have of driving off the spleen, and regulating the circulation. Whenever I find myself growing grim about the mouth; whenever it is a damp, drizzly November in my soul; whenever I find myself involuntarily pausing before coffin warehouses, and bringing up the rear of every funeral I meet; and especially whenever my hypos get such an upper hand of me, that it requires a strong moral principle to prevent me from deliberately stepping into the street, and methodically knocking people's hats off—then, I account it high time to get to sea as soon as I can. This is my substitute for pistol and ball.

When writing in the first person, it is the voice that must reach out and grab. Melville's does.

PLOT & STRUCTURE

The famous first line, "Call me Ishmael," had perhaps a deeper meaning to nineteenth-century American readers, steeped as they would have been in the Bible. Ishmael was the son of Abraham by Hagar, a servant. Thus, he was not the child of God's covenant, as Isaac, son of Sarah, was. Ishmael was sent away by Sarah so he would not share in Isaac's inheritance. He was an outcast. That is what Melville establishes immediately.

Then the narrator goes on, in this haunting passage, to say, basically, that he goes to sea to keep from killing himself. But Melville is poetic—*damp, drizzly November in my soul.*

There's also a touch of humor to keep things from getting too maudlin—Ishmael says he sometimes wants to methodically knock people's hats off.

He's got an attitude. That's one key for literary novelists. If you're doing the book in first person, then give us a voice that intrigues us.

Earlier, I warned about not starting with descriptions of setting, weather, and the like. That is not an ironclad rule, but simply a helpful tip. Readers today are impatient, and want to know why they should keep reading.

So if you want to use description to start, make sure it does three things: (1) sets mood; (2) gets a character involved early; (3) gives us a reason to keep reading!

Here is how Janet Fitch's *White Oleander* begins:

> The Santa Anas blew hot from the desert, shriveling the last of the spring grass into whiskers of pale straw. Only the oleanders thrived, their delicate poisonous blooms, their dagger green leaves.

Already we have a mood. The weather does not just exist; it portends. The first sentence gives us desolation. The second gives us something that thrives, but it is dangerous. Read the rest of the book to find out how this applies!

Now Fitch gives us the narrator, getting the character involved early:

> We could not sleep in the hot dry nights, my mother and I. I woke up at midnight to find her bed empty. I climbed to the roof and easily spotted her blond hair like a white flame in the light of the three-quarter moon.
>
> "Oleander time," she said. "Lovers who kill each other now will blame it on the wind."

Now this is a character I want to know more about. Who says things like this? We read on to find out.

In *The Big Rock Candy Mountain*, Wallace Stegner gives us a character who is literally in motion:

> The train was rocking through wide open country before Elsa was able to put off the misery of leaving and reach out for the freedom and release that were hers now.

Why wasn't Elsa free before? What is she going to do with this new freedom? Where is she headed?

> She tucked her handkerchief away, leaned her shoulder against the dirty pane and watched the telegraph wires dip, and dip, and dip from pole to pole, watched the trees and scattered farms, endless variations of white house, red barn, tufted cornfield, slide smoothly backward. Every mile meant that she was freer.
>
> The car was hot; opened windows along the coach let in an acrid smell of smoke, and as the wind flawed, the trailing plume swept down past her eyes, fogging the trackside. Two men up ahead rose and took off their coats and came back toward the smoker. One of them wore flaming striped suspenders and stared at her.

A small detail—the man staring. It adds to the sense of vulnerability of this woman, and that, as we have seen, is a subtle form of jeopardy. Our sympathy is beginning to build.

W. Somerset Maugham begins *Of Human Bondage* with description, but then gets us immediately to that change-disturbance that is so crucial:

> The day broke gray and dull. The clouds hung heavily, and there was a rawness in the air that suggested snow. A woman servant came into a room in which a child was sleeping and drew the curtains. She glanced mechanically at the house opposite, a stucco house with a portico, and went to the child's bed.
>
> "Wake up, Philip," she said.

Why is Philip being awakened? The mood is somber (gray, dull, heavy clouds, raw weather). We want to find out what's happening:

> She pulled down the bed-clothes, took him in her arms, and carried him downstairs. He was only half awake.
>
> "Your mother wants you," she said.
>
> She opened the door of a room on the floor below and took the child over to a bed in which a woman was lying. It was his mother. She stretched out her arms, and the child nestled by her side. He did not ask why he had been awakened. The

woman kissed his eyes, and with thin, small hands felt the warm body through his white flannel nightgown. She pressed him closer to herself.

"Are you sleepy, darling?" she said.

Her voice was so weak that it seemed to come already from a great distance. The child did not answer, but smiled comfortably. He was very happy in the large, warm bed, with those soft arms about him. He tried to make himself smaller still as he cuddled up against his mother, and he kissed her sleepily. In a moment he closed his eyes and was fast asleep. The doctor came forwards and stood by the bed-side.

"Oh, don't take him away yet," she moaned.

The doctor, without answering, looked at her gravely. Knowing she would not be allowed to keep the child much longer, the woman kissed him again; and she passed her hand down his body till she came to his feet; she held the right foot in her hand and felt the five small toes; and then slowly passed her hand over the left one. She gave a sob.

A mother being separated from her child. Why? Emotional jeopardy is here in force.

So what have we seen?

Any type of novel can hook a reader, set tone, give a sense of motion, connect us with a character, and set the wheels in motion.

Why would you want your plot to begin any other way? The only alternative is that you start with none of this, hoping the reader will stick with you.

But even if you write with a style that makes angels weep, you're not going to keep readers interested for too long on style alone.

Why not make angels and readers both happy?

Grab 'em from the start.

EXERCISE 1

Go over the opening chapter of your work in progress (or write one now). What techniques will you use to grab the reader from the very first paragraph? Are you establishing a feeling of motion? If not, rewrite it using the techniques you have learned in this chapter.

EXERCISE 2

What is your story world? How well do you know it? How are you giving the reader a sense of it in detail, without just dumping blocks of description?

EXERCISE 3

How are you introducing your Lead character? What is going to make your Lead memorable? Brainstorm five possibilities for your Lead in each of the following categories:

- **Identification.** How is the Lead "like us"?
- **Sympathy.** Think about jeopardy (physical or emotional); hardship; underdog status; and vulnerability.
- **Likability.** Witty? Cares about other people?
- **Inner conflict.** What two "voices" are battling inside your Lead?

EXERCISE 4

What is disturbing your Lead's ordinary world? What change is causing ripples or waves?

EXERCISE 5

Give your opposition character his due. Dean Koontz once wrote:

> The best villains are those that evoke pity and sometimes even genuine sympathy as well as terror. Think of the pathetic aspect of the Frankenstein monster. Think of the poor werewolf, hating what he becomes in the light of the full moon, but incapable of resisting the lycanthropic tides in his own cells.

How can you justify, from the opposition's standpoint, what he's doing? What is there in his background that explains the way he is? What aspects of his character are charming, attractive, or seductive?

chapter 5

[MIDDLES]

> *There are no second acts in American life.*
> —F. SCOTT FITZGERALD

Maybe so, Scott. But as you well knew, there are in novels. And that's the big, long middle part that you have to fill.

What you do in Act II, the middle, is write scenes—scenes that stretch the tension, raise the stakes, keep readers worried, and build toward Act III in a way that seems inevitable. Chapter seven on scene writing will cover this in greater detail. Here we want to take a look at the big picture.

And for that I'd like to start with death.

DEATH

I am convinced that the most compelling fiction has death hovering over the Lead throughout.

Death you say? As in somebody getting knocked off?

Not exactly. There's that old song that says, "I die just a little when he plays piano in the dark." In other words, there are deaths that are not physical. We can die on the inside.

Besides physical death, which is the staple of the action thriller, there is psychological and professional death.

Psychological Death

Why has *The Catcher in the Rye* had such staying power over the years? Part of the reason has to be that so many of us relate to the adolescent twilight between childhood and adulthood. And in that gray world, many go on a search for a reason to live.

If Holden doesn't find it, he will die inside. And maybe that will lead to a physical death through suicide.

If someone has the object of his desire close at hand, and not having it will mean everlasting loss, we can understand that there will be some dying inside if the objective is not realized.

That is really what we mean by the objective being absolutely crucial to the happiness of the Lead (see O in the LOCK system on page 11 of chapter one). Set this up right and you'll create the intense experience readers crave from great fiction.

Professional Death

Our work world is essential to our lives and happiness. Most of us hope to find meaning in our work, and if there is a professional duty that is a major part of our existence, we are in good territory for fiction.

We can set up a situation where a loss in this duty can mean the end, or at least a massive dilution, of our professional life.

Think of the lawyer, down on his luck, who gets a case that could redeem him. Or the cop who has a chance to stop a killer.

What keeps the reader reading is worrying about what the Lead is going to lose.

THE OPPOSITION

How do you know what obstacles to throw? The first step is to conceive an opposition character. I use this term rather than "villain" because the opposition does not have to be evil. The opposition merely has to have a compelling reason to stop the Lead.

Three keys will help you come up with good opposition:

- Make the opposition a person. (A master like Stephen King can make the opposition nonpersonal, as in *Tom Gordon*, where it's Trisha against the woods. But don't try this at home until you've had lots of practice.)
- If it is a group, like the law firm in *The Rainmaker*, select one person in that group to take the lead role for the opposition.
- Make the opposition stronger than the Lead. If the opposition can be easily matched, why should the reader worry?

Then ask yourself, "Why do I *love* my opposition character?" Climbing into the opposition's skin will give you an empathetic view, and a better character as a result.

Adhesive

Your confrontation still needs one more crucial ingredient: *adhesive.* Because if your Lead can simply walk away from the opponent and still be able to realize her objective, the reader will be asking, "Well, why doesn't she?"

An adhesive is any strong relationship or circumstance that holds people together.

If the Lead can solve his problem simply by resigning from the action, the reader will wonder why he doesn't do so. Or if there is not a strong enough reason for the Lead to continue, the reader won't be all that worried about him.

There needs to be a strong reason for the Lead to *stick around*, to keep the characters together throughout that long muddle.

If you have carefully selected an objective that is essential to the well-being of the Lead and an opposition with an equally valid reason to stop the Lead, your adhesive will usually be self-evident.

You must figure out a reason why the Lead and opposition can't withdraw from the action.

Writing your novel will then be a matter of recording various scenes of confrontation, most ending with some sort of setback for your Lead, forcing her to analyze her situation anew and take some other action toward her objective.

Think of the long middle of your book as a series of increasingly intense battles. Sometimes your Lead will be out of action to regroup, but most of the time she'll be fighting toward her ultimate goal.

Back and forth, parry and thrust.

That's the heart of your novel.

Here are a few tips to make that adhesive strong:

- Life and death. If the opposition has a strong enough reason to kill the Lead, that's an automatic adhesive. Staying alive is essential to one's well-being.
- If there is a professional duty involved, that's adhesive. The readers understand why a lawyer who takes a case cannot just walk away. Same for a cop assigned a case.
- Moral duty is also a strong adhesive. If a mother's child is kidnapped, for example, we understand why she doesn't walk away from the action. She will do whatever it takes to get the child back.
- Obsession is another strong adhesive. In *Rose Madder*, the psycho hus-

band is simply not going to stop hunting down his wife. He's obsessed with seeing her dead.

- Sometimes the physical location can operate to keep the opponents bonded. *The Shining*, by Stephen King, is an example. A husband, wife, and child live and work at a mountain hotel that gets snowed in every winter. They physically can't walk away. (*Casablanca* is another such story. No one can get out of Casablanca without permission or "Letters of Transit.")

As an example of the crucial importance of adhesive, consider the Neil Simon play *The Odd Couple*. Oscar Madison is a happy slob. He lives in a bachelor pad where he and his friends can be as sloppy as they want. They can smoke cigars, play cards, and make a mess.

Felix Unger, Oscar's friend, is a neat freak. When he moves into Oscar's apartment, sparks fly. The two do not get along. This is the engine of the conflict.

The obvious question, however, is why doesn't Oscar just kick Felix out? It's Oscar's apartment, after all. If he can't stand Felix, why not show him the door?

Simon, recognizing the need for adhesive, cleverly sets it up from the start. Felix's wife has left him, and he is suicidal. Oscar and the others are worried about Felix being left alone. Thus, Oscar, Felix's friend, undertakes an understandable moral task—watching out for Felix.

Of course, the humor of the play occurs as Oscar reaches the point where he feels like killing Felix himself.

In literary fiction, the adhesive will sometimes be self-generating. A Lead must change on the inside or suffer psychological loss. Or she must get away from an influence (the opposition) that threatens to squelch her growth. In *White Oleander*, for example, Astrid struggles throughout the book to find her own identity, apart from a domineering mother.

Some other examples:

- In *Jaws*, Brody has a professional duty to protect the residents of his town.
- In *The Catcher in the Rye*, Holden is dying inside in the world he inhabits and must find another reason to live.
- In Dean Koontz's *Intensity*, Chyna spends much of the book trapped in the back of a killer's van (a physical location). Later, she tries to save a tortured hostage (a moral duty).

- In the movie *The Fugitive*, the adhesive is the law. Richard Kimble (Harrison Ford) is innocent of his wife's murder. It's not only self-interest that keeps him on the run; he also has a moral duty to find the man who killed his wife. On the other side, Sam Gerard (Tommy Lee Jones) is a U.S. Marshal, and thus has a professional duty to catch the fugitive. We well understand why neither character can just walk away.

ARM YOURSELF FOR CONFRONTATION

ARM stands for *Action, Reaction, More action*. It is the fundamental rhythm of the novel.

Think about it. Unless your Lead character is doing something, you have no plot. Plot results from the action of the character to solve the problems in front of him, all with the aim of gaining his desire.

Action requires that the character has decided upon an objective and that he has started toward it. This action must be opposed by something or the scene will be dull. So pick an obstacle, an immediate problem to overcome.

What About a Passive Lead Character?

Someone who doesn't really do much? My advice again: Don't try this at home until you're practiced and skilled like Anne Tyler, who manages to pull it off (for some readers) in *A Patchwork Planet*. The Lead, Barnaby, is a thirty-year-old man who seems to float through the novel as things happen around him and to him. Tyler uses details and her perceptions of character to keep interest aroused.

Most often the right choice is another character who, for whatever reason, is standing in the way of the character. Conflict results.

Let us take a few examples.

Suppose we're writing a legal thriller, and a young lawyer has just been assigned to help on a case. The case involves one of the firm's big clients and the SEC. The young lawyer's first task is to gather information, and he sits down with the client's chief accountant.

If the scene becomes merely a question-and-answer session, with the lawyer asking and receiving what he wants, we have a lifeless scene. Not much interest. This can happen when you have characters on the same side, with similar interests.

How do you spice up such a scene?

You find ways to add conflict or tension.

One way to do it is through the surroundings. Perhaps the session is constantly interrupted by other business around the office. Before any of the crucial information can come out, the session is ended when the accountant is called to another task.

But tension from the characters themselves is often the surest way to generate interest.

The accountant trusts the lawyer, but he is afraid. Instead of answering the questions directly, he keeps asking about what might happen to him. The lawyer has to keep trying to calm him down.

What the lawyer doesn't get is the information he needs. That's conflict, a frustration of his goal in the scene.

Or the lawyer goes over to the accountant's house. As he begins to ask questions, the accountant pulls a gun on him. Is that conflict? You bet.

But why does he pull the gun? You'll have to figure that out for yourself.

And that's what novelists do. They write actions and justify them.

At the end of an action scene, the character might have overcome the various obstacles in his way and attained his scene goal. But keeping in mind that worrying the reader is the primary goal of the middle of the book, it is actually much better if the character does *not* attain his goal. In fact, if the situation can be made worse, then so much the better for us, your readers.

So now we have our young lawyer looking down the barrel of a gun. The accountant says that if he comes around again, he's going to be shot. "Now get out."

We have reached the end of our action unit with a nice kick in the pants to our character. Now what does he do?

He *reacts*.

That's how the human being operates, isn't it? When a nasty situation hits us, we react to it.

First we react emotionally. This depends upon our psychological makeup. It's the same for your character.

Our young lawyer might be angry, confused, scared, or some other variation on these themes.

Then what happens? Well, the character might give up and go home. He might decide to leave the firm and look for a new job.

But then your story is at an end. If the action involves the main plot, your character cannot give up. Therefore, he is going to take *more action* after he's thought about what to do. It may be a few seconds of time, or it may require longer rumination. But at some point, he will decide to take further action, and the pattern repeats itself.

Action, reaction, more action.

It keeps your story moving forward. Chapter seven covers scene writing and will expand on how you do this, beat by beat.

KEEP THEM READING

Writers sometimes refer to the infamous "Act II Problem," which boils down to this: How do you keep the readers interested through that long portion of the novel? Yes, we write action, reaction, and more action. But what sort of action?

It will help enormously if you think about two principles all the time: (1) stretching the tension and (2) raising the stakes.

Learn to do these two things, and you'll save yourself a lot of plot headaches. And you'll have those readers anxiously flipping the pages.

Stretching the Tension

One of my great movie-going experiences was watching *Psycho* in high school in an auditorium during a storm. The place was packed. The mood was right. And from the shower scene on, people were screaming their heads off.

I'm glad my first exposure to the movie was not on television. I got to see it uncut (which is more than we can say for Janet Leigh after the shower scene). But more importantly, I got the full effect of the suspense without commercial interruption.

When Vera Miles started walking toward *the house*, the audience shrieked. Most people were shouting *Don't go in there! Stop! NOOO!* My skin erupted in a million pin pricks.

Of course, Vera didn't listen. And it seemed like it took forever for her to get inside the place, and then down to the basement to see, ahem, Mrs. Bates.

The screaming did not stop during the entire sequence. The anticipation was unbearable. The surprise-twist climax actually changed my body chemistry. I didn't sleep right for a week.

Which demonstrates why Alfred Hitchcock was called the master of suspense. What he did better than any other director was *stretch the tension*. He never let a thrilling moment escape with a mere whimper. He played it for all it was worth.

And so should fiction writers. Learning how to stretch tension is one of the best ways to keep your readers flipping pages, losing sleep, and buying your books.

Set up the Tension

Before you can stretch anything, of course, you need the raw material. You don't fashion a clay pot without clay. The clay for a novelist is trouble. The question you have to keep asking is this: What problem has the potential to lay some serious hurt on my character?

If your Lead has misplaced his pajamas, you could write several pages about it, throwing obstacle after obstacle in his path (a roller skate, a phone call, the postman ringing twice). But the hunt is unlikely to engage your readers. There just isn't enough at stake at the end of the line (unless, of course, your hero has hidden the mafia's money in the pajama bottoms and has five minutes to find it).

So the first rule is simple. Always make sure scenes of tension have something to be tense about.

When you've got a handle on the trouble for your character in a given scene, you're ready to stretch it. You can do that with two aspects of your fiction—the physical and the emotional. Each presents an opportunity to transform your story from the mundane to the thrilling.

Stretching the Physical

Physical peril or uncertainty is perfect material for the big stretch. The way to do it is simple—*slow down*. Go through the scene beat by beat in your imagination, as if you're watching a movie scene in slow motion.

Then, as you write the scene, alternate between action, thoughts, dialogue, and description. Take your time with each one. Milk them.

Let's say you have a woman being stalked by a man with assault on his mind. It could start this way:

[**Action**] Mary took a step back.
[**Dialogue**] "Don't be afraid," the man said.
[**Thought**] *How did he get in here? The doors are all locked.*
[**Action**] He swayed where he stood, and [**Description**] she could smell the beer on his breath.
[**Dialogue**] "Get out," she said.
[**Action**] He laughed and slid toward her.

Want to stretch even more? Good. Do it. Each item—action, thoughts, dialogue, description—can be extended:

[**Action**] Mary took a step back, bumping the end table. [**Description**] A vase crashed to the floor.
[**Dialogue**] "Don't be afraid," the man said. "I don't want to hurt you, Mary. I want to be your friend."
[**Thoughts**] *How did he get in here? The doors are all locked.* And then she remembered she'd left the garage door open for Johnny. *Stupid, stupid. You deserve this, you always deserve what you get.*

Extending beats can even stretch tension when a character is alone. The secret, once again, is in the setup material.

In *One Door Away From Heaven*, Dean Koontz has a scene early in the book where Leilani, a nine-year-old girl, walks through a trailer home to find her drugged-out mother. Doesn't seem like much of a problem, except Koontz sets the scene up with this description: "Saturated by silence, the house brimmed also with an unnerving expectancy, as though some bulwark were about to crack, permitting a violent flood to sweep everything away."

From there, for seven pages, Leilani continues step by step. The suspense builds until the revelation at the end of the scene. This section, which many writers would have dealt with in a paragraph, adds enormously to the overall tension.

Your ability to orchestrate beats so they conform to the tone and feel of the story you're trying to tell is one of the most important skills you can develop. Here are three key questions to ask before you write a tense scene involving physical action:

• What is the worst thing from the *outside* that can happen to my character? This may be in the form of another person, a physical object, or a circumstance outside the character's control.

- What is the worst trouble my character can get into in this scene? You may come up with an instant answer. Pause a moment and ratchet it up a notch. This may suggest further possibilities.
- Have I sufficiently set up the danger for readers before the scene? Remember, they need to know what's at stake before they start worrying.

Stretching the Emotional

Of course, a scene does not have to involve physical peril to have tension worth stretching. Trouble can be emotional as well.

When a character is in the throes of emotional turmoil, don't make things easy on her. We humans are a circus of doubts and anxieties. Play them up! Give us the whole show.

In chapter one of *The Deep End of the Ocean* by Jacquelyn Mitchard, Beth's youngest son, Ben, disappears in a crowded hotel. The next forty pages cover hours, not days. Emotional beat after emotional beat is rendered as Beth goes through the various manifestations of shock, fear, grief, and guilt.

For example, when the detective, Candy Bliss, suggests Beth lie down, Mitchard gives us this paragraph:

> Beth supposed she should lie down; her throat kept filling with nastiness and her stomach roiled. But if she lay down, she wanted to explain to Candy Bliss, who was holding out her hand, it would be deserting Ben. Did Detective Bliss think Ben was lying down? If Beth ate, would he eat? She should not do anything Ben couldn't do or was being prevented from doing. Was he crying? Or wedged in a dangerous and airless place? If she lay down, if she rested, wouldn't Ben feel her relaxing, think she had decided to suspend her scramble toward him, the concentrated thrust of everything in her that she held out to him like a life preserver? Would he relax then, turn in sorrow toward a bad face, because his mama had let him down?

Notice how Mitchard uses physical descriptions that show rather than tell: *throat kept filling with nastiness; stomach roiled.*

She places us in Beth's mind as her thoughts come one after another, accusing her. Then Mitchard goes back to the action of the scene. And so the beats continue.

In Brett Lott's story "Brothers," the beats come mainly through dialogue. During a drive through the desert after picking up a chair for someone, the narrator tries to understand his younger brother: "Tim had been chewing on something since we'd picked up the rocker recliner." What Tim is chewing on is the subject of the story, related through Tim's emotional account of a neighbor's death.

We keep reading to find out what impact this has on the narrator. Does he really know his brother? What will the revelations do to him? Lott keeps up the tension by delaying answers until the end.

To stretch inner tension, ask these questions to get your raw material:

- What is the worst thing from the *inside* that can happen to my character? This encompasses a whole universe of mental stakes. Hint: Look to the character's *fears*.
- What is the worst information my character can receive? Some secret from the past or fact that rocks her world can be stalking her through the scene.
- Have I sufficiently set up the depth of emotion for readers before the scene? We need to care about your Lead characters before we care about their problems.

Stretching the Big and the Small

Think of tension stretching as an elongation of bad times. This can be on a large scale, as in Jeffery Deaver's *A Maiden's Grave*, a novel about a one-day hostage crisis. Each chapter is marked by a clock reading, for example, 11:02 a.m. The chapters then give the full range of dramatic beats.

The tension can also be stretched on a micro level. Usually this happens when you're revising. You come across beats that pass a little too quickly for the rhythm you're trying to create.

In *A Certain Truth*, featuring my early 1900s Los Angeles lawyer, Kit Shannon, I have Kit sharing a meal with the temperance champion Carry Nation. The first draft of the scene had this:

> Their laughter was interrupted by the figure of the Chief of Police, Horace Allen. He stood at their table with one of his uniformed officers. Kit knew immediately this was not a social call.
>
> "Kathleen Shannon." The Chief's voice was thunderous.
>
> "Good evening, Chief."

I felt the moment, for dramatic purposes, needed a little more time. I rewrote it, adding more beats:

> Their laughter was interrupted by the figure of the Chief of Police, Horace Allen. He stood at their table with one of his uniformed officers. Kit knew immediately this was not a social call.
>
> "Kathleen Shannon." The chief's voice was thunderous, causing all conversation to cease within the place.
>
> Kit felt the silence, sensed the social opprobrium flowing her way from the gentile patrons. A pleasant evening was being rudely interrupted, and that was not why people came to the Imperial. "Good evening, Chief."

The best way to get the right amount of tension into your novel is to stretch it as much as possible in your first draft and then look at what you've got.

Go for it, and don't worry about overdoing it or wearing out the reader. You have that wonderful thing called *revision* to save you. If you write *hot*, packing your scenes with physical and emotional tension, you can always revise *cool*, and scale back on rewrite. That's much easier to do than trying to heat things up the second time around.

Of course not every scene should be a big, suspenseful set piece. A novel can sustain only a few of those, and you want them to stand out. But any scene can be stretched beyond its natural comfort zone. Get in the habit of finding the cracks and crevices where troubles lie and burrowing in to see what's there. You may strike gold. And your readers will be thankful for the effort.

Raising the Stakes

In the classic Warner Bros. cartoon *The Scarlet Pumpernickel*, Daffy Duck is earnestly pitching his new script to the unseen Jack Warner. As Daffy tells the story, we see it unfold, performed by the great stock company of Daffy, Porky Pig, Sylvester, and Elmer Fudd.

But it soon becomes clear that Daffy does not have an ending for his movie. Warner presses him. "Then what happens?" Daffy keeps reaching, and Warner keeps asking for more.

In desperation, Daffy says, "The price of foodstuffs skyrocketed!" And we see a picture of a little bitty kreplach on a plate.

Poor Daffy. In his zeal, he forgot that adding any old plot development is not enough to make a gripping story. You've got to have something important on the line, something that matters. Daffy should have been asking himself, *Who cares?* That's a question all novelists must repeat, over and over, as they write. Is there enough going on to make readers care about what happens? What does the Lead character stand to lose if he doesn't solve the central problem of the novel? Is that enough?

If you can create a character worth following and a problem that must be solved—and then along the way raise the stakes even higher—you're going to have the essential elements of a page-turner.

There are three aspects of stakes that you should consider—those flowing from plot, character, and society.

Plot Stakes

Commercial fiction, which is sometimes called *plot driven*, needs to have large stakes. Something that is a threat to the Lead character from the *outside*. Almost always this is in the form of another person trying to do the Lead harm—physically, emotionally, or professionally.

In Jack Schaefer's famous Western, *Shane*, the homesteaders in 1889 Wyoming are a thorn in the side of rancher Luke Fletcher. Fletcher wants them off what he considers his cattle range. The homesteaders, led by Joe Starrett, want to stay.

Here the stakes are high to begin with. On the ranchers' side is a whole way of life, earned by blood and toil over a long period of years. On the other side is a new way of life, a chance to own and work a piece of land, and raise a family. Both values are worth fighting for. A loss by either side is going to severely impact a number of people.

A lot of posturing goes on between the two factions, especially when Starrett hires a mysterious man named Shane to help work his place. Tensions rise until a fight occurs between Shane and Fletcher's men. Joe Starrett intervenes to help, and the fight is won.

Starrett's son, Bob, the narrator of the story, thinks the fight means that Fletcher is finished. But his father explains:

> Fletcher's gone too far to back out now. It's a case of now or never with him. If he can make us run, he'll be setting pretty for a long stretch. If he can't, it'll be only a matter o' time before he's shoved smack out of this valley.

And Shane adds, "By talking big and playing it rough, Fletcher has made this a straight win or lose deal."

Indeed, shortly thereafter a gunfighter named Wilson arrives in town "carrying two guns, big capable forty-fives, in holsters slung fairly low and forward."

So now the stakes have been raised to the highest level—this conflict is going to end with somebody dead.

Stakes can also be raised in a plot by arraying an ever stronger opposition force against the Lead.

Early in James Grippando's *The Pardon*, Jack Swyteck, a lawyer, is being threatened by a man who may be a killer. The stakes are raised when the man murders Jack's former client and sets Jack up as the prime suspect.

Now Jack doesn't have to deal with one man. He's got the police force and the prosecutor's office after him as well.

Naturally, the threat of death is high stakes. But note that the "death" can be professional as well. The down-and-out lawyer who gets one final (seemingly hopeless) case; the disgraced cop who has one last chance to do it right—these are a couple of examples of those who must win or leave the world they know.

Sometime during your plotting—whether you outline extensively or fly by the seat of your pants—spend some time asking questions like these:

- What physical harm can come to my Lead? How far can I take that threat?
- What new forces can come into play against my Lead? What other characters can I introduce that will make things worse? How would these outside forces operate? What tactics would they use?
- Is there some professional duty at stake here? What's the worst thing that can happen to my Lead's career life?

Character Stakes

What goes on inside a character can be just as important as what happens outside. In literary fiction, the stress is usually on this inner aspect. But the question remains the same—what problem is big enough to make the readers care?

In J.D. Salinger's *The Catcher in the Rye*, the danger to the Lead, Holden Caulfield, is not physical but psychological. He needs to find some sort of reason to live in the world, a world occupied primarily by what he deems "phonies."

When he leaves his prep school one night to begin an odyssey through

New York City, it is an obvious quest for meaning. The psychological stakes get raised as the story moves along.

We know from the intensifying language just how perilous this inner search is. "I swear to God I'm a madman," Holden says at one point. And by the end of the book, he just may be.

The inner world of the Lead character is an opportunity for commercial novelists to add more dimension to their stories—by raising the *inner* stakes for their leads. Quite often this comes down to a matter of choice. By sharpening the horns of a dilemma, one can raise the stakes for the character.

In *The Pardon*, Grippando also raises the stakes for the main subplot character. Jack's estranged father is the governor of the state. When it looks like Jack could be convicted of capital murder, the law-and-order governor will have to decide whether to issue a pardon, at the cost of his political life. It's a deeply personal anguish.

In Deborah Raney's *Beneath a Southern Sky*, the Lead, a widow named Daria, is happily remarried and newly pregnant—then discovers that the beloved husband she thought dead has been found alive in the Colombian jungle. Now she's married to two men, each of whom is the father of one of her daughters. Her pregnancy raises the emotional stakes for all involved.

So ponder things like this:

- How can things get more emotionally wrenching for my Lead?
- Is there someone the Lead cares about who can get caught up in the trouble?
- Are there dark secrets from the past that can be revealed?

Societal stakes

When social trouble is big enough, it can raise the stakes by adding a huge layer of complication to the Lead's woes. Readers will wonder whether the Lead's personal problems will worsen because of the dire conditions in her immediate world.

Consider Scarlett O'Hara, whose desire is to get Ashley Wilkes to marry her. The first part of the book is built around her scheme to get Ashley alone at the big barbeque at Twelve Oaks, declare her love, and receive his troth in return.

Her immediate problem is Melanie Hamilton, whom Scarlett finds out is now pledged to Ashley. Scarlett cannot believe that Ashley really loves this mouse and is determined to step in. Her plan fails. Not only does Ashley refuse to leave Melanie, but Scarlett's secret is found out by a snoozing eavesdropper—the rogue Rhett Butler.

Now what to do? As Scarlett considers her setback, explosive news hits the party—war has begun. Ashley, along with all the other young men of the county, will be going off to fight. (Hint: Whenever war breaks out, stakes are raised!)

Scarlett is going to face all the challenges of a woman on the home front, even as she continues to obsess about Ashley.

Use these questions to help you develop your own societal stakes:

- What are the social aspects of the story that swirl around the characters?
- Are they dealing with some huge issue? If not, can you find one?
- What other characters can line up on either side?

To get your novel to that next level of stakes, train yourself to think of deeper tribulation for your Lead. Get really mean. Using questions like the ones in this chapter, create a list of things that can go wrong for your poor character. Stretch yourself at this stage.

Next, take your list of answers and sort them by their degree of trouble, from least to worse. As a general rule you want the trouble to increase as the story moves along.

You now have a "stakes outline," which can be used to invent scenes and turning points for your novel. Of course you don't have to use every bit of trouble, nor the biggest. But at least with a stakes outline you will have a packed storehouse of material to access when you need it.

Come to think of it, skyrocketing foodstuffs could, in the right story, be a massive social problem that makes things a lot worse. My apologies to Daffy. That Duck could write.

HOW TO ENERGIZE A LETHARGIC MIDDLE

It happens to even the best writers. They're writing along, well into Act II, when all of sudden everything starts to crawl. The plot begins to feel like a lazy uncle outstaying his welcome, sitting on the couch and boring you with pointless anecdotes.

How do you pump new life into a plot? We have ways. Here are a few of them:

[1] **Analyze the stakes.** Looking to the tips in this chapter, ask yourself

what the main character will lose if he does not achieve his objective. Unless it is something that threatens tremendous loss, either physically or emotionally, readers won't care what happens.

[2] Strengthen the adhesive. What is it that bonds the Lead and the opposition together? If the adhesive is not strong enough, the readers will wonder why the plot should continue at all. Look at the possible adhesives in this chapter and find at least one that fits your plot.

[3] Add another level of complication. In Robert Crais's thriller *Hostage*, burned-out hostage negotiator Jeff Talley is suddenly faced with a tense standoff in an otherwise placid bedroom community.

Fine and dandy on its own, but Crais then adds another level: The hostage inside the house has in his possession incriminating financial evidence against the mob because he is the mob's accountant! The mob needs to get that evidence before the cops do.

To put pressure on Talley, the mob kidnaps his ex-wife and daughter and holds *them* hostage. This added level of complication supercharges the entire book.

[4] Add another character. Not just any character, but one that will make the Lead's life that much more difficult. It might be a surprise character from the past, who knows something the Lead wants to keep hidden.

Or it could be a character who, on the surface, supports the Lead. But that support is not helpful for one reason or another.

A love interest can work for added complication, too.

[5] Add another subplot. Use this one sparingly. Subplots (see chapter eight) must be organic and relate to the main plot. You don't want to tack one on that seems merely to take up space.

A romantic subplot, as mentioned above, is always a possibility.

Think also of family issues the Lead may have. Or something mysterious—the shadow subplot—which is haunting or hunting the Lead.

[6] Push on through the Wall. Sometimes, the Act II Problem is merely writer's exhaustion. A temporary loss of confidence. Maybe even the fear that what you're writing is total garbage.

This is the Wall, and it should help you to know that most novelists hit it at some point in their first drafts.

For me, it is around the thirty-thousand-word mark. I get there and suddenly think all the worst things about my novel: the idea stinks and is beyond redemption; my writing is lame, the characters uninteresting, and the plot virtually nonexistent. I can't possibly go on. Career over. The anxiety is only magnified when there is an advance already half spent.

Here is a simple prescription I've come up with:

- Take one whole day off from writing.
- Try to spend some time at a peaceful location—a park, a lakeshore, a deserted parking lot. Anywhere you can be alone.
- Spend at least thirty minutes sitting without doing anything. Don't read, and don't listen to music. Breathe deeply. Hear the world around you.
- Do something for pure fun. See a movie. Shop for hours without buying. Eat ice cream.
- In the evening, drink a glass of warm milk and fall asleep reading one of your favorite writers.
- First thing the next day, write at least three hundred words on your novel, no matter what. Don't edit, and don't slow down. Just write. You'll start to feel excited again.
- Push on until you complete your first draft.

And know this: Your first draft is never as bad as you thought it was at the Wall.

HOW TO TRIM AN OVERWEIGHT MIDDLE

Here we have the opposite problem. Instead of wondering what to put in, we have too much going on. The novel is starting to sink under its own weight.

If that's your conundrum, rejoice! Almost always, cutting stuff improves your book (see chapter eleven for more on revision).

Here are three ways you can get a leaner, meaner Act II:

[1] **Combine or cut characters.** Is it possible to take two characters who are serving two different purposes (or somewhat overlapping in their purposes) and combine them?

Look to the Lead's allies first. If there are too many people on his side, it's a good idea to combine because a novel stresses opposition.

Or it may just be that a character has to go. Sometimes this happens with minor characters we fall in love with. We start to give these colorful walk-ons more and more stage time. And like ham actors, they take it.

You may need to politely ask them to leave the show. If they put up a fight, maybe you can write another novel, this time about them.

Minor characters love that.

[2] Absorb a subplot. In the same way, there may be a subplot that isn't really adding to the plot. The actions may interest you, but are they distracting to most readers?

Combine the best parts of a soggy subplot to create a stronger main plot.

[3] Trim the dullness. Look to your scenes themselves. Is there enough conflict? Is there too much talk without tension? Are the reaction scenes lasting too long?

Recalling Hitchcock's Axiom, put yourself in the editor's chair. Constantly ask yourself if there is enough interest in what you're writing to hold an editor's attention. Is there any place he would be tempted to put it down and go get lunch?

Cut that part to the bone or altogether if need be.

Act II is the biggest challenge the novelist faces. But if you have laid a solid foundation through the LOCK system and you use the principles in this chapter, you'll find you actually enjoy the writing. You're creating a plot that works.

EXERCISE 1

Define how your Lead will die, either physically, professionally, or psychologically, if she does not achieve her objective. If you can't, ask yourself if the objective is truly crucial to the Lead's well-being. Find a way to make it so important readers will understand why the objective must be achieved.

EXERCISE 2

Deepen your opposition character. Find an answer to the question, "Why do I love this character?" Have you given him justifications for what he does? Is he as strong, or stronger than the Lead? If not, make him so.

EXERCISE 3

Select a scene from your novel that is fraught with conflict or tension. Isolate the part of the scene where the tension is at its peak. It may be a few paragraphs or a few pages. Whatever it is, try to stretch the tension further. Use *each* of the tools suggested in this chapter to accomplish this. Come back to the scene a day or two later and read it again. Does it hold your interest throughout? You can always cut back if you need to, but most often you'll find that you've found a way to add to the reading experience in a positive manner.

EXERCISE 4

What are the stakes in the novel? Look at each aspect—plot, character, and society. If you are missing one, consider adding it to the mix. And then consider how you can raise each one to its maximum level in the course of the novel.

EXERCISE 5

Reread a novel that didn't work for you. As you do, play the role of editor and look for ways to improve it, based on what you've read in this chapter. Write a long letter to the author (you don't have to mail it) suggesting the changes you'd like to see before submitting the manuscript to the publishing committee.

chapter 6

[ENDINGS]

Your first chapter sells your book. Your last chapter sells your NEXT book.
—MICKEY SPILLANE

A weak ending can ruin an otherwise wonderful book.

A strong ending can redeem an otherwise mediocre book.

So take your endings seriously. Wrap up your books so they knock your readers out. That is how you make a writing career as a novelist.

One of my favorite thriller writers is David Morrell (he's also the author of a terrific book on the craft, *Lessons From a Lifetime of Writing*). His novel *Burnt Sienna* is one of his best. If the test of a thriller is its can't-put-it-down quotient, this book passes the test.

But what truly stands out, in my view, is the non-Hollywood and quite poignant ending. I won't give it away now. Read the book to see how a master craftsman deepens the reading experience.

A great ending does two things above all else: First, it feels perfect for the kind of novel it is appended to. Second, it surprises the reader. It is not so familiar the reader has the feeling he's seen it somewhere before.

Why are endings so hard? Because the novelist is like the plate spinners I used to watch on the old *Ed Sullivan Show*. These guys would have seven or eight plates spinning at the same time, sort of like a wild Act II, and then they'd have to come up with a big finish that got all the plates off safely and with a little flourish.

Your plot will have lots of plates spinning by the time you get to the end. You need to get them off safely. You need a little flourish. And you need to do it in a way that is not predictable. You don't want readers finishing your book thinking, "I've seen that so many times before."

Which brings up another challenge: With each passing year—with every new book, movie, and television show—more endings are thrown out into popular culture.

What was once a fresh approach may now actually be getting a little stale. We all know the old *we-think-the-bad-guy-is-dead-but-he-really-is-not-and-comes-back-for-one-last-stab-at-the-hero ending*. It wasn't old in the movies twenty years ago. But if a filmmaker tries it now, everybody in the audience is going to be thinking, "He's not really dead, and if the hero turns his back he's an idiot."

That's why endings are hard, and why we need to work on them with all the creative juices we can muster.

KNOCKOUT ENDINGS

The most exciting boxing matches are those where it looks like one fighter is going to lose, only to draw on reserves of strength to deliver a knockout blow to his opponent.

Do that with your novel. Maintain the tension in the story until the last possible moment. As you near the end, it should look as if the opposition is the one who will win. He has everything going for him. The Lead is up against the ropes.

Only when the Lead reaches deep within and makes her move will the knockout blow be thrown.

Near the ending, you want the readers to ask, "Will the Lead fight or run away? Will the forces marshaled against the Lead simply be too much for her to face?"

To stay and fight, your Lead will have to call upon moral or physical courage, just as in the examples below:

- In *Jaws*, Brody must finally head out to sea and, with help, kill the shark. He does.
- In *The Rainmaker*, Rudy must go all the way through a trial even though he has no experience. He wins.
- In Dean Koontz's *Intensity*, Chyna must find a way to kill her tormentor. She finds it.
- In *The Silence of the Lambs*, Clarice stays with the case in order to stop Buffalo Bill. She stops him.

Readers like to have the hero decisively defeat the opposing force. But that doesn't always have to be the case.

A good example is Jonathan Harr's *A Civil Action*, which we discussed in chapter four. The nonfiction book tells the story of lawyer Jan Schlichtmann's obsession to get justice for the residents of a small town whose water supply was poisoned by two huge companies. Of course, the other side, with unlimited funds, does everything to crush him, both personally and professionally. They do. But we are left with a sense of awe at how long the hero stood up under the gun.

ADDING THE *AH!* AND THE *UH-OH!*

There is one more thing you need to do to leave the reader with the ultimate reading experience. I call these the "Ah" and the "Uh-Oh."

You get the "Ah" once the main action of the story is wrapped up. With the knockout blow administered, you need to give the reader a final scene in which something from the hero's *personal* life is resolved.

In *Midnight*, Sam Booker has brought down the villain's evil plan. But the book ends with Sam returning to try to make amends with his rebellious son. Sam embraces him, and even though their issues aren't resolved, at least the process has begun. "That was the wonderful thing," goes the book's last line. "It *had* begun."

This emotional resolution in the Lead's personal life makes us go "Ah." It's like the perfect last note in a great piece of music. Look at the very last scenes in a number of thrillers, and you'll see how often this is done.

Dickens strikes this chord of personal resolution at the of *David Copperfield*:

> And now, as I close my task, subduing my desire to linger yet, these faces fade away. But one face, shining on me like a heavenly light by which I see all other objects, is above them and beyond them all. And that remains.
>
> I turn my head, and see it, in its beautiful serenity, beside me. My lamp burns low, and I have written far into the night; but the dear presence, without which I were nothing, bears me company.
>
> Oh Agnes, oh my soul, so may thy face be by me when I close my life indeed; so may I, when realities are melting from me like the shadows which I now dismiss, still find thee near me, pointing upward!

A book can also leave the reader with a sense of foreboding, perhaps even uttering, "Uh-oh," as he turns the last page. Charles Wilson's *Embryo* has such an ending. The book details the search for a mad doctor and the process he uses to bring forth children outside the womb. They become evil children who actually *smile* when contemplating how bad they can be.

The main story is resolved when the hero and love interest end up with what they think is a normal child. All is well. But in the final scene their little girl, Pauline, is alone outside. She finds some matches and, curious, lights one. She pitches it and it lands on her dog's back.

> He suddenly jumped and whirled and tried to look back across his shoulder at what had stung him. Pauline realized what she had done and looked sad for a moment.
> And then she smiled.

Uh-oh! Wilson has left us to contemplate the horror starting all over again.

CHOOSE YOUR ENDING

There are three basic types of endings shown in the graph below are: (1) the Lead gets his objective, a positive ending; (2) we don't know if the Lead will get his desire, an ambiguous ending; and (3) the Lead loses his objective, a negative ending.

A positive ending is found in *Jaws*. Brody kills the shark.

An ambiguous ending is found in *The Catcher in the Rye*. We don't know if Holden Caulfield will be able to make it in the world after he leaves the sanitarium.

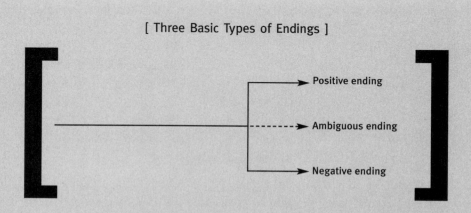

[Three Basic Types of Endings]

Positive ending

Ambiguous ending

Negative ending

The test of a good ambiguous ending is that it causes strong feeling, feels right, and can generate discussion. Indeed, that's what happened with Holden. Take the haunting last line: "Don't ever tell anybody anything. If you do, you start missing everybody."

Will Holden therefore detach and never speak of anything deeply again? Will he then become a "phony" like those he deplores? Or is this some sort of Zen *koan* that shows a step toward a new grasping of life, a healing through trial?

A negative ending occurs in *Gone With the Wind*. Scarlett loses her true love, Rhett. (Margaret Mitchell cleverly added a *note* of ambiguity, with Scarlett thinking surely she will be able to get him back.)

To the three basic endings, we can add a couple of complexities, which are outlined in the graph below. For it may be that in gaining his desire, the Lead really has a negative *result*. Similarly, the Lead may lose his desire, yet gain something better.

An example of the first type, a gaining of desire but at a terrible cost, is found in Jack London's *Martin Eden*. Human achievement and Nietzche's will to power do not bring Eden what he's looking for. Rather, life as he chose to live it is "an unbearable thing." He jumps off a ship into the ocean:

> He filled his lungs with air, filled them full. This supply would take him far down. He turned over and went down head first, swimming with all his strength and all his will. Deeper and deeper he went. His eyes were open, and he

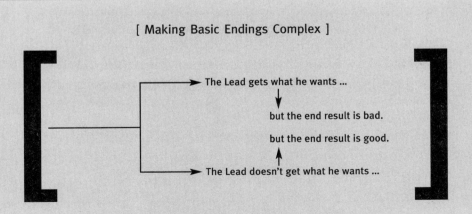

[Making Basic Endings Complex]

The Lead gets what he wants ...

but the end result is bad.

but the end result is good.

The Lead doesn't get what he wants ...

watched the ghostly, phosphorescent trails of the darting bonita. As he swam, he hoped that they would not strike at him, for it might snap the tension of his will. But they did not strike, and he found time to be grateful for this last kindness of life.

Down, down, he swam till his arms and leg grew tired and hardly moved. He knew that he was deep. The pressure on his ear-drums was a pain, and there was a buzzing in his head. His endurance was faltering, but he compelled his arms and legs to drive him deeper until his will snapped and the air drove from his lungs in a great explosive rush. The bubbles rubbed and bounded like tiny balloons against his cheeks and eyes as they took their upward flight. Then came pain and strangulation. This hurt was not death, was the thought that oscillated through his reeling consciousness. Death did not hurt. It was life, the pangs of life, this awful, suffocating feeling; it was the last blow life could deal him.

His wilful hands and feet began to beat and churn about, spasmodically and feebly. But he had fooled them and the will to live that made them beat and churn. He was too deep down. They could never bring him to the surface. He seemed floating languidly in a sea of dreamy vision. Colors and radiances surrounded him and bathed him and pervaded him. What was that? It seemed a lighthouse; but it was inside his brain—a flashing, bright white light. It flashed swifter and swifter. There was a long rumble of sound, and it seemed to him that he was falling down a vast and interminable stairway. And somewhere at the bottom he fell into darkness. That much he knew. He had fallen into darkness. And at the instance he knew, he ceased to know.

What about the other kind, the loss that is really a gain? I must use an example from *Casablanca*, which has perhaps the most famous ending in film.

As the Lead, what is Rick Blaine's desire? Simple. He wants Ilsa, who is married to war hero Lazlo. By the end of the film, Rick can have Ilsa; she's consented to go away with him, but Rick gives her up and insists she go off with her husband.

He actually sacrifices his greatest desire for a greater good. The war effort. And for a marriage. Had he taken Ilsa away from Lazlo, it would have been at a moral cost.

So Rick is freed from the ghost of Ilsa ("We'll always have Paris"), comes back into the fight, and joins the human family again. And he gets a new friend in the bargain, the little French prefect, Louis.

Sacrifice

What makes the ending of *Casablanca* so popular?

The element of sacrifice. Rick gives up his object of desire for a greater good.

Why is that theme so powerful? Because it is wired into our cultural consciousness. In giving up our own well-being for a greater good, we tap into the deepest yearnings of man.

As Viktor E. Frankl, author of *Man's Search for Meaning*, argued, man is on a lifelong search for meaning. Meaning does not come from isolation. Meaning is a community thing.

When someone sacrifices himself for the good of someone else, that is powerful on a gut level.

In our Western culture, the idea of sacrifice is embedded in our foundational texts and myths. Abraham was willing to sacrifice Isaac. For that he received a reward, becoming blessed by God.

Yet even Ayn Rand, the atheistic voice of "rational selfishness," included this philosophy in her novels.

The Fountainhead is about a man who is willing to sacrifice his own career and work, rather than let either be changed by the collective. In *Atlas Shrugged*, her heroine, Dagny Taggart, gives up the power and prestige of her railroad to uphold the dignity of human worth.

Whether you buy Ayn Rand's philosophy or not, as a fiction writer, she tapped into the right fictional dynamic.

In the *final choice* type of ending, the hero is on the horns of a terrible dilemma. He can choose a course that gets him to his objective, but at a moral cost. Or he can "do the right thing" but lose the most important goal, the thing he's hoped for throughout the novel.

As illustrated above, in *Casablanca*, Rick sacrifices his love for Ilsa for the greater good.

In the *final battle* type of ending, the hero has to sacrifice his own safety and well-being. He has very good reasons not to stay and fight. He's probably going to lose.

The great Frank Capra film, *Mr. Smith Goes to Washington*, is a perfect example. Jefferson Smith (played by James Stewart) is appointed to the United States Senate on a fluke, to be a simpleton puppet of a state machine. He just doesn't know it.

When he finds out that his dream of setting aside land for a boys' camp conflicts with the plans of the machine, he discovers what a stooge he's been.

When Smith makes an attempt to buck the machine, it kicks into high gear to destroy him by getting him booted from the Senate on a trumped-up fraud charge.

There is no way he's going to be able to beat this.

But with the help of a savvy politico (played by Jean Arthur), Smith is convinced to give it one more try. He has to sacrifice his fear to do this. He has to put himself into harm's way.

Two Types of Sacrifice

Here is a simple comparison of the sacrifices in each of the two principle endings. Notice what kind of courage is required for each:

FINAL CHOICE	FINAL BATTLE
Lead sacrifices his *goal*	Lead sacrifices his *safety*
Moral courage	Physical courage

TWIST ENDINGS

So how do authors come up with those fantastic twist endings, the ones you don't see coming but sense are inevitable? The ones that leave you breathless and thrilled and unable to wait until the author's next book?

I'll tell you. I don't know.

I wonder if the authors themselves know. I suspect some do, but I also believe this is not a part of plotting that can be reduced to a formula.

However, I do believe there are some things you can do that will help your own inner writer generate possible twists for the ending.

First, you probably already have an ending in mind. You've been writing toward that ending, especially if you prefer to work with outlines (see chapter ten for more on outlining systems). And that's okay. Keep writing.

But as you get closer to the end of your first draft, pause and come up with ten alternative endings. Yes, I said ten.

And I don't mean take four weeks to do this. It should take less than thirty minutes. Brainstorm. The quicker the better. Let yourself go, and don't worry about justifying every one of them.

Once you've got your list, let your imagination cook the possibilities for a day or two.

Come back to your list and take the top four. Deepen them a little bit. Let them cook some more.

Finally, choose the one alternative ending that seems to work best as a twist—not an alternative ending at all, but an added surprise.

Figure out how to work that into your ending, and then go back into your novel and justify it somehow by planting little clues here and there.

There is your twist ending.

It is impossible to get more specific about technique here because every plot is going to be different. Remember that an ending must resolve all of the important plot issues, and those are going to vary from book to book.

Draw on the plot material sloshing around in your head. When it comes time to contemplate a little twist, you'll be ready. Give it some time and go for it just the way Harlan Coben does on the very last page of *Tell No One*. Trickster!

TYING UP LOOSE INFORMATION

You may get to the end of your novel and find some loose threads hanging. There are a couple of things you can do to tie these up and prevent an infamous anti-climactic ending.

First, determine whether these loose threads are crucial or ancillary. What happened to a minor character's pants is probably not crucial to know. What he did with the stolen money probably is. There is no hard and fast way to do this. You just have to have a sense that your readers will be more concerned about some things and only vaguely interested in others.

But vague interest can turn to real frustration if those loose ends aren't tidied up.

If a loose thread is something major, you need to create a major scene, or a series of scenes to deal with it. This might necessitate extensive rewriting, but that's okay. Do it. Make it work.

With minor threads, it is often enough to have a character explain what happened. For example, in some of my law thrillers I'll have a character mention the legal fate of a character who did something bad in the middle of the book: "Oh, and they caught Smithers trying to escape into Canada. He goes on trial next month."

Another technique is the short epilogue, though this must be well written and not merely an information dump.

In *Gone for Good*, author Harlan Coben ties up a major loose end with an epilogue that is a short excerpt from a newspaper story. It gives the feeling of real resolution without "author intrusion."

The best way to catch loose ends is to have a couple of people read your manuscript. If they end up asking you questions like, "Hey, whatever happened to this guy?" or "What about the submarine they found off the coast of Maine in chapter two?" then you know you have some loose ends.

LAST-PAGE RESONANCE

You want to leave your readers with a last page that makes the ending more than satisfying. You want it to be memorable, to stay with readers after the book is closed.

This is a matter of *resonance*. In dictionary terms, it is like the musical effect that comes from an *intensification and prolongation of sound that is pleasing to the ear*. It's that last note in a magnificent symphony that produces a feeling that affixes itself to the soul.

Working to make your last page like that is worth every ounce of your effort. It's the last impression, what psychologists call the *recency effect*. Your audience will judge your book largely by the feeling they have most recently, namely, *the end*. Leave a lasting impression and you will build a readership.

Think about the following.

Language

Each word must be carefully chosen here. Not that this isn't a consideration elsewhere in your novel, but it is especially crucial here. Sometimes the words are clipped and to the point, as in this example from J.D. Salinger's *The Catcher in the Rye*: "Don't ever tell anybody anything. If you do, you start missing everybody."

Sometimes a bit of the poet is called for, as in this excerpt from *Jewel*, by Bret Lott:

> Only letters, rows of them, the first letter of her name. She's written thousands of these before, filled tablet and tablet and tablet, but on this night, they are

enough. More than enough, the sky now black outside the kitchen window, the train tracks gone quiet until sometime late tonight, when the house will shudder once again, and God might wake me from my sleep, bring me to the bedroom window to see the train moving outside, that black shadow moving forward on into the night and leading me away from here, from Brenda Kay alone and asleep in the next room, from the rest of my children, from the ghosts of the lives I've been blessed enough and cursed enough to have led.

Only letters, labored, indifferent, yet full as she can make them of herself. Letters, I finally hear, singing with all they have, scores of them swirling round me in voices I'll never understand, but beautiful all the same, god smiling and smiling and smiling.

Dialogue

Often, dialogue works as a resonant ending, so long as it doesn't feel tacked on. How do you avoid that? By planting, earlier in the novel, similar dialogue.

In one of my novels, *The Nephilim Seed*, I have a bounty hunter helping a mother find her kidnapped daughter. He has a rather loose approach to his work. At one point, the mother asks him what they are going to do to get out of a particularly bad situation. The response: *"Improvise," he said.*

As the novel progresses, they are drawn to each other, but each has personal reasons for not wanting to get involved. At the end, however, the mutual attraction can't be denied. The last lines:

> He took her hand then, and faced her. "I've been alone for so long," he said. He didn't have to go on. Janice knew that this was his way of asking her if there was any way she could find a place in her life for him. In his voice and look were the collected vulnerabilities of a man who had been fleeing from life for years and didn't quite know what stopping would mean for him.
>
> "It's been so long I guess I just don't know what to do next," he said.
>
> Janice smiled. She reached her hand behind his neck and pulled him gently toward her, kissing him softly on the cheek. It was warm and a little stubbly, but resilient. Then she whispered something in his ear.
>
> "Improvise," she said.

Description

If there is a particular description of setting or character that is just right, this can make for a perfect ending.

In Stephen King's *The Girl Who Loved Tom Gordon*, the rescued girl, Trisha, taps the visor of her cap and points her index finger up at the ceiling, a gesture that resonates because it has been explained earlier in the novel. She doesn't have to say a thing for the meaning to be clear.

Or a description can carry haunting reminders of what's been, and what may be to come. As in Daphne du Maurier's *Rebecca*:

> He drove faster, much faster. We topped the hill before us and saw Lanyon lying in a hollow at our feet. There to the left of us was the silver streak of the river, widening to the estuary at Kerrith six miles away. The road to Manderley lay ahead. There was no moon. The sky above our heads was inky black. But the sky on the horizon was not dark at all. It was shot with crimson, like a splash of blood. And the ashes blew towards us with the salt wind from the sea.

A Summing Up

There is a way to sum up the feelings of a character without making it seem like author intrusion. As we saw earlier, this is exactly how Dean Koontz does it in *Midnight*. Sam Booker has had a hard time with his teenage son, Scott. After all that has gone on in the novel, Sam returns home with people he has come to care for, and is able to embrace his son. Both begin to cry:

> Looking over Scott's shoulder, he saw that Tessa and Chrissie had stepped into the room. They were crying too. In their eyes he saw an awareness that matched his, a recognition that the battle for Scott had only begun.
>
> But it *had* begun. That was the wonderful thing. It *had* begun.

AVOID THE RUSH

It is a tough slog to write a novel, so it's understandable that near the finish line writers might want to take a short cut.

Sometimes writers rush through their endings because they're so anxious to finish the novel after being at it so long. Professional writers working on deadline are especially prone to this.

How can you avoid getting tired and rushing your ending? Here are some suggestions:

[1] **Dream.** The most original material in our entire writer's body dwells in dreamland. And the nice thing is it can happen all the time. You can dream at night involuntarily, or you can daydream at will.

So as you go through your novel, carve out times when you allow your imagination to feed you images, even if you already have mapped out an ending.

Get in the habit of jotting down your dreams when you get up in the morning. Keep a dream journal. Ask yourself how that dream might relate to your ending. Maybe it won't have any direct bearing, but it will give you a starting point for thinking more deeply about the ending.

You can encourage daydreams by listening to music. I like movie soundtracks for their various moods. Do some daydreaming and make notes. What you come up with may be the perfect image or scene for your ending.

If you do this periodically when writing your novel, you won't feel like you have to rush toward the ending.

[2] **Think big.** Don't pull your punches at the end. Pour everything you have into it. You can always scale back during the rewrite. But you need good material to work with, and that comes from being passionate and working at optimum creativity on your ending.

[3] **Take your time.** This requires discipline. Don't back yourself into a tight deadline corner. If you need to take a daylong break before you begin writing your ending, have the flexibility to take it. I don't recommend longer than a day because you want to keep the flow of your material coursing through your veins. But you don't want to feel like you have to break the sound barrier in order to finish.

EXERCISE 1

Reread the last couple of chapters from five novels you love. Analyze each of them. Is it closed-ended? Up or down? Does it have a twist? Why does it work for you? This will help you understand your own writing preferences.

EXERCISE 2

What sort of ending do you have in mind for your novel? Try writing the climactic scene. This does not have to be the scene you'll actually use, but it may be. At the very least it will get your writer's mind working on the end and allow yourself to understand your characters more deeply. Use this information in your writing.

Come up with two or three alternative endings. List as many as ten one-line possibilities. Then choose the two or three most promising, and sketch out the scenes in summary form (250 words maximum). If an alternative seems stronger than the one you've had in mind, use it. Keep the old ending as a possible twist at the end. Or keep your original ending, and use one of the alternatives as a possible twist.

Make a list of all the loose ends in your novel. You can do this as you write by keeping a separate document and recording the items as they come up. Create a strategy for tying them up with plot developments, minor characters, or using a newspaper story.

chapter 7

[SCENES]

The novel of a thousand pages begins with a single scene.

—PROVERB IN WAITING

A good plot is about disturbance to characters' inner and outer lives.

Scenes are what we use to illustrate and dramatize those disturbances. Scenes are the essential building blocks of plot. And a plot is only as strong as its weakest block.

Readers may be willing to forgive other writing sins if they are reading scenes that plop them down on an emotional roller coaster. On the other hand, flat scenes are like the trams that take us to and from the park—slow, crowded, and hardly worth the ride. And readers aren't likely to take a ride like that more than once.

So make your scenes count, every one.

WHAT IS A SCENE?

A scene is a fictional unit. If you string scenes together and they somehow relate, you can write a novel.

If you can make each one of your scenes truly unforgettable, you can write an unforgettable novel.

An unforgettable scene has something fresh. It has something surprising, and emotionally intense. It has characters we care about doing things that we *must* watch. You create unforgettable scenes by freshening what is forgettable, making the scenes come alive with tension and originality.

Write a scene for all it's worth, and then look at it again later. Change the dull parts. Try something new.

Most often, the best way to create an unforgettable scene is to intensify the *clash*. Two characters oppose each other. They have the strongest possible reasons to do so.

THE FOUR CHORDS OF A SCENE

Scenes do four things. I call these the *four chords of fiction*.

The two major chords are: (1) action and (2) reaction.

The two minor chords are: (1) setup and (2) deepening.

These chords are often played together. Action and reaction tend to dominate, with the minor chords dropping in.

But these four chords will enable you to write any scene to serve any purpose in your plot.

Let's also distinguish between a *scene* and a *beat* (both of these terms come from the theater). A scene is the longer unit. Much of the time a scene takes place in a single location, and almost always is played out in real time. If you change location or jump ahead in time, you may jar the reader—but a scene can also be designed to do just that.

A beat is a smaller unit within a scene.

In *The Wizard of Oz*, there is the scene where Dorothy is confronted by the Cowardly Lion. The scene begins with threat and ends with the lion's agreement to join the group on the way to Oz. There is obviously action and conflict. But there is also an emotional beat after Dorothy slaps the lion's nose. And it deepens the character of the lion.

Let's take a closer look at the chords:

Action

Action happens when a character does something in order to attain his main objective. In a given scene, he has a *scene purpose*.

A scene purpose may be anything that is a step toward achieving the story goal.

A lawyer wants to prove his client's innocence. He goes to the home of a witness for an interview. His purpose in that scene is to get information that may help his client.

That's action.

But a scene needs conflict, or it will be dull.

So the witness doesn't want to talk to the lawyer. Now we have confrontation (an essential element of the LOCK system), and we can write an action scene.

Commercial fiction will feel like it is mostly action scenes.

Here is a straight action scene from a novel of mine called *Final Witness* (it was easier to grant myself permission to reprint than jump through financial and legal hoops to get access to another novel. I beg the reader's indulgence). The point-of-view character in this scene is a Russian immigrant who has built up a nice little life for himself in America with a bit of trafficking in drugs:

> Now, sitting in stocking feet in the living room of his own stylish home, he could pop in a little platter and watch virtually anything he wanted.
>
> Tonight it was *Independence Day*.
>
> Sarah was out at her weekly social gathering. Dimitri was proud of her accomplishments, too. ... She had become a fixture in the upscale community where they both lived. Best of all, she didn't ask detailed questions about his enterprises. They were a perfect fit.
>
> With a vodka in hand Dimitri clicked the remote and started the movie. ...

[A simple objective to start. A man wants to watch a movie. He's having a quiet night at home.]

> He thought he heard a sound from the garage just after the credits finished. It was a thump of some kind, as if someone had dropped a soft bag on the floor. But no one could be in the garage, fixed as it was with a double security system. No one except Sarah could get inside without tripping the alarm.
>
> Maybe she was home early. No, it was too early. She hadn't been gone more than half an hour. ...
>
> Something told him he wasn't alone. It was instinct, born of the Soviet system where someone was always looking over your shoulder.
>
> Dimitri Chekhov hadn't felt that in a long time, but he felt it now.

[An obstacle arises to his objective. A feeling that he is not alone.]

> "Sarah?" he called.
>
> No answer.
>
> He got up from his easy chair and turned toward the front of his house. There was only darkness and shadow. Again, his mind told him no one could be inside. He had the finest security system money could buy. He needed it. The business he was in was not free from cutthroat competition—literally. ... But his house was secure. He decided to sweep through the house once, put his fears behind him, and get back to the talking toys.
>
> He had a .38 in the antique desk in his study. He went for it just in case. As he walked through the hallway he flicked on the lights. No sudden image of an intruder. Nothing but cold emptiness. ...

Feeling more confident than fearful, he strode toward the kitchen.

[Action taken to overcome the obstacle, which is his fear.]

> He turned on the lights and, as he expected, saw only the glistening tile and pine of his wife's newly remodeled kitchen. ...
>
> A hand covered his face and pulled his head back. A searing pain shot through his neck. Dimitri felt another hand grab the gun from him, twisting his wrists until he thought they might break. He was pulled backward, off his feet, dragged across the kitchen floor. ...

[The confrontation now is physical.]

> Dimitri pumped his arms, trying to hit his assailant with an elbow. He made contact with the body, but with hardly any force. He tried to twist out of the grasp but the man snapped his head back again, causing incredible pain. In the next instant Dimitri felt himself being shoved in a chair, and rope being thrown around him.
>
> The hand on his face released him for an instant. But before Dimitri could turn his head a heavy cloth was snapped over his eyes and pulled tight. Dimitri tried to move his arms, but the rope restrained him. It took only a few seconds more before he was completely incapacitated and blind to the world. ...
>
> One of the men turned his chair around. He heard activity on the other side of the garage, as if the other man were moving something.
>
> "You can have it all," Dimitri said. "Both of you. I'll leave. I'll take my wife and go back to New York. I won't come back."
>
> The only sound he heard was the tinny knock of a large can of some kind. And then he knew, suddenly, the whole thing. As he cried out, "Don't do this!" he felt the gasoline being poured on his head, smelled the sickening smell. ...
>
> Then Dimitri felt the sodden blindfold being lifted from his head. He blinked, his eyes burning from the gas. He coughed as the fumes assaulted his lungs. Shaking his head, he tried to focus. The lights were on, blindingly bright. Sensing his assailants behind him, he turned his head, but couldn't see them.
>
> He looked forward, finally able to make out images, and saw someone sitting across from him. Perhaps one of the men, ready to talk, to negotiate. Perhaps they were not unreasonable men after all.
>
> And then Dimitri Chekhov screamed. It came through muffled, the thick rope in his mouth muffling his sound.
>
> Dimitri screamed again.

In a chair, secured with ropes, was the lifeless body of his wife. Her head hung limply to one side. ...

He jerked himself violently in his chair, tipping himself over, falling hard on the concrete. His head hit with sudden force. He almost blacked out. He wished then for death. He cried out once more.

Then he closed his eyes and began to cry. When the flames came, instantly covering his entire body, it was almost a relief. Dimitri Chekhov did not scream again.

[The prompt at the end: Who was behind this grisly death?]

Reaction

A reaction scene is how a Lead character feels emotionally when something (usually bad) happens to him.

The lawyer doesn't get anything helpful from the witness. In fact, the witness says she saw his client pull the trigger at point blank range.

Now the lawyer is going to have to mull that one over. How does he feel about it? What's he going to do about it?

When he finally decides what he's going to do, you can write another action scene.

A literary novel may feel like a lot of reaction scenes because they are generally more about the interior life of a character.

Reaction is often done in beats. Here is a short reaction beat from my novel, *Final Witness*. Rachel Ybarra is a paralegal who is helping on a big case at the United States Attorney's Office. A reporter named Stefanos has made her acquaintance and told her she must meet with him. We get a peak into Rachel's thought process here:

Rachel arrived at the marina at half past six. She parked on the street near the Red Lobster, grabbed her briefcase and checked it. She had a legal notepad and a hand-held tape recorder inside.

Stefanos had told her they would meet at his office, but had to connect first by the seafood restaurant. Wind was whipping off the ocean as the sun set in the west, casting an orange wake across Marina del Rey and the entire southern California coast. Rachel thought momentarily how nice it would be to live near the beach. The glory of creation, the cleansing of the sea breeze, the purity of it—what a lovely contrast it would be to the cold lines and dark corners of downtown.

The thought of peace brought on a sudden urge to jump in her car and drive away. What was she doing here? She had no business getting involved at the investigatory level on a case as big as Supevsky.

[Internal questioning.]

But she gave herself two reasons for staying. The first was to find out why she was in danger. The second was to see if there was really something Stefanos had to help the Supevsky case. In her mind, the latter reason was the most important. She wanted to help Lakewood get his case back. She wanted another chance.

[Her justifications.]

Her chance came walking up from the side of the restaurant a few moments later. Stefanos wore a dark red windbreaker and blue jeans, looking more like a weekend sailor than anything else. He smiled and waved, then indicated to Rachel to walk his way.

"Thanks for coming," he said, shaking her hand.

Placing the Reaction Beat

You can put a *reaction beat* in the middle of an action scene so we know how the character is feeling. Dean Koontz's *Intensity* is pretty much a nonstop cat-and-mouse game with a killer. Chyna, the Lead, is in a store, trying to avoid being seen:

She could not at first see the killer, who was at one with the night in his black raincoat. But then he moved, wading through the darkness toward the motor home.

Even if he glanced back, he wouldn't be able to see her in the dimly lighted store. Her heart thundered anyway as she stepped into the open area between the heads of the three aisles and the cashiers' counter.

The photograph of Ariel was no longer on the floor. She wished that she could believe it had never existed.

The last line is a reaction beat, a moment of reflection in the midst of intense action (thus the title of the novel).

These major chords, action and reaction, were called *scene* and *sequel* by writing teachers Dwight Swain and Jack M. Bickham. They allow the narrative to unfold in a logical fashion.

Character takes action, is frustrated by conflict, and usually ends up with a setback. He reacts to this development, thinks things over, and decides on another action.

It is not necessary to ping pong between these two chords every time. As shown above, you can place reaction (or sequel) as a beat within action. There are other variations (see Bickham's *Scene & Structure*). But if you handle action and reaction well, your plot will move along smartly.

Setup

Setup scenes, or beats, are those units that must occur in order for subsequent scenes to make sense.

All novels need a certain amount of setup.

We have to know who the Lead character is, what he does, and why he does it. We have to see how he gets into whatever predicament is going to dominate the book.

Further, there may need to be some setup beats in the course of the story.

How, then, do you do this without writing dull exposition?

You simply build in a problem, however slight, to the setup scene. It can be anything from the character feeling anxious, to an argument, to a problem that must be dealt with immediately.

Setup scenes are minor chords, and should be kept to an absolute minimum. Usually they occur early in the book.

The opening pages of *Gone With the Wind* are for setup. They give us Scarlett O'Hara and reveal her character. How? She is having a coquettish *argument* with the Tarleton twins. We get some setting and the flavor of the book to come.

Then Stuart Tarleton declares that Ashley Wilkes is going to marry Melanie Hamilton, producing the following reaction beat:

> Scarlett's face did not change but her lips went white—like a person who has received a stunning blow without warning and who, in the first moments of shock, does not realize what has happened.

Deepening

Deepening is to the novel as spice is to food. This chord of fiction is generally not a full scene. It is, instead, what you add to the mix to deepen the reader's understanding of character or setting. Make it fresh, drop it in strategically, and the flavor will be exquisite.

But like spice, deepening must not be overdone or it will ruin the taste.

In his novella, *The Body*, Stephen King takes a short, spicy break from the narrative to have Gordie tell one of his famous stories to his friends. It concerns a certain large boy named Hogan, some castor oil, a number of pies he eats at a contest and the "revenge" he exacts on the town as a result. (One might pick a better metaphor than *spice* for this particular deepening episode.)

Why did King take this digression? Because it is just the kind of story these boys would like. It deepens their relationship as they continue their journey. It adds something to the story that straight narrative would not.

What a Scene Isn't

Summarizing is when the author tells us what has happened "off scene." Think of this as the stuff that is not unfolding for the reader in linear time, beat by beat. A scene is like this:

> John took a step toward her.
>
> "Stop," she said. She picked up a hammer.
>
> Laughing, John shook his head. "That's pitiful."

Summarizing would look like this:

> He had tried to attack her, but she had picked up a hammer. When he laughed about it, she actually used it on him. His headache lasted five weeks.

You use summarizing primarily as a short cut, to get you from scene to scene as quickly as possible. In the following summary, we are in linear time but we're skipping the beats that would make a scene:

> Holding his head, John drove to the hospital. Traffic was terrible. It took him two hours to get there.

Then you get back into a scene:

> "Hoo boy, what happened to you?" the nurse said.
>
> "I attacked a hammer with my head," John said.

GET HIP TO YOUR SCENES

In order to be successful, you must write scenes that always give readers their money's worth. You can do it if you master these three essentials: hook, intensity, and prompt (HIP).

Capture Them at the Beginning

The *hook* is what grabs the reader's attention from the start and gets him pulled into the narrative. And here is where many a writer stumbles.

Feeling there needs to be an adequate description of the location first, then the characters, a writer may tend to start his scenes slowly. This is, of course, a logical choice. We think in a linear fashion, and figure we have to get the readers seeing the location, then the characters *in* the location, before we can get to the good stuff, like action and dialogue.

Don't fall into this trap. Readers don't care about the natural order if they are intrigued. You have a number of options to choose from in order to make that happen.

Here is an example of the linear way:

> We were back in his office. I sat in the armchair in front of Pistillo's desk. His chair, I noticed this time, was set a little higher than mine, probably for reasons of intimidation. Claudia Fisher, the agent who'd visited me at Covenant House, stood behind me with her arms crossed.
> "What happened to your nose?" Pistillo asked me.

In *Gone for Good*, however, Harlan Coben starts the scene like this:

> "What happened to your nose?" Pistillo asked me.
> We were back in his office. I sat in the armchair in front of Pistillo's desk.

Dialogue is the stronger hook here. It starts the scene off with a question, and makes us want to know what the narrator is going to answer. Coben then drops in one paragraph of setting and gets back to the action.

Another hooking technique is the teaser. This is a subtle promise to the reader that a tense scene is about to occur. Coben begins a *Gone for Good* chapter thus: "I fell into such a deep sleep that I never heard him sneak up on me."

Who is *he*? What happened after he snuck up on the narrator? Coben teases first, then unfurls the answers.

Still another hook is action, pure and simple. Again Coben: "Claudia Fisher burst into the office of Joseph Pistillo."

This raises the question of why Claudia burst into the office, instead of knocking or strolling. We read to find out.

Even description can work as a hook, so long as you make it do double duty. Each place or character you describe should not only create a picture for the reader but also establish the proper mood. In "All That You Love Will Be Carried Away," a story about a man's darkest moment, Stephen King begins this way:

> It was a Motel 6 on I-80 just west of Lincoln, Nebraska. The snow that began at midafternoon had faded the sign's virulent yellow to a kinder pastel shade as the light ran out of the January dusk. The wind was closing in on that quality of empty amplification one encounters only in the country's flat midsection.

Even though this is description, notice the mood created by fading light, dusk, wind, emptiness. We are being set up to feel the inner life of the character even before we meet him. And when readers feel something, they want to keep reading.

So work hard to grab readers at the start of every scene. Try different opening paragraphs. Vary your methods. Alternate dialogue with action, description with teaser. You'll soon happen upon the hook that feels right.

Hold Readers Tight

Once you have the reader's attention, you can concentrate on the second essential of scene—*intensity*. Every scene must have it, to a greater or lesser degree. Without it, your scene will sit there like a deflated blimp—it may have potential, but it ain't gonna fly.

Masters of the craft know this. Dean Koontz's aptly titled *Intensity* is filled with scenes of impending danger as a woman tries to escape a sadistic killer. As the story builds, so does the possibility that she will be discovered by the villain. Virtually every scene in the first half of the book is built on the chance she'll be found out:

> He stood just outside the cab door, thirty feet from her, stretching almost lazily. He rolled his big shoulders as if to shake weariness from them, and he massaged the back of his neck.
>
> If he turned his head to the left, he would see her at once. If she didn't remain absolutely still, he would surely spot the slightest movement even from the corner of his eye.

The intensity level of your scenes should increase as the story moves toward the climax. In the Koontz novel, the heroine, Chyna, is captured. The last half of the book chronicles her attempts to escape with another prisoner before they are killed.

> Chyna stretched out on her stomach, leaned into the skylight, and used the
> mop to push the stepstool toward the back of the hall and out of the way.
> Dropping down onto it, one of them might have broken a leg.
> They were so close to escape. They couldn't take any chances.

This occurs just before some killer dogs come after them (Dobermans are intense by definition) and we're moved to a scene of even greater intensity. Koontz holds us in his grip by increasing the physical peril as the book progresses.

Literary fiction, on the other hand, usually concentrates more on the emotional turmoil of the characters. John Fante's classic novel, *Ask the Dust*, has numerous evocative scenes showing us the yearnings of the young writer Arturo Bandini:

> Now I prayed to St. Teresa again. Please, sweet and lovely saint, gimme an
> idea. But she has deserted me, all the gods have deserted me, and like
> Huysmans I stand alone, my fists clenched, tears in my eyes. If someone only
> loved me, even a bug, even a mouse, but that too belonged to the past ...

The language here is fiercely personal (*gimme an idea; if someone only loved me*) with emotional images (*fists clenched; tears*). The tension level is just as great as a scene about physical actions.

So pack your scenes with tension. How? Primarily through the writer's best friend: conflict. When two characters with opposing agendas meet, you have built-in tension. A cop tries to question a witness who doesn't want to talk; a would-be lover tries to get a woman to give him the time of day and she won't; a parent tries to find out what his wayward teenager is doing but can't. Your novel's central story should present endless possibilities for conflict—if it doesn't, this isn't the novel you should be writing.

Even scenes with allies—two characters who agree on a goal—should have tension. Otherwise, you'll end up with dull exchanges of informational dialogue.

That's how the best buddy movies work. *Lethal Weapon* partnered a straight-arrow, soon-to-retire cop (Danny Glover) with a suicidal wild man (Mel Gibson). The tension in their scenes elevates the movie above the standard cop thriller.

And we all remember the scene in *Butch Cassidy and the Sundance Kid* when Butch is trying to get Sundance to jump into the river. The heat in their argument rises until Sundance lets loose his dark secret: "I can't swim!"

Always go over the scenes you've written with an eye for intensity level. If it isn't strong enough, try to ratchet it up. Even a relatively quiet scene (which you use to modulate the pace of your novel) can give us the thoughts of the viewpoint character, showing us her worries or anxieties, thus allowing for emotional intensity.

If a scene still doesn't provide adequate intensity, use the writer's next best friend: the delete key. Your readers will be happy you did.

Make Them Read On

Finally, you need to end scenes with a *prompt*, something to make readers turn the page. So often new writers let their scenes fizzle out, ending on a boring note: People walk out of rooms, drive off in cars, or offer dull parting phrases like "Good-bye" and "Nice talking with you."

Don't ever let your scenes droop at the end. You have many ways to move the reader along.

One of the best "read-on prompts" (ROPs) is impending disaster. In *Intensity*, Chyna is hiding from the villain in a convenience store. Koontz ends the scene this way:

> As she stepped out of the aisle to hide at the end of a row of display cases, Chyna heard the door open and the killer enter. A growl of wind came with him, and then the door swung shut.

The danger can also be to the emotions, as when Arturo in *Ask the Dust* leaves the woman he longs for:

> As I closed the door all the desire that had not come a while before seized me. It pounded my skull and tingled in my fingers. I threw myself on the bed and tore the pillow with my hands.

Another ROP is *portent*, which can be given through a haunting image. In Stephen King's *Needful Things*, Hugh Priest has fallen under the spell of Leland Gaunt, the mesmerizingly creepy proprietor of a shop that has items people feel they must have. Hugh Priest feels that about a foxtail that brings back warm memories.

Gaunt refuses money for it. Instead, he asks about a woman named Nettie Cobb, or "Crazy Nettie" to the town:

> "Now listen to me, Hugh. Listen carefully. Then you can take your fox-tail and go home."

Hugh Priest listened carefully.

Outside it was raining harder, and the wind had begun to blow.

Here are some other great ROPs to end scenes with:

- A mysterious line of dialogue
- A secret suddenly revealed
- A major decision or vow
- Announcement of a shattering event
- Reversal or surprise—new information that turns the story around
- A question left hanging in the air

If a scene seems to sputter to a close and you're not sure what to do, here's a great tip: try cutting the last paragraph or two. You don't have to write every scene to its logical conclusion. In fact, it's often the best choice not to. Cutting creates interest, a feeling of something left hanging—and that makes readers want to find out why.

Remember Hitchcock's Axiom. Get HIP and you won't have to worry about dull parts showing up in your fiction.

THE INTENSITY SCALE

One of the best plot rules, of course, is *show, don't tell*. But this is not a law. Sometimes a writer *tells* as a shortcut, to get on to the meaty part of the scene. *Showing* is essentially about making scenes vivid. But if you try to do it constantly, the parts that are supposed to stand out won't. And your readers will get exhausted.

So when do you show and when do you tell? A little tool called the Intensity Scale will help you answer that question. Every scene in your story is going to vary in emotional intensity. And the intensity level *within* each scene will shift around. This is the natural ebb and flow of fiction.

In fact, one could argue that the skill of the fiction writer boils down to the ability to *exploit intensity*. The most intense moments, the places where you want the reader to feel the greatest emotion, must not only come at the right time; they must also stand out as the most vivid parts of the narrative.

With the Intensity Scale, you have a way to accurately gauge those moments. Simply put, you judge each scene you write on a shifting scale from 0–10. A 0 means there is no intensity at all; a 10 is over the top. As your scene moves along in time, the intensity level will move around.

As a general rule, your scenes should never drop to a 0 and rarely get to a 10. Almost all of your scenes should be written somewhere in between.

Furthermore, most scenes will have a natural build. They will start in the lower intensity range, then elevate to the higher.

There is room for variation, of course. Sometimes you may want to jump into a scene *in medias res* (in the middle of things) and stay there. Another technique is to start high, drop back to low, and build again. Whatever your choice, the Intensity Scale helps make the decision regarding show and tell.

The diagram illustrates a common pattern: A scene that begins around 1 or 2, gradually builds to a 7 or 8. It doesn't go over the top (a book can only sustain one or two such scenes), nor does it fall into coma land (a reader can stand *no* such scenes).

Now look at a scene you've written and gauge it by the scale.

The simple rule is this: when your scene goes above the median line (5), you are in the "show zone." Lean toward showing as much as you can.

When you are below the median, in the "tell zone," you can err on the side of tell. Why? Because the reason your scene exists, if you are doing it correctly, is what happens in the show zone. If it is not, then you seriously need to think about cutting that scene.

Some Examples

In Greg Iles's thriller, *24 Hours*, there is a little setup scene with Karen and Abby, a mother and her young daughter. The father, Will, has just left for a trip:

> Abby clapped her hands and burst into laughter. Breathing hard from the singing, Karen reached down and punched a number into her cell phone. She felt guilty about the way she'd spoken to Will at the airport.

This part of the scene is not intense. It does not need to be. It is a relatively short beat that lays the groundwork for later emotional impact. We don't need a drawn-out segment full of show. It is enough here to tell us that Karen felt guilty.

Soon, however, the intensity is ratcheted up near the top of the scale. Abby has been kidnapped from the house. Karen is confronted by a stranger in the house who tells her, "Abby's fine. I want you to listen to me." Karen's reaction requires show, and Iles obliges:

> At the word "Abby," tears filled Karen's eyes. The panic that lived beneath her skin burned through to the surface, paralyzing her where she stood. Her chin began to quiver. She tried to scream, but no sound came from her throat.

By showing us through physical description what Karen is feeling, Iles enables the reader to experience the emotion directly.

Another example in the same vein is from Ridley Pearson's *The Pied Piper*. A woman worries about having left her four-month-old with a babysitter for the first time. Near the beginning of a restaurant scene, we have an intensity level of about 3. So Pearson merely says of the mother, *She was sick with anxiety.*

Later, after calls home have gone unanswered, the tension level moves to around 7. Thus, we are given a more vivid description: *The knot in her stomach twisted more tightly. Her fingers went cold and numb.*

Raymond Carver, whom some might call the king of show (he was a master at finding the right, illuminating detail), naturally followed this strategy. His story "Neighbors" begins by quickly telling us the condition of the characters: *Bill and Arlene were a happy couple. But now and then they felt they alone among their circle had been passed by somehow. …*

By the end of the story, however, Carver writes: *They held each other. They leaned into the door as if against the wind, and braced themselves.* The context of the story is in these lines, left to work their magic in the reader's imagination.

Using the Intensity Scale for Balance

A good plot is an exercise in proper balance. For example, a thriller needs some relief from the action so a reader can catch his breath. A literary novel that delves deeply into character should find respite on occasion through comic relief, action, or some other change of pace.

The Intensity Scale can help you with this balancing act.

A novel usually revolves around a few big scenes. These act like guideposts as the novelist moves from one to the other up through the climax. In between, scenes of differing degrees of intensity are used to vary the pace.

Determine which chapters or scenes in your novel are the ones that your story cannot do without. There are no hard and fast rules, but a novel of 100,000 words might contain half a dozen big scenes.

Write these scenes for all they are worth. Get the narrative quickly into the show zone and stay on the high side, in the 8–10 range. Scenes that are transitional can be a mix. They might be quiet and reflective, moving from 2 to 5 or 6. Or they may have a seething inner conflict that feels like a 7 or 8 to the character.

You can actually graph each of your scenes on cards, lay them next to each other, and step back for a look at your novel as a whole.

The simple point is this: By staying aware of your scenes' levels of intensity and writing accordingly, you'll make your own novels fresh and memorable to your readers.

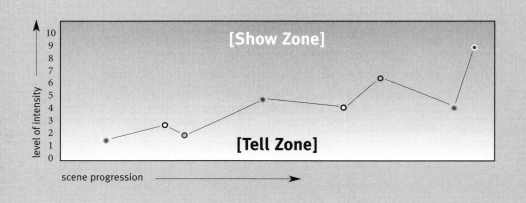

10: Over the top! Use with care; only two or three scenes per book should hit this level.

8, 9: Good range for your big scenes, those turning points that every novel needs.

6, 7: Conflict, important emotions, sharp dialogue, inner turmoil.

5: A good place to start scenes that build to the higher ranges.

3, 4: Setup scenes (short) and other transitions.

1, 2: If you start here, get out quickly.

0: Don't even think about it. For instance, lengthy descriptions (e.g., weather, place), especially in the first chapter, will flatline your novel and induce yawns (and rejections) from editors.

Pull a novel at random from your shelf. Open to any scene and read it. Now analyze:

- Was this an action scene? Identify the places where you learn about the character's objective in the scene and the conflict. How does the scene end? Do you want to read on? Why or why not?
- Is this mainly a reaction scene? What is the emotion the character is feeling? How does the author show it? At the end of the scene, what has the character decided to do, if anything? Is the character different? Stronger? Weaker?

EXERCISE 2

Now find an action scene and chart its intensity using the blank Intensity Scale that is provided above.

EXERCISE 3

Look at one of your chapters and analyze the hook, intensity level, and prompt at the end. How can you strengthen each aspect?

chapter 8

[COMPLEX PLOTS]

> *Writing is very much like bricklaying. You learn to put one brick on top of another and spread the mortar so thick.*
>
> —RED SMITH

And brick by brick, you can add levels of complexity to your plot. Because while a fast-moving story is a good thing, a story that lingers inside the reader long after the last page is another accomplishment entirely.

A memorable plot requires that you take your writing to the next plateau. There are numerous ways to add complexity to your plots. We'll look at a few of them in this chapter.

But first, we ought to ask, "Why complex? Isn't the prevailing rule in life KISS—Keep it Simple, Stupid?"

Not when you consider the beauty of complex structures. They seem simple because they work so well. That's the effect you want to achieve in your own work.

DEVELOPING YOUR THEME

At some point in your plotting, ask yourself what *the take-home value* of your story is going to be. What is the lesson or insight—the new way of seeing things—that you want the reader to glean?

Put it into one line. This will be your theme.

Think of theme as the *meta-message*, the one big statement about the world your work of fiction will convey. A novel should have only one meta-message, though it may offer several submessages.

Dostoevsky's *The Brothers Karamazov* propounds numerous messages, such as the futility of pure intellect and the burden of free will. But it has only one main theme, which might be phrased *faith and love are the highest values of human existence.*

Themes deepen fiction, but you must beware of a common danger. It is tempting for a writer to take a theme and *force* a story into it. This results in a host of problems, including cardboard characters, a preachy tone, a lack of subtlety, and story clichés.

How can you avoid these novel killers? Here is one simple rule to remember: *Characters carry theme.*

Always.

Develop your characters fully and set them in the story world where their values will conflict with each other. Allow your characters to struggle naturally and passionately. Theme will emerge without effort.

Subplots

Weave theme into plot. Like a tapestry, thematic strands must come together in a seamless way to create an overall effect. The feel must be organic. This is most often done through subplots.

A subplot can be primarily thematic, concerned with what the Lead character *needs to learn.* While the outer action of the main plot is going on, causing all sorts of problems for the Lead, the thematic subplot focuses on issues that are personal and interior.

For example, you have a detective who is trying to solve a murder. In the main plot, he is going to interview witnesses, follow leads, avoid death, fight with his partner, run up against his captain, and so forth.

At the same time, he is having trouble at home. His wife has started drinking because of the stress. This is affecting the kids. The detective's marriage is falling apart because he has not learned how to give his wife what she needs.

This is the subplot that carries a theme, which might be *learning to love is as important as success at a job.*

A thematic subplot can end on a positive or negative note and still carry the meta-message.

If the wife leaves the detective at the end, that's a negative, but the Lead has learned the lesson in a bitter fashion. He may not accept the lesson, but it has hit him in a personal way.

Or the detective figures out he must sacrifice something of his professional life to keep his marriage alive. He and his wife reconcile, a positive note. Same lesson.

A thematic subplot adds depth and meaning to a story. It allows you to make a statement about the important things in life, even if the main character isn't thinking about them most of the time.

Symbols and Motifs

Symbols and motifs deepen your plot, but only if they are not larded on. Again, naturalness is the key.

A symbol is something that is representative of another thing. A motif is a repeated image or phrase.

Norman Maclean's "A River Runs Through It" is a story where water is a central motif. It begins: "In our family, there was no clear line between religion and fly fishing. We lived at the junction of great trout rivers in western Montana. ..."

From the start, we have a connection between water, religion, and family (not to mention the symbolic significance of fishing). The river becomes the central image repeated throughout the story. When the narrator watches his brother fly-fishing from a boulder, he reflects "the whole world turned to water."

And at the end, the narrator tells us "all things merge into one, and a river runs through it. The river was cut by the world's great flood and runs over rocks from the basement of time. ... I am haunted by waters." The motif was literal at the beginning, symbolic at the end. It frames and defines the story.

Janet Fitch weaves symbols and motifs into *White Oleander*. The oleander plant—tough, attractive, poisonous—represents Astrid's mother, who tries to control Astrid's life from prison. The tomato plants "groping for a little light" signify Astrid herself as she faces various challenges. These elevate the story from a collection of plot incidents to a commentary on life, love, and human resiliency.

Whales become a symbol of hope in Lisa Samson's *The Living End*. The grieving narrator, Pearl Laurel, is having doubts about life. She goes on a whale-watching trip, and someone tells her it would be awful to go through all this trouble and see no whales. This causes Pearl to reflect. "I am convinced. This life is more than just the face value. It has to be. There have to be whales at the end." In the next scene, Pearl gets a look at the whales and takes pictures, "the first pictures I've taken on this camera in years."

Here is an opening moment from my novel *Breach of Promise*. The father of a girl named Maddie is looking back on happier times:

And then the time we were watching *It's a Wonderful Life* on TV one Christmas. Maddie was four. Donna Reed and Jimmy Stewart started singing "Buffalo Gals" as they were walking home from the high school dance. I glanced at Maddie and she seemed mesmerized.

... *aaaannnd dance by the light of the moon.*

Jimmy and Donna, singing.

Maddie looked at me then. "Can we do that?" Paula was on the phone in the kitchen. I alone had to field this one, and knew from experience that Maddie's questions sometimes threw a bolo around my head.

"Do what, honey?"

"Dance by the guy in the moon?"

"By the light of the moon."

"Whatever, Daddy."

"You bet we can."

"Now?"

It was one of those things you don't stop and analyze. I think God implants a certain instinct in fathers (who are somewhat slow on the uptake) which tells them to heed their children without extensive cross-examination.

"Sure," I said. I lifted her off the couch—she in her soft cotton PJs with rabbits and me in my cutoffs and Dodger tee-shirt—and went to the kitchen to tell Paula we were going up on the roof of the building. Paula, phone at her ear, put her finger in the air, telling me to be quiet.

I carried Maddie up to the roof.

The moon was almost full. It seemed huge. It cast a glow over the hills, where million dollar homes gawked somewhat incredulously at the apartment buildings below. The kind of homes I dreamed of living in, with Paula and Maddie and a big, fat $20 million contract to star in the next Ridley Scott movie.

But tonight I did not care that I was on an apartment building roof. Maddie had her warm arms around my neck, and I held her and swayed, swayed, swayed. Time went completely away as we danced by the light of the moon.

The moon and the dance became a motif that was to repeat in memory, and in a final image of the novel. I had not planned it that way, but after writing the above decided this was exactly what I was looking for. It held the whole book together for me and gave me an image in my mind as well.

You find symbols and motifs in your work by paying attention. Write scenes rich in sensory detail and look closely at what you've created.

LONG NOVELS

Length of novel, especially when it involves expanse of time, presents another layer of complexity. One challenge for the novelist of long books—epics, histories, and the like—is how to keep the reader interested for 500, 800 or 1,000 pages. With such scope there is plenty of room to go wrong, pad, or overstay your welcome. Even some of our best novelists have fallen into the abyss of prolixity from time to time.

Style alone is not enough to pull the reader through.

Furthermore, the episodic nature of some long novels seems to defy the LOCK system and three-act structure. But, as we'll see, this is mere illusion.

Let's take a historical novel as an example. Suppose the author wants to tell the story of young boy in Ireland in the 1860s and end with him being a crooked and successful politician in the 1920s. There will be settings in Ireland, England, on board a ship, in Boston, and eventually in New York. In New York, there will be several parts chronicling the Lead's climb to the top.

Along the way, too, the Lead's objectives may change. In the early parts of the book, his struggle is to survive. In the middle, it is to make friends with the powerful. In the latter parts, he is trying to gain power.

There will be different opponents over the course of time. A villainous neighbor, an oppressive sea captain, a crooked cop, a Town Hall mayor.

You get the idea. Loads of material and plenty of ways to stall.

How do we keep a plot of such complexity paced for readability?

The same way you eat an elephant: one bite at a time.

Each bite, in this instance, is a major section. And the jaws of mastication are the old reliables, the LOCK system and three-act structure.

Simply treat each section as a mini-plot.

Let's say the Ireland section of our proposed historical novel is to take our Lead through his hard youth to his setting off for London. Let's say, further, that this section will be about 20,000 words.

Think of this section as a 20,000-word novelette. Use the LOCK system, only turn the L for Lead (which in our example remains constant) to Locale and turn the K from Knockout to Kick-in-the-pants prompt—you want the reader to be compelled to read the next section. At the end of the novel, you will write a knockout ending.

In the following table, the Lead is always going to be Connor, an Irish lad:

LOCALE	OBJECTIVE	CONFRONTATION	KICK
Ireland	Get out of Ireland	Father, Neighbor	Beats up father and runs
England	Find work; survive	Constables, crime boss	Framed; he flees
Ship	Avoid punishment	Evil captain	Jumps ship
Boston	Find a niche	Prejudiced cops, Irish rivals	Kills cop
New York 1	Make money	Cheating partner	Gains business
New York 2	Get power	Political bosses	Knock out ending

Within each section, you may construct subplots, adding further to the complexity. A subplot character may also span the sections, making connections with the main plot.

The movie *Forrest Gump* is like that. There are several sections, beginning with Forrest as a boy. He goes to Vietnam, later becomes a Ping Pong champion, then makes it as a shrimper, and so on.

But consistent throughout is his relationship with the girl, Jenny.

Now let us subject our sections to the three-act structure. We'll use the first New York section as an example.

In Act I of this section, Connor arrives in New York and finds lodging with a friend of his family, an Irish immigrant. There is some equilibrium established here. The rundown tenement on the East Side becomes Connor's new "ordinary world."

But then the friend is forcibly evicted for not paying the rent, and Connor is out in the street. This is the new inciting incident, the disturbance in the ordinary world we've established.

Connor's objective becomes to make money. He believes that money is the key to everything in America.

He meets a fellow who convinces him to become business partners.

Connor signs an agreement with the man, linking the two—a "doorway of no return."

Over the course of this section's Act II, however, Connor becomes suspicious of the way the business accounts for its money. There are ups and downs as Connor pursues his objective, money. He runs across a major clue or suffers a major setback that puts him in direct conflict with his partner, who has been cheating him. This becomes the second doorway, leading us into Act III.

Through some clever ruse or with the help of a lawyer, Connor cheats the cheater and gains control of the business. Suddenly he has a taste of power. What will he do with it?

That's the kick that propels the reader forward.

The LOCK system and three-act structure will never let you down, no matter how long or short your novel.

PARALLEL PLOTS

In a parallel-plot novel, you switch back and forth between the plot lines. If you can manage to end each section in a fashion that makes readers want to read on, you're going to achieve that magical effect—*I couldn't put it down!*

Parallel plots are just that: two or more plot lines that run along the same forward path. You may have a main plot—featuring a lead character you wish to emphasize—and one or more parallel plots to go with it. Or you can equalize among the plot lines.

The Fan, a thriller by Peter Abrahams, is a simple, two-track story. The first track is about Gil Renard, a salesman, and how his life is slowly coming apart. The second part is about Bobby Rayburn, a millionaire star baseball player, and what he is going through.

Gil does some bad things, but we keep reading because what happens to him could happen to us. He starts losing his edge in sales, his child is a disappointment to him, he has a key sales meeting that he misses and loses the client. He attacks the man his ex-wife has married. He is let go from his job at the company his father had started. His wife gets a restraining order preventing him from being around her or his son.

So he goes back to his hometown and takes up with a childhood friend who is now at the criminal end of the spectrum. He starts burglarizing with him, and eventually that leads to murder.

While this is going on, we cut from time to time to Bobby's troubles as a star baseball player. Back and forth until Gil makes his way into Bobby's life by killing his rival on the team, then eventually getting a job working as a landscaper for him after saving Bobby's kid from drowning in a pool. The supreme stalker. How will it end?

Stephen King's *The Stand* has several plotlines that run along the same path. Gradually these plotlines converge, eventually all coming together for a shattering climax.

Dean Koontz produces the same effect in *Strangers*. When you unpack the book's plot, it's really about a fifty-page science-fiction suspense story. But by adding several parallel plots, Koontz transforms the book into a seven-hundred-page epic.

You Must Make Each Plot Work On Its Own

Of course, to make this type of complexity work, each of the plotlines has to carry its story weight. If one of the plotlines sags, it will dilute the effect. You'll have readers giving a sigh of disappointment every time they come back to that line.

So how do you do that?

You use the LOCK system on every plot. You make sure you create a Lead readers will want to follow, with an objective that is crucial to her well-being, and forces that confront her all the way until that knockout at the end.

COMPLEXITY FROM PLAYING WITH STRUCTURE AND STYLE

Some novels and movies are told in *nonlinear* fashion. They jump around in time, and things don't unfold in the way we normally think of for three acts.

But you will notice that the best of these work because the LOCK elements and the information necessary for the beginning, middle, and end *eventually* line up to create a coherent story.

As a trial lawyer and teacher of trial advocacy, I would stress to students that the jury is looking first of all for *the story*. They don't care about the law during the taking of testimony. They want to know *what happened*.

Evidence comes to them in a choppy way. They'll hear from various witnesses on different aspects of the facts, usually in a nonchronological fashion. But what they are doing all the time is trying to fit the pieces into a coherent narrative.

In closing arguments, the lawyers—if they are doing their job—weave a narrative and only then apply the law to the facts.

Your readers will be doing the same thing if you write a nonlinear plot. It can work, so long as you help them fit it all into a coherent pattern.

A classic example of a nonlinear narrative that works well is the Orson Welles film *Citizen Kane*. The story of Charles Foster Kane is told through the flashback remembrances of various characters who knew him, jumping around the various stages of his life. Each remembrance brings us a little closer to the full story.

Another example is the cult favorite *The End of the Night*, by John D. MacDonald. It is a story of four young people on a cross-country killing spree. It could have been told in a straight line, but MacDonald lets the story unfold in another way.

The prologue is a letter written by a prison guard to his friend Ed. It describes the electrocution of four murderers. It is written in a singular voice ("All I can say is, I'm damn glad they didn't spread the four out, say about two weeks apart. A man would hardly have no love life at all. Ha, ha."). So, in a unique way, we get the end of the story first.

Chapter one is written in the omniscient point of view (POV). It has the feel of a documentary in describing the lawyer, Riker Deems Owens. Language such as "Should the discerning reader detect ..." is almost Victorian. Then the chapter switches to a memorandum Owens wrote, so it is naturally a first-person POV. The memo describes the killers who became his clients, known as the Wolfpack.

Chapter two is a third-person account of Helen Wister, who became the last victim of the Wolfpack murderers.

Chapter three introduces the death-house diary of Kirby Stassen, one of the Wolfpack. In first person, he tells about himself and the events leading up to the murders.

The chapters then bounce back and forth among the Owens memo, third-person accounts, and Stassen's death-house diary.

Each chapter gives us a little more of the story, until we have it all by the end. And by changing styles in each chapter, MacDonald creates different tones that also add to the effect. I highly recommend you hunt this little gem out at your local library or used bookstore. MacDonald was a master plotter.

Another great plotter is David Morrell. In *Lessons From a Lifetime of Writing*, he explains his thinking about the structure of *Double Image*. His hero, Coltrane, is a photographer, and the events of the book reveal that his life has a "double image."

The novel starts out in the past, in Bosnia, with Coltrane photographing Ilkovic, a war criminal. Coltrane barely escapes from the experience with his life. We then cut to present-day Los Angeles, where photographer Coltrane meets Randolph Packard, an old, dying, legendary photographer. Packard suggests doing a project with Coltrane. Eventually, this project leads to the old house of Packard's that Coltrane wants to buy. Within that house is a mystery: photos of a beautiful woman. Who was she?

Coltrane starts getting strange messages on his machine. Like someone is playing with him. Who? On page 95, he figures out it's Ilkovic, back to hunt him. From there until about page 215, there is stalking and action until Ilkovic is killed by Coltrane.

So the Ilkovic plot has intruded on the mystery plot. Now Morrell moves back to the "who is the woman" plot. Double plots. Double image.

The range of play within structure is wide. Just remember that when the reader gets to the final page, he's going to want to know what happened.

EXERCISE 1

Make three columns on a sheet of paper. In the first column, record the rich details that stand out in your scenes. In the middle column, list your main characters. In the last column, catalogue the significant settings. Now look for connections between the columns. Connect a detail with a character and place. Or work the other way, from place to character to detail. Pick the strongest two or three connections, and see if you can weave them into your plot as motifs or symbols.

EXERCISE 2

Determine the take-home value for your novel, and put it into one line. This can be done at any stage of your plotting. If you do it early, keep it in mind as you develop your scenes. But be careful of heavy-handedness when you do. The message must come out naturally.

EXERCISE 3

Music is a great way to brainstorm images for your novel. Relax and do some deep breathing. Put on a piece of music that moves you—perhaps a movie soundtrack, classical music, or jazz. Don't play anything with lyrics. You want the music to wash over you. As it does, close your eyes and let images and even scenes suggest themselves to your imagination. Stop and record these on paper or in the computer. Repeat this exercise from time to time as you write.

chapter 9

[THE CHARACTER ARC IN PLOT]

Great plots have great characters. While this is not a book on character creation and implementation, we can't let the subject of plot go without touching on at least one aspect of character work that is all important: character change.

What makes a plot truly memorable is not all of the action, but what the action *does to the character*. We respond to the character who *changes*, who endures the crucible of the story only to emerge a different person at the end. It may be a major difference, as with Ebenezer Scrooge in Charles Dickens's *A Christmas Carol*. Or it may be a subtle change, as when Scarlett O'Hara finally matures at the end of *Gone With the Wind* (just not soon enough to keep Rhett).

What deepens a plot is when characters grow. Events happen and should have impact on the characters. Are there novels where the characters don't change? Sure. But these are not usually classified as "enduring." In a detective series, for example, the main character may remain rather static, the only change from book to book being the nature of the case.

Even in a series, however, subtle changes in the character over time can elevate the books from mere entertainments. Sue Grafton's Kinsey Millhone and Robert B. Parker's Spencer are examples.

So look to create character change in your novels in a way that deepens the plot and expresses a theme. For when a character learns something or suffers because he changes for the worse, it is an expression by the author about the larger canvas—not merely what happens in the novel, but what happens in life.

THE CHARACTER ARC

As opposed to the *plotline*, the character arc is a description of what happens to the inside of the character over the course of the story. He begins as one sort of person in the beginning; things happen to and around him, gradually moving him in an "arc" that ends when the story is over.

Your lead character should be a different person at the other end of the arc.

For example, in the film version of *The Wizard of Oz* Dorothy begins as a dreamer, a farm girl with her head in the clouds. She dreams of finding a better life "over the rainbow."

At the end, she realizes "there's no place like home." We might describe this arc as going from *discontentment* to *contentment*, an arc of 180 degrees. Or from *dreamer* to *realist*.

However we put it, we are saying that Dorothy has grown because she has learned a life-changing lesson.

The character arc has a build to it. It must, or the change will not be convincing. A good character arc has:

- A beginning point, where we meet the character and get a sense of his interior layers (more on layers in a moment)
- A doorway through which the character must pass, almost always reluctantly
- Incidents that impact the layers
- A deepening disturbance
- A moment of change, sometimes via an "epiphany"
- An aftermath

Let's take a look at each step in more detail. We'll use the example of Ebenezer Scrooge in Dickens's *A Christmas Carol* as our prime example. This is the greatest character-change story ever written. It's a good model.

Beginning Point

When we first meet Ebenezer Scrooge, he is described as a "squeezing, wrenching, grasping, scraping, clutching, covetous old sinner!" Dickens goes on to provide a biting physical description of Scrooge, and then proceeds to *show* us what Scrooge is like. In one instance, some men have stopped by Scrooge's place of work to seek donations for the poor. Scrooge snaps:

"Since you ask me what I wish, gentlemen, that is my answer. I don't make merry myself at Christmas and I can't afford to make idle people merry. I help to support the establishments, I have mentioned: they cost enough: and those who are badly off must go there."

"Many can't go there; and many would rather die."

"If they would rather die," said Scrooge, "they had better do it, and decrease the surplus population."

A bit later, Scrooge's clerk, Bob Cratchit, once more requests the day off after Christmas. It is, after all, only one day a year. As you know, however, Cratchit's simple request is denied, further illustrating the heartless nature of Scrooge.

The Layers

We all have a *core self*. It is the product of many things over the years—our emotional makeup, our upbringing, our traumas and experiences, and so on. Most of the time we're not really thinking about who we are. Yet the core is there.

And we will do what we can to protect this core because, by and large, people resist change. So we surround that core with layers that are in harmony with our essential self. Working from the core outward, these layers include: (1) beliefs; (2) values; (3) dominant attitudes; and (4) opinions.

If you think about it, these layers get "softer" as they move away from the core. Thus, the outer layers are easiest to change. It is much easier to change your opinion, for example, than one of your deeply held beliefs.

But there is always a ripple effect when a layer experiences change. If you change an opinion, it will filter through to the other layers. Initially, there may not be much effect. But change enough opinions, and you start to change attitudes, values, and even beliefs.

On the other hand, suddenly changing a core belief automatically affects the other layers because it's such a strong shift.

How might we describe Scrooge's core self at the start of *A Christmas Carol*? He is a miser and a misanthrope. He loves money and hates people.

His *beliefs* include the pointlessness of love and charity.

He *values* money over people.

His *attitude* is that profit is more important than good works.

In his *opinion*, Christmas is a humbug, clerks are always trying to take advantage, and so on.

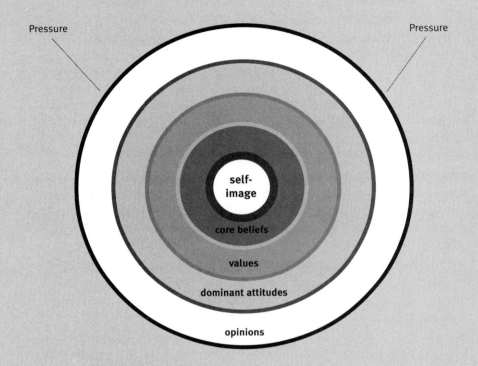

[The Force Field of Character Change]

Pressure

Pressure

self-image

core beliefs

values

dominant attitudes

opinions

Pressure from the outside penetrates the layers. When all the outer layers are sufficiently changed, the core—self-image—changes automatically.

To make Scrooge into a new person, these layers are going to have to be disturbed. How is that to happen?

Ghosts, of course.

Scrooge is to be visited by three ghosts. The first, the Ghost of Christmas Past, takes Scrooge to a familiar scene:

> "Good Heaven!" said Scrooge, clasping his hands together, as he looked about him. "I was bred in this place. I was a boy here!"
>
> The Spirit gazed upon him mildly. Its gentle touch, though it had been light

and instantaneous, appeared still present to the old man's sense of feeling. He was conscious of a thousand odours floating in the air, each one connected with a thousand thoughts, and hopes, and joys, and cares long, long, forgotten.

"Your lip is trembling," said the Ghost. "And what is that upon your cheek?"

Scrooge muttered, with an unusual catching in his voice, that it was a pimple; and begged the Ghost to lead him where he would.

Scrooge is crying! This hard-bitten man who seems so intractable has, at a scene from his boyhood, connected with long-forgotten emotions. They affect him. He attempts to divert the Ghost's attention. It is the first, small indication that somewhere inside Scrooge's cold, uncaring body is a warm person who may re-emerge.

The Ghost takes Scrooge to see the shop where he was a young apprentice, Old Fezziwig's. Scrooge remembers how generous Fezziwig was to his employees, how he brought joy into their lives. This brings Scrooge to another moment of reflection on his own relationship with his employee, Cratchit. The moment results in a softening toward Bob Cratchit, whom we met earlier in the story when Scrooge barked at him. Some of the outer layer of Scrooge has been affected.

And the plot advances.

Impacting Incidents

The Ghost of Christmas Present takes Scrooge for a look at the Cratchit family. What Scrooge witnesses there is the joy of Christmas as shared by a poor family, including Tiny Tim:

"God bless us every one!" said Tiny Tim, the last of all.

He sat very close to his father's side upon his little stool. Bob held his withered little hand in his, as if he loved the child, and wished to keep him by his side, and dreaded that he might be taken from him.

"Spirit," said Scrooge, with an interest he had never felt before, "tell me if Tiny Tim will live."

"I see a vacant seat," replied the Ghost, "in the poor chimney-corner, and a crutch without an owner, carefully preserved. If these shadows remain unaltered by the Future, the child will die."

"No, no," said Scrooge. "Oh, no, kind Spirit! say he will be spared."

We are starting to get into deeper levels with Scrooge here. There is an interest "he had never felt before." The shadows are doing their work.

Before the Ghost of Christmas Present leaves, Scrooge sees one more image that sears into him—under the Spirit's robe are two young children tainted by poverty and want:

> "Have they no refuge or resource?" cried Scrooge.
>
> "Are there no prisons?" said the Spirit, turning on him for the last time with his own words. "Are there no workhouses?"
>
> The bell struck twelve.

Notice how Scrooge's own words (the references to prisons and workhouses), planted early in the story, now come back to haunt him.

This is a powerful technique for character change. If you can repeat a motif, or have the character somehow come face to face with his "earlier self," the reader will see the pressure to change powerfully conveyed.

It is best to underplay such moments. In Dickens's time a bit more on-the-nose writing was acceptable. Don't overdo it, or you may lapse into melodrama. We'll say more about that later in this chapter.

Deepening Disturbances

We are fast coming to the point where Scrooge will try to become a new man. The ultimate disturbance is when the Ghost of Christmas Yet to Come shows the dismal aftermath of a despised man's death.

And then Scrooge is shown the Cratchit family again, where he learns that Tiny Tim is dead.

The Ghost next takes Scrooge to a graveyard, and points to a headstone. With this shock to his system, Scrooge finally snaps:

> "Spirit!" he cried, tight clutching at its robe, "hear me! I am not the man I was. I will not be the man I must have been but for this intercourse. Why show me this, if I am past all hope?"
>
> For the first time the hand appeared to shake.
>
> "Good Spirit," he pursued, as down upon the ground he fell before it: "Your nature intercedes for me, and pities me. Assure me that I yet may change these shadows you have shown me, by an altered life!"
>
> The kind hand trembled.
>
> "I will honour Christmas in my heart, and try to keep it all the year. I will live in the Past, the Present, and the Future. The Spirits of all Three shall strive within me. I will not shut out the lessons that they teach. Oh, tell me I may sponge away the writing on this stone!"

In his agony, he caught the spectral hand. It sought to free itself, but he was strong in his entreaty, and detained it. The Spirit, stronger yet, repulsed him.

Holding up his hands in a last prayer to have his fate reversed, he saw an alteration in the Phantom's hood and dress. It shrunk, collapsed, and dwindled down into a bedpost.

Aftermath

Scrooge has declared that he is a changed man. But that is not enough. We must see some action that demonstrates the change, shows that it has truly taken effect.

First, we see a Scrooge we haven't encountered before, bounding out of bed and rejoicing in his own happiness. Then he goes to the window and stops a boy running by. He engages the lad to buy a prize turkey:

"I'll send it to Bob Cratchit's!" whispered Scrooge, rubbing his hands, and splitting with a laugh. "He shan't know who sends it. It's twice the size of Tiny Tim."

There is an action. Now we know Scrooge is different. We've been shown. The showing continues when he finds the two men whom he rebuffed who had solicited a donation from him the day before and makes it up to them. Scrooge then dines with his nephew, and the next day raises Bob Cratchit's salary and asks to assist him with his family.

So, when we get to the final words of the great Dickens classic, we believe them:

Scrooge was better than his word. He did it all, and infinitely more; and to Tiny Tim, who did not die, he was a second father. He became as good a friend, as good a master, and as good a man, as the good old city knew, or any other good old city, town, or borough, in the good old world. ... [A]nd it was always said of him, that he knew how to keep Christmas well, if any man alive possessed the knowledge. May that be truly said of us, and all of us! And so, as Tiny Tim observed, God Bless Us, Every One!

The Epiphany

Since *A Christmas Carol* is a character-change story, the beats are clearly designed for that purpose. In many novels, the character arc may be quieter and shown in a subtler fashion.

That's fine. You can still use the steps above. But be ready to work hardest on that *moment of change*, which we might call the *epiphany*—that realization that comes to us and shifts our way of viewing the world.

What we want to avoid with such moments is melodrama—the overplaying of the emotion involved. Epiphanies and realizations are often best when underplayed.

In fact, it is quite possible not to play it at all! Yes, the moment of change can be *implied* by what happens *after it*. In other words, the proof of the change (what author Nancy Kress calls "verification" in her book *Dynamic Characters*) can follow pressure. That is one way to avoid being "on the nose" with the change.

In my novel *Deadlock*, a Supreme Court Justice, Millie Hollander, is an atheist. But pressure has been applied in a big way. So much so that something major happens on her plane trip back to Washington D.C. Let's take a look:

> The plane rose into fog, a gray netherworld. Millie took a deep breath, looked out the window, feeling as uncertain as the outside.
>
> In so many ways this day should have been a relief. Her body was good again. She'd spent precious hours with her mother, connecting with her in a way that she'd never dreamed was possible. And she was going back to Washington to assume the job of a lifetime—Chief Justice.
>
> So why the disquiet?
>
> She put on the earphones the flight attendant had passed out earlier, clicked the dial until she got classical music. And what music. They were right in the middle of Beethoven's Symphony No. 9 "The Ode to Joy." The beauty of Beethoven.
>
> Beauty.
>
> She put her head back, just letting the music wash over her. And then she looked outside again. Bright sunlight hit as the ascending plane topped the fog. Suddenly, there was clear sky, the bluest of blue, and soft clouds seen from above, like an angel's playing field.
>
> The music swelled.
>
> Inside her something opened up. There was a flooding in, an expansion, as if she were a sail filling with wind. And it terrified her.
>
> She put her hands on the earphones, pressing them in, making the music even louder to her ears, as if she could crowd out all thought, all sensation.
>
> But she could not. For one, brief moment—but a moment of almost

unendurable intensity—she felt like a door was opening, and thought she might go crazy.

That's where the scene ends. The book then cuts forward in time, and we see the results of this moment. Instead of spelling out the change when it happened, the writer leaves room for suspense, and only later pays off the scene.

A Character's Changing Beliefs

Another way a character can change is by learning a lesson that will change the way he looks at life. At the end of Harper Lee's *To Kill A Mockingbird*, Scout, the narrator, realizes what her father Atticus has been trying to teach her. Most people are decent "when you finally see them."

Consider your character's primary beliefs. Can you design incidents that will teach the character a new "life lesson"?

Character-Arc Table

A simple way to map character change is to create a table that covers the main beats of your story. This will enable you to describe the character's inner life at each juncture.

Let's say your novel is going to emphasize four major incidents in the life of a criminal—the crime, time in jail, a trial and sentence, and an aftermath in prison. Create a table with four columns.

Begin with the first column, "the crime." Describe in a few words who your character is on the inside. Next, go to the last column, "prison." Describe how you want your character to be at the end. What will be his life lesson? How will he have changed?

Now you can fill in the other columns to show a progression toward that final point. Come up with adequate pressure in these places to justify the outcome.

The character-arc table will give you ideas for scenes that illustrate what's happening inside the character, which in turn will help you deepen your story.

THE CRIME	JAIL	TRIAL AND SENTENCE	PRISON
Without pity, cynical	Mistreated here, but helped by another con Changes his opinion of other prisoners	Has to face the victims of his crime Witness testimony shows him how he's wasted his life so far His inner layers are affected	Compassion and empathy are what is needed in the world Proved by how he treats a prison guard

A strong character arc will enhance any plot. It is well worth your time to create memorable changes that flow naturally from the story. It is not always easy, but your readers will thank you for the effort.

EXERCISE 1

Analyze a favorite novel or story that has a big change happening to the Lead. *A Christmas Carol* is a classic. Underline all the passages where the Lead is being challenged in significant areas of his life. Put a checkmark next to those passages that show how the challenges are affecting character change.

EXERCISE 2

Write a short profile about your Lead character's personality at the beginning of your plot. Describe his:

- Beliefs
- Values
- Dominant attitudes
- Opinions

Now ask what things will happen in the course of the plot to change or challenge these elements.

Make your own character-arc table like the one on page 150, and fill in the top row with the major incidents that challenge your character's inner life. In the lower rows, describe what happens to the character as a result.

chapter 10

[PLOTTING SYSTEMS]

> Dramatic characters, inventive plotlines, exciting
> and intense situations are not achieved through
> accident or "good luck." The writers of great books
> zealously learn the craft of their profession so
> they can release the power and depth of their
> imagination and experience.
>
> —LEONARD BISHOP, DARE TO BE A GREAT WRITER

In 1173, the architect Bonanno Pisano began construction of his dream project: the bell tower for the cathedral in Pisa, Italy. It wasn't until two years later that a horrible problem was discovered. The tower was beginning to lean.

There was nothing wrong with the design of the tower. The problem was the foundation. The soil was too soft. And all the subsequent work could not correct the mistake.

That's what can happen with a work of fiction. If certain foundational elements are missing, the story is going to sag. You can avoid major problems by some focused thinking about your story before you write.

TO OUTLINE OR NOT TO OUTLINE

One of the most common questions new fiction writers ask is, Should I do a complete outline before I write? And if so, how extensive should it be?

To put this in a little historical perspective, let us look at a long-standing feud between the NOPs and the OPs.

The NOPs are the "no outline" people. These happy folk love to frolic in the daisies of their imaginations as they write. With nary a care, they let the characters and images that sprout in their minds do all the leading. They follow along, happily recording the adventures.

Ray Bradbury is a NOP. In *Zen in the Art of Writing* he says:

PLOT & STRUCTURE

> Plot is no more than footprints left in the snow after your characters have run
> by on their way to incredible destinations. Plot is observed after the fact rather
> than before. It cannot precede action. That is all Plot should ever be. It is
> human desire let run, running, and reaching a goal. It cannot be mechanical. It
> can only be dynamic.

The joy of being a NOP is that you get to fall in love every day. But as in love and life, there is heartache along the way.

The heartache comes when you look back and see nothing resembling plot. Some fresh writing, yes, but where is the cohesion? Some brilliant word gems flash, but they may be scattered over a plotless desert.

The OPs—outline people—seek security above all. They lay out a plot with as much specificity as possible. They may use 3" x 5" cards, spread out on the floor or pinned to corkboard, and rework the pattern many times before writing.

Or they'll write a plot treatment, forty or fifty pages written in the present tense. Then they'll edit that like they would a full manuscript. And only then will they begin the actual novel.

Albert Zuckerman, an OP, says in *Writing the Blockbuster Novel*:

> No sane person would think of setting out to construct a skyscraper or even
> a one-family home without a detailed set of plans. A big novel must have the
> literary equivalent of beams and joists strong enough to sustain it excitingly
> from beginning to end, and it also must contain myriad interlocking parts fully
> as complex as those in any building type.

The value of the OP approach is that, with experience, one can virtually guarantee a solidly structured plot. The highs and lows will come at the right time. There are no unhappy tangents.

The danger, however, is the lack of that freshness and spontaneity the NOPs are known for. An OP may get to a place where one of the characters is screaming to do something other than what's written down on a scene card. The OP fights the character, whipping him back into submission. But in doing so, he may have missed the exact angle that would make his plot original.

Even Experts Differ

There is no single, inviolable way to lay a fictional foundation. Some of the best writers out there have different approaches.

Robert Crais, author of *Hostage* and *The Last Detective*, is an OP, a self-described "plotter." He likes to know as much as he can about the story and scenes he's going to write before he gets going. But his books are still action packed and full of surprising twists.

On the other side of the fence is NOP Elizabeth Berg, author of such titles as *Range of Motion* and *Never Change*. She starts with a *feeling* rather than a roadmap. For her, the joy in writing fiction comes with the daily discoveries of things she did not know were inside her.

David Morrell, author of numerous bestsellers, takes a middle path. He likes to start a free-form letter to himself as the subject takes shape in his mind. He'll add to it daily, letting the thing grow in whatever direction his mind takes him. What this method does is mine rich ore in the subconscious and imagination, yielding deeper story structure.

But when it comes to the writing, says Morrell, "I try to let the story's drama carry me along and reveal surprises. Often, the best moments in a scene are those that I never imagined ahead of time. In a way, I try to entertain myself as much as I hope to entertain the reader."

Jerry Jenkins is the author of the best-selling fiction series of all time, Left Behind. Ultimately, it will be fourteen books, with a prequel and sequel. Naturally for a project of that length, Jenkins must have constructed a huge outline, so as not to get lost.

He didn't. "My structure is intuitive," Jenkins says, "and I write the whole manuscript, beginning to end, chronologically, bouncing from perspective to perspective by instinct. I'm gratified people think it looks carefully designed, but it's not blueprinted in advance."

When readers ask him why he chose to kill off their favorite character, Jenkins responds, "I didn't kill him off; I found him dead."

A Little of Both

My personal message to the OPs and the NOPs—be true to yourself, but try a little of the other guys' method. You may be delighted at what you come up with.

For example, NOPs could look at their first drafts as if they were big outlines! That first draft might be the exploratory notes for a plot that works. Once it is done, the NOP can step back and see what's there and reformulate the outline into something that is more plot solid.

A simple way to do this is to read over your first draft, then write a two- or three-page synopsis. Now put on your plotting hat and edit that synopsis until you come up with a roadmap for your story.

Then you're ready to do a second draft in NOP style. As Bradbury advises, don't rewrite it, *relive* it.

You OPs could work on your outlines as if they were first drafts. If you do a manuscript-style outline, write it with passion and a sense of play. Let things happen that you don't plan.

If you work with cards, generate whole bunches of scene ideas, even crazy ones. Then put the cards all together and shuffle them. What sort of pattern does this suggest?

You can tighten your outline then, according to your OP instincts. But you'll have generated some things that couldn't have come from a strictly left-brained regimen.

Any method will work so long as it is *your* method. But I would counsel you to do two things before you write.

[1] **Use the LOCK system.** As explained in chapter one, these are the elements that give you a solid foundation for your novel. If there is a glaring weakness in your story, it will probably be revealed here.

Work with the elements until they are strong enough for you to consider writing a whole book.

[2] **Write the back cover copy.** When you are comfortable with your LOCK elements, move on to the writing of your back cover copy. This is the marketing copy that compels a reader to buy your book. This is what you see on the back of paperback novels in your bookstore.

What you want to do is create a few paragraphs that excite your own interest, enough to compel you to move on to the next step. You can even pause at this point and share your back cover copy with some trusted friends to get their take on it. If no one can see the excitement in the story, you have the chance to rework things before spending all that time writing an outline. For example:

> Sam Jones is a cop who has fallen from grace. He's battling the bottle and losing his family. Then he is assigned to the biggest murder case in years—the mayor has been killed in a gruesome way.
>
> It seems open and shut, with a prime suspect—a political rival—being the target of the investigation. It may just be the case that brings Sam out of his darkness.

But as he gets closer to the truth, things are not as clear as they first appeared. Not only that, but the killer is stalking him and his family. The message is clear—drop the investigation or lose your life.

Will Sam be able to stay alive long enough to find out who really killed the mayor? Can he save his own family?

And if he does, what will the cost be?

Add plot elements to the back cover copy. You are getting more specific. Hone these paragraphs until you are bubbling over with excitement.

So important is the back cover copy to your plotting—it is the very least you should have before you when you begin to write—that I've created a worksheet found in Appendix B for your own use.

Now you're ready for the next step—employing a plotting system.

A SYSTEM FOR NOPS

You may think that if you are a pure NOP, there is no such thing as a plotting system.

Not necessarily. In fact, you will benefit greatly by going at your wild flights of literary genius with a little bit of good old left-brain discipline.

Don't worry, you will be allowed all the freedom and joy of creation you desire. But you'll be happy in the long run that you added a little order to your creative chaos.

[1] **Set yourself a writing quota.** Each day you write—and preferably that is every day—you should not leave your writing desk until you have completed your quota. The magic number for many writers seems to be one thousand words. You'll have to find the number that works best for you. Frankly, that is easier for those of you who are pure NOPs because you are discovering your writing as you go along and as it pours out of you.

In fact, writing quickly is the best way for a NOP to go. What you love is getting those wonderful, stream-of-consciousness words flowing out of your flying fingers.

Further, you may want to attempt to write first thing in the morning, in order to take advantage of what author Dorothea Brande called the "unconscious on the ascendant." Those first images in your mind as it emerges from sleep into the conscious state are gold.

So you do your quota, and if it's going good, you press on and do more. You have fun; you let your characters tell the story.

Can you go on and finish a whole novel this way? Certainly, but you will have a lot of rewriting and rethinking to do. That's all right. Some writers like to do it that way.

The Nifty 350

I like a kick start in the morning. For my body it is the medium of the coffee bean. For my writing it is 350 words knocked out before I do just about anything else.

There are any number of things I can do besides write. If I don't watch it, my day can fill quickly with little tasks, distractions, interruptions, phone calls and crises of various magnitudes.

But if I set down those "nifty 350" early on, I find I am immediately motivated to do more. Often I'll press on and get even closer to my quota. Even if I stop at 350, I still feel good because I've got those words under my belt, and finishing up my quota later on doesn't seem so daunting.

[2] Begin your writing day by rereading what you wrote the day before.

I recommend you read your previous day's work in hard copy. You are not to make major changes at this time; you can only clean up minor things or add to what you have written.

Here's how you add. When you reach a place in the previous day's pages where you want to add something, put a letter with a circle around it. Start with the letter A. You may have an A and a B and a C. (This, by the way, is a Natalie Goldberg idea.)

Now begin your new writing by doing the added portions. For example, you're writing a story about growing up in Los Angeles. You decide that in the section describing your street you want to add something about a creepy neighbor who lives around the block. You have placed an A where you want this copy to be inserted.

Write about the creepy neighbor. Let yourself go. This section could be one paragraph or it could turn into an entire chapter. When you're done with it, cut and paste it into the master document. Or you may not want to add anything to your previous day's work, and that's fine. After reading it over, begin writing today's pages.

[3] One day per week, record your plot journey. Take time to record what you have done using a plot grid. What you are doing is, using Ray Bradbury's terms, recording the characters' footprints in the snow. This will be incredibly useful to you later on.

You also use this grid to record dates and times so you know at a glance how your plot is stacking up logically.

There you have it. That wasn't so painful, was it? Be glad. You are still a NOP. Now you can use the plotting suggestions in the rest of this book to make what you have in front of you that much stronger. It's a win-win situation.

SYSTEMS FOR OPS

There are as many ways to outline as there are writers. Most working OPs develop their own systems over the years, picking and choosing from what other writers do.

I've written novels every which way, from NOP to OP and in between. So I feel qualified to offer a selection of systems for you to choose from. Try them out. See what works for you. That's the way to go and grow.

Index Card System

Writers have been using index cards since index cards were invented. I suppose they used slips of paper before that. Blaise Pascal, the great genius of the seventeenth century, was planning to write a huge treatise in defense of Christianity. He kept his notes on pieces of paper tied up in little bundles. He died before he could start his magnum opus, but his notes were published as the *Pensées*, one of the great books of the Western world.

So index cards may be just right for you.

There are software programs that simulate index cards and allow you to manipulate them on the screen. Some writers find it a little too constricting, however, to be bound by the parameters of a computer monitor.

Personally I like the feel of the cards in my hands. I can take them with me anywhere. (There's nothing wrong with being a bit of a Luddite when it comes to writing.)

With index cards, you can then spread them out before you on the floor, pin them to a big corkboard, or do whatever else you want to do with them. Cards can be easily switched around or thrown away. You can put them in your pocket and work on them while you're sipping your morning coffee at the local cafe. If inspiration hits you while you're in the shower, you can towel off and jot a note on an index card, and throw it on the pile.

Flexibility is the key with index cards, and if you tend to be somewhat more right-brained most of the time, index cards are a great way to harness your frequent bursts of genius. Later, with the help of your left brain, you can lay out a solid story.

Beginning stages
You can begin your scene cards at any point in the planning process. Perhaps you want to do some work on your LOCK elements or your characters. It doesn't matter. What matters is that you create a stack of scene ideas and then arrange them for structure.

Here is one suggested method. Spend a few hours coming up with vivid scenes in your mind and recording these scenes on index cards. You don't have to do this all in one sitting. In fact, it's better if you don't. You'll find as you start collecting scenes that your writer-mind will work in the back-ground, and when you come back to the cards, you'll have ideas bubbling up to the surface that will be exciting to you.

A scene card can be as simple as this:

Monica drives to John's house;
chased by bikers. Saved by Fireman Dan.

Carry around blank index cards in an envelope or small file pocket. When you have some free time or scheduled creative time, take out the stack and start writing scene ideas.

Don't think about structure yet. You'll come up with scenes in random order. Just let your mind play.

And don't think about what scenes you'll keep. Later you'll toss out the ones that don't work (only don't toss them out for good; put them in a discard pile because you may want to come back to them at some point).

On the previous page, there's an example of a fairly simple scene card. You also can make them more formal, with a setting as the key indicator:

STARBUCKS

Bill confronts Stan about Monica.
Fight.
Ex-Green Bay Packer Lyle throws Bill and Stan through window.

Ending First

Eventually, you'll have a stack of scenes. You've done your LOCK work and written the back cover copy. You're ready to start getting serious about structure.

Think about your ending. You should have a possible climactic scene in mind. Perhaps all you know is that you want your Lead to win in a big way and you want a certain kind of resonance. Fine. Put that down on a card. This will be your last, or next-to-last scene card. Give it as much detail as you're comfortable with.

The point is to have something to shoot for.

Major Scenes

Now spend some time thinking about the major scenes that your plot will require. You will no doubt have in mind a number of these. They may be less than fully formed, but you have a feeling about them. Give them as much detail as possible, but don't sweat it.

Come up with a gripping opening scene (if you haven't already), and put that on a card.

Then figure out the disturbance, and put that on a card.

Next, create the doorway of no return that leads into Act II, and the second doorway that leads into Act III.

The Layout

You are now ready to lay out your cards for the first time. Use the floor or a large table or wherever else you're comfortable being the hovering god over your story.

Put your opening scene card on the left, and your climactic scene card on the right. Put the disturbance card near the opening, and the first doorway a bit after that. Put the second doorway card near the end.

Now fill in your story in between. Space out your big scenes in the most logical order, usually meaning that the scenes grow progressively more intense as you move toward that last card.

If there seems to be a gap between scenes, space that needs filling, put a blank card or cards there. Try to get a *feel* for the rhythm of the story this way.

You should be getting an idea of the big picture now. Your plot will begin to feel like a cohesive whole.

Playing Around

Play with these cards for at least a week. Add scenes and take scenes out. If you have the sense that a certain scene is going to go in a certain place, but you're not sure yet what the details will be, put a blank card there. Maybe you want to have a reaction scene following some intense action. You can write "Reaction scene" and move on.

That's the beauty of the index card system.

You can get even fancier. If your plot involves multiple leads or numerous subplots, each of these can be recorded on different colored cards. Or you can get sticky notes of different colors to put on the cards as codes. You can lay out the cards by color in straight lines, so the plots all run parallel to each other. Then, from above, you can integrate the different cards at different points in a single line, and there is your master plot.

Or you can put your cards out in a plotline and character line. The plotline records the action, and a character line records what's going on inside the character along the way. You can then create a nice character arc for your story.

Once you've got a pretty solid order, number the cards in pencil. Then you can get them back in order after you shuffle the cards!

That's right. Shuffle them like a Vegas poker deck. This is a cool idea from Robert Kernan's excellent *Building Better Plots*. Now go through the cards two at a time in this random order.

What you're looking for are new connections between plot elements, some fresh perspectives on the story. You may then want to revise your structure accordingly.

There are variations upon the index card system. One writer friend of mine, a very successful novelist, takes a long section of butcher paper and along the top puts down the various beats of the three-act structure and hero's journey. She makes a long column out of each of these beats. Then she gets different colored Post-It notes, representing her major characters, and records scenes on these. She then sticks them on the paper until it becomes a symphony of colors.

At the end of the day, she rolls up the butcher paper and places it in a tube that is usually used to hold large maps. This tube has a strap so she can carry it over her shoulder. When she wants to work on it again, out it comes, unrolling in all its glory.

Writing It

Finally, you begin writing, scene by scene. I suggest that after each group of three or four scenes, you lay out your cards again. New ideas and twists may come to you. Create new cards if you want. Rearrange others. Add to what you've written on the cards.

It's all up to you. You'll find this system highly flexible and creative.

The Headlights System

I believe it was E.L. Doctorow who compared his plotting to driving at night with the headlights on. You have an idea as to your direction, but you can see only as far as the headlights. When you drive to that point you can see a little farther. And so on, until you reach your destination.

In other words, you can outline as you roll along. And why not? Nothing in the writers' rule book—even the OP's rule book—says you have to outline completely before you begin writing. In fact, even for an OP, that may not be the way to go.

Why not? Because there is so much you discover about your story and characters *as you write* that it is sometimes best not to have a comprehensive outline chiseled in stone. That might cause you to resist the fresh material that has come up and get back to your preset ideas.

With the headlights system, you don't face that tendency. Here's how it can work.

Begin your journey, as always, with the LOCK system and back cover copy. You should have an idea of where you want to end up. That would be the final chapter. What sort of feeling are you going for? It can be vague and may even change radically, but it's always nice to start a journey with a destination in mind.

Using scene dynamics (see chapter seven) and the principles for starting off strong (chapter three), write your opening chapter.

When you get to the end of the chapter, *immediately* jot down your ideas for the next few chapters.

You should have plenty of story material cooking in your mind at this point. Now look at what your headlights see up ahead.

Generate scene ideas by asking the following questions:

- What is my character's emotional state at the end of the scene? How will he react in the next scene?
- What is the next action my character needs to take?
- What strong scene up ahead needs transitional scenes before it?
- Do I need to add any new characters? Has a character in the scene I've just written suggested other plot developments?

Your notes can be as full or as scanty as suits your preference. For example, let's say you've written an opening to your coming-of-age story, which has your lead character, a teenager named Sally, moving into a new house in a new town. At the end of the chapter, she sneaks a peek out her bedroom window and sees a boy from across the street staring at her.

Now what? You write the following:

Chapter 2: Next day, Sally walks to store where she sees the boy again. He tries to talk to her. She runs away.

Chapter 3: That night, Sally's father lectures her on how to make friends. They don't communicate well. Blow up.

Chapter 4: Monday. First day at new school. Sally is harassed by a jerk. The mystery boy saves her.

And there you have your outline for the next few scenes. If you want to flesh out the scenes a little more before writing them, go ahead. For example:

Chapter 2: Next day. Raining. Sally walks to the store to get some school supplies. She is at once enchanted by and somewhat afraid of her new environment. There are contrasting images of beautiful gardens and rundown homes, of fresh smells and the odor of dirty, wet streets. She thinks about her friends back in Connecticut. At the store, she is about to grab some notebook paper when she sees the boy. Once again, he's staring at her, this time with a smile on his face. He comes toward her. Frightened for some reason, Sally tries to get out of the store, bumping into people, etc. She is sure she's being stalked.

That's how, step by step, you both discover and outline your novel. You drive as far as your headlights allow. Enjoy the ride!

The Narrative Outline

Some very successful writers, like Ken Follett, create long narrative outlines for their books. This is also called a *treatment*. It can run between twenty and forty pages, maybe more.

The narrative outline is written in the present tense. It can include a bit of dialogue, but only what is crucial to the story. What you're trying to create is a large canvas overview of the story.

Here is what a treatment might look like:

Randy Miller is a big man at Taft High School. He is the star of the football team and hangs around with all the right people.

So why should a scrawny little guy like Bob be of any interest to him? Because Bob is teased mercilessly by the bigger guys, yet seems to have a serene way of taking it. There is a serenity inside Bob that Randy wishes he could figure out.

Randy would like to talk to him, but doing so would be socially unacceptable—uncool! There is a real class system at school. This is especially evident at lunch time. There is only one cool table, where Randy and friends sit; and one definite outcast table where Bob sits, often alone.

One day Randy observes as his buddies pull down Bob's pants and stick him head first in a garbage can. As Bob struggles out amidst the laughter all around, Randy just shakes his head at him. "Man, you are such a dweeb. Why don't you stop being dweeby?"

"What do you mean?" Bob says.

"Everybody's got potential. You want me to teach you?"

Bob doesn't answer, and Randy just waves him off as a lost cause.

Meanwhile, Randy is struggling in American Lit, taught by the tough Mrs. Agnes. Tough because she cares about these kids, and will not let them just skate by. She tries to bring out of every student deeper insights than they otherwise have, through poetry and books. Bob does well in this class …

This narrative outline will be revised and edited several times until you feel you have a solid story.

The David Morrell Method

As you already know from earlier chapters, I'm a big fan of the books of David Morrell, especially *Lessons From a Lifetime of Writing*. Morrell's method is geared toward getting deeper into your story idea, finding out why you really want to write it. It's a trip into the subconscious and the place where real writing power resides.

It's a simple concept. You write a letter to yourself. You ask yourself questions about your idea. The most important question is, *Why?* Keep asking that one over and over.

I used this method for my novel *Breach of Promise*. Here is the first part of what I wrote:

Why am I writing this? I am writing this because I want readers to *feel* the story of a man coming to learn what it is to be a father, only to have the system tear his guts out. And the fact that he's discriminated against even while doing what's right … wow. What does he do?

Is that all? Well, I want readers to love Mark and follow his spiritual journey. And why do people love someone? If he *cares* about someone else (his daughter, of course; another character?). If he is *vulnerable* (worries, fears, hopes—and he's the *underdog*).

What, exactly, is the journey about? He goes from being a guy trying to be an actor, to someone who discovers deeper values—-his daughter, for one. He really loves his daughter.

Why? What is it about having a daughter that is so important to *this guy*? Maybe he had a kid sister? Who died in a terrible way? And maybe Maddie helps him cope with that. (Or maybe that's too much. It detracts from the real part of the story, which is just him trying to get Maddie back?)

Is there some other reason for Mark to be so attached to Maddie? Maybe because he's never been really successful at anything—he failed at baseball, even though injured, and his acting deal isn't coming along. There might be a moment where Mark realizes that he had better be a success for his own daughter. Too many other people mess this job up. Let's get back to the spiritual journey.

Every day I would add to this journal, deepening my understanding of the material. This is a powerful technique even NOPS will love.

The Borg Outline

If you are a pure OP, if you desire to know just about everything that is going to happen in your novel before you begin writing, here's a simple plan to help you get there. I call it the Borg outline.

The Borg, as *Star Trek* fans know, is a cybernetic life form that assimilates all life forms it can in order to create a collective, advanced consciousness. If you are a super OP and you want that kind of all-encompassing system, this will work for you.

You go from the general to the specific, and then you tweak the specifics until you're ready to write.

Here are the steps for you to follow:

[1] **Define the LOCK elements.** As discussed in chapter one, a solid plot needs at least four things:

- A Lead
- An objective for the Lead
- Confrontation in the form of an opposing force
- An idea of what kind of knockout ending you want

So spend a good deal of time defining your LOCK elements. It can be as simple as this: *Sam Jones is a cop who wants to find out who really murdered the mayor. He is opposed by the killer, who turns out to be the mayor's wife. In the end he is triumphant, but I want the feeling to be bittersweet.*

That's very general, as it should be. If you're going to construct a complete outline you don't want to commit yourself too quickly at any point in the proceedings. Stay fairly loose to give your imagination some breathing room.

[2] Write your back cover copy. As mentioned elsewhere, begin by getting your summary statement into shape. See Appendix B for a worksheet for this part of your outline. This will be your overall story guide as you continue to put together the outline.

[3] Create the overall structure. Using the principles in chapter two, begin to get a sense of your overall structure. Think in terms of three acts. For example:

> **Act I:** Sam gets the case.
> **Act II:** Sam struggles to solve the case.
> **Act III:** Sam solves the case.

Next, think about the two doorways of no return. Ask yourself why Sam must solve the case. What incident is going to force Sam to take the case? It might be as simple as being assigned the case. That means he has a duty that he must obey. That would be the first doorway.

Then Sam comes across a major clue or suffers a possible setback, which becomes the second doorway. This may be a vague scene at first, but write it down in general terms either on an index card or however else you like to keep track of your scenes.

Come up with a possible ending scene and add that to your list.

[4] Do some character work. If you like to do extensive character biographies, now would be the time to work on those. You should at least know the minimum information as laid out in chapter four and the character arc as discussed in chapter nine. Take a few days just to work on characters. Make them colorful and unique because this will suggest possible scenes.

I find it handy to distill all, my character work into a one- or two-page grid with the following information:

[Character Grid]

Name	Description	Role	Objective & Motive	Secret	Emotion Evoked

[5] **Create act summaries.** You have three acts already laid out. Give a summary of each act. What is going to be accomplished in each? We are getting more specific now. For example:

ACT 1

Sam Jones is a New York cop. He has been on the job nearly twenty years, the last five as a detective. He has a wife and daughter, but things are not so good at home. His wife has been hitting the bottle pretty hard for the last few years but won't go to seek treatment. His daughter is thirteen and rebellious. Sam is from a family of four boys and is clueless about how to raise or relate to a daughter. This is affecting his work. He has not been as sharp on the job lately, and he has heard about it from on high.

When the mayor of New York City is murdered in a particularly grisly fashion, Sam gets the case. This is the doorway of no return because this is Sam's duty.

ACT 2

Sam and his partner, Art Lopez, begin at the crime scene and encounter a sloppy ME who seems new. A series of witness interviews follows, each one adding perplexity to the case.

Meanwhile, his daughter has started smoking and staying out at night. Sam's wife is beside herself and seems to be cracking up. Sam has no idea what to do about either one of them.

PLOT & STRUCTURE

A clue points to the mayor's office as the source of a possible hit on the mayor. How could that be? As Sam and Art close in on some answers, trouble comes their way in the form of an assassination attempt. The two of them figure out that there is something very big going on behind the scenes. A conspiracy? This clue is the second doorway. Sam is going to be forced to confront a much bigger problem than he thought.

ACT 3

Sam begins to focus on the mayor's chief of staff. He follows him around, but is not satisfied with what he sees.

He gets a call from the hospital informing him that his wife has overdosed on sleeping pills and nearly died.

Torn between his personal and professional obligations, Sam almost gives up his job. But then he discovers that the chief of staff is having an affair with the mayor's window. The clues fall into place.

Sam confronts the two of them and is almost killed by their hit men accomplices. But he survives.

Sam quits the force to dedicate himself to his family.

[6] Create chapter summary lines. For each act, start creating one-line summaries of possible chapters. Again, you can put these on index cards or simply list them. You will be manipulating them a lot, so be flexible. Some of your chapter lines for act one might go like this:

Prologue: The mayor is murdered.
Chapter 1: Sam questions a witness in an unrelated homicide. The witness freaks out.
Chapter 2: Sam is dressed down by his captain for being overzealous.
Chapter 3: Sam gets drunk and complains to his partner. Doesn't want to go home.
Chapter 4: At home, Sam yells at his wife and daughter. His wife drinks.
Chapter 5: A newspaper reporter corners Sam about the witness incident. Sam is assigned the case with a partner, Art Lopez.
Chapter 6: The killer's point of view: watching the news on TV.

And so on. This part of your outlining can take a long time, and it should. Give yourself a realistic deadline and strive to meet it.

Lay out your plot on index cards or in some other form so you can get the big picture. Give yourself some time away and then come back to your plot once more for fine-tuning. Maybe you're going to want to add or subtract scenes. In fact, you should.

[7] **Do full chapter summaries.** Expand your chapter lines into short summaries of the scenes you are going to write. Put down the locations, times, and characters involved. See chapter seven on scene writing.

Strive to keep these summaries to less than 250 words. For example:

CHAPTER 1

We meet Sam Jones as he is in the middle of questioning a Korean store owner who witnessed a shooting outside his store. The perpetrator was black and the victim apparently white, though the storeowner is unclear about who was who. This neighborhood has been the scene of racial tensions, and Sam feels the need to get a quick solution. Sam is also a little on edge, thinking about his wife and daughter at home. Things have not been going well there lately, and it is affecting his work. Sam is resentful about that. But he keeps his attention on the store owner, a middle-aged man who is full of fear. Sam knows that this witness is withholding information because he is afraid of retaliation. Despite Sam's assurances that he will be safe, the storeowner resists. Sam has had it and starts yelling at the store owner that he better be worried about what Sam will do if he doesn't cooperate. The store owner freaks out and starts screaming. He runs out of his store where he is nicked by a kid on a bike. This freaks him out even more and he starts threatening, "Lawsuit! Lawsuit!" Sam rolls his eyes. Another wonderful night as a New York cop.

[8] **Take a breather.** You deserve it.

[9] **Write your novel.** Follow the chapter summaries, step by step, as you write your book. If you come to a place where you're absolutely compelled to deviate from your outline, pause and think about it, and if need be, change the outline from that point forward. Yes, it involves work and new chapter summaries. But you are an OP, and you love this.

[10] **Revise your novel.** See the next chapter.

EXERCISE 1

Answer the following questions quickly, recording your first response:

[A] When you go to a party, you most look forward to:
   1. Seeing old friends   2. Meeting new people

[B] If you had to choose which music to listen to, you would choose:
   1. Classical   2. Rock

[C] What subject were you better at in school:
   1. Math   2. Art

[D] How would your closest friend place you between:
   1. Control freak   2. Wild child

[E] Whom would you rather spend an hour with:
   1. William F. Buckley   2. Jack Black

[F] You most like:
   1. Security   2. Surprises

[G] You would be happier as a:
   1. Software developer   2. Poet

All right, this was a little unscientific. But honestly, if you have mostly ones, you probably fall on the OP side of the continuum. If you have mostly twos, you might very well be a NOP. Choose a system that fits your "profile" and give it a try.

EXERCISE 2

Make a list of your favorite novels. Put down at least ten titles. Now look at the list. Is there a similarity to them? Are they heavy on plot and action, or do you prefer more character-driven books? Or is there a mix?

There are more NOPs on the literary/character-driven side, and more OPs on the commercial/plot-driven side. Take this into account in choosing a system. You should be writing the type of novel you most like to read.

chapter 11

[REVISING YOUR PLOT]

> *Let your characters have their way. Let your secret life be lived. Then at your leisure, in the succeeding weeks, months or years, you let the story cool off and then, instead of rewriting, you relive it.*
> —RAY BRADBURY

We've all heard that writing is rewriting. True. But *how* do you rewrite? What do you work on first? What do you decide to keep and what do you toss?

This chapter is an attempt to give you a systematic approach to revision. Whether you are a NOP or an OP, left-brained or a righty, your plot will only get stronger if you give it some cool, rational attention.

Ernest Hemingway had a rather personal way to describe first drafts. To paraphrase, he said all of them are like, ahem, biological waste.

I don't think I'd go quite that far. Hemingway, after all, ran with the bulls, so he knew how to fling it. There is some truth in what he said, however. The first draft exists to be rewritten.

GETTING THE FIRST DRAFT DONE

You've got to have something to revise, so rule number one is finish that first draft!

What's the best way to do that?

Follow one of the systems in this book (see chapter ten). Then write it as quickly as you comfortably can.

This means you don't spend hours, Proust-like, laboring over pages and words. You can do that later. Oh, you can linger a little, looking for just the right style, but keep pushing ahead. Set a good-sized word quota for each day, and then write on through to the end. This is the "what's happening" draft.

The reason you press on is that your heart will be eager to take your imagination in hand and explore fictional possibilities. If you stop and get too technical, too concerned with getting it exactly right, you may never find the most original parts of your story. A promising road or rivulet may lie forever undiscovered! Even if you're an OP, be a little like Lewis and Clark on that first draft. Try things.

You can edit your previous day's work before moving on, but that's it. Fight the temptation to go back and do more.

You can also use the step-back technique (see chapter fourteen) but only to make sure you have your bearings—use the LOCK system to analyze your story so far.

Keep writing. Get to the end. Don't allow yourself to abandon the project. You must finish what you write.

But what, you ask, if I have a chaotic mess at the end?

Celebrate. This is the way it usually is, even for veteran novelists. Stephen King describes seeing his first draft as "an alien relic bought at a junk-shop or yard sale where you can hardly remember stopping."

You OPs may feel you've got things pretty well in hand at the end of the first draft. If you have followed your outline, the LOCK system, and the three-act structure, chances are it will indeed have a solid foundation.

But now's your chance to change things for the better. Here are the steps in the revision process.

Step 1: Let It Cool

Your first draft needs a cooling-off period. So forget all about your novel and do something else. You might try some different forms of writing during this period, just to stretch and grow. Write some poems, essays, or op-ed pieces. Or begin work on your *next* novel. You're a *writer*, not someone who has written a book.

All the while, your first draft is cooling in the recesses of your brain, where a lot of good stuff happens, unnoticed.

After two or three weeks you're ready for the revision process to really kick in.

Step 2: Get Mentally Prepared

Writers vary in their embrace of revision. "I don't like writing," some say. "I like having written."

For others, the rewriting process is like getting to take the final exam over again. And again. And each time your grade gets better.

Whatever camp you fall into, do some things to get mentally ready for revision. And by that I mean try to get pumped about it.

Tell yourself these things before you sit down with the manuscript and red pencil:

- Rewriting strategically is only going to strengthen my book.
- Rewriting strategically is fun because I know what to do for each step.
- Rewriting is what separates the real pros from the wannabes.
- I don't wannabe a wannabe. I wannabe a pro.

With all that in mind, get ready to work on your plot.

Print a fresh copy of your novel. Yes, on paper. You want to re-create the conditions a reader will be in when she reads your book.

Step 3: Read It Through

Take this copy to a quiet spot and read. If you can read it all the way through in one long sitting, great. If not, make time to get through it as quickly as you can. Do not get bogged down in details at this point. What you want is the big picture, the overall impression. You can take very brief notes if you wish, but try not to slow down for any considerable period.

Develop a System for Your Read-Through

It helps to have an orderly approach at this point. One of the worst things you can do is start at page one and just tinker with each problem you see as it comes up. I use a red felt-tip pen and some symbols to help me mark up the manuscript quickly as I go:
- A checkmark (√) for pages where I feel the story is dragging.
- Parentheses around incomprehensible sentences.
- A circle in the margin where I think material needs to be added.
- A question mark for material I think might need to be cut.
And that's it. Otherwise, I plow through the manuscript as fast as I can.

You should work from the big issues down through the small ones. Sol Stein calls this the *triage* method, which the *American Heritage Dictionary* defines as: *A process for sorting injured people into groups based on their need for or likely benefit from immediate medical treatment. Triage is used on the battlefield, at disaster sites, and in hospital emergency rooms when limited medical resources must be allocated.*

Got it? View your first draft as a disaster (does wonders for your ego, doesn't it?). Actually, just understand your first draft needs attention. Using *triage*, get to the most important questions first.

The first big question to ask is, *What is the story I'm trying to tell?*

Wait! Shouldn't I know by this time what my story is? Maybe. But there might be a deeper story trying to get out, something you were writing even though you weren't fully aware of it yet.

Stephen King has a nice metaphor for this. He refers to the *boys in the basement*, the writer's mind working down below. Now's the time to take a peek at what they've been doing.

So analyze your story, asking the following questions:

- Are there places that surprised you as you read the draft? Why do you suppose that is? Is there material there you'd like to expand?
- What are the characters really doing in this story? Might they have issues you haven't explored fully yet?
- Look to the places that drag. These might be scenes where you have avoided dealing with something deeper. What are the characters *really* thinking in these places? What are their passions, frustrations, and desires?
- Imagine alternative plotlines. How might your plot be different if it headed off on another tangent from various points in the story? You don't have to follow them, but they might suggest other streams that can flow into the main plot.

If any of the answers resonate with you, try writing a summary of your plot, but with the additional plot material the above questions have suggested. Write a two- or three-page synopsis, then rework it, adding new thoughts, characters, and themes. Think of this as getting closer to the story you really want to tell.

Next, think about structure:

- Does your story play out naturally in three acts?
- Is there an immediate disturbance to the Lead's world?
- Does the first doorway of no return occur before the one-fifth mark?

- Are the stakes being raised sufficiently?
- Does the second doorway of no return put the Lead on the path to the climax?
- Does the rhythm of the story match your intent? If this is an action novel, does the plot move relentlessly forward? If this is a character-driven novel, do the scenes delve deeply enough?
- Are there strongly motivated characters?
- Have coincidences been established?
- Is something happening immediately at the beginning? Did you establish a person in a setting with a problem, confronted with *change* or *threat*?
- Is the timeline logical?
- Is the story too predictable in terms of sequence? Should it be rearranged?

All of this thinking is guaranteed to make your basic plot stronger. Now you're ready to consider the other big questions. Be sure to take notes as you answer these questions:

QUESTIONS ABOUT YOUR LEAD CHARACTER
- Is the character memorable? Compelling? Enough to carry a reader all the way through the plot? A lead character has to jump off the page. Does yours?
- Does this character avoid clichés? Is he capable of surprising us? What's unique about the character?
- Is the character's objective strong enough?
- How does the character grow over the course of the story?
- How does the character demonstrate inner strength?

QUESTIONS ABOUT YOUR OPPOSITION
- Is your opposing character interesting?
- Is he fully realized, not just a cardboard cutout?
- Is he justified (at least in his own mind) in his actions?
- Is he believable?
- Is he as strong as or stronger than the Lead?

QUESTIONS ABOUT YOUR STORY'S ADHESIVE NATURE
- Is the conflict between the Lead and opposition *crucial* for both?
- Why can't they just walk away? What holds them together?

- Are the big scenes big enough? Surprising enough? Can you make them more original, unanticipated, and draw them out for all they are worth?
- Is there enough *conflict* in the scenes?
- What is the least memorable scene? Cut it! Now we have a *new* "least memorable scene." Consider cutting it, too.
- What else can be *cut* in order to *move the story relentlessly forward*?
- Does the *climactic scene* come too fast (through writer fatigue)? Can you make it more, write it for all it's worth? Set a ticking clock?
- Do we need a new *minor subplot* to build up a sagging midsection?

QUESTIONS ABOUT YOUR MINOR CHARACTERS

- What is their purpose in the plot?
- Are they unique and colorful?

Step 4: Brood Over What You've Done

Just walk around thinking about your draft. Be careful not to bump into walls or other people.

Do this for five to seven days. Each day when you first wake up, jot down some more notes about your novel, or write things down in a journal. Take one last look at all your notes.

Step 5: Write the Second Draft

Some writers begin their second draft at page one and write the whole thing as if new. Others cut and paste and use lots of the original material. You'll have to see what works best for you. Only don't resist a massive rewrite just because it looks like a lot of work.

Great writing *is* a lot of work, but that being said, I don't know of any more satisfying labor.

Step 6: Refine

The good news is from here on it gets easier. After the second draft is completed, set it aside for a week. Then come to it fresh and read it through. This time you will tighten or cut scenes, deepen characters, and expand or revise subplots. You have a solid story. This draft only refines it so the big elements—character, plot, scenes, theme—come through exactly the way you want them to.

Some teachers advise that you "kill your darlings." If you are so in love with a line, they say, it probably sticks out too much. You're no longer objective. So kill it. Take it out.

"But the poor darlings," you plead.

Use common sense. Always ask yourself if a "darling" serves the story or if it makes the reader momentarily aware of the author. If it's the latter, you know what to do: Cut it.

Step 7: Polish

Finally, move on to the polish. As the name suggests, you go through and give everything that last bit of shine. Do a *scene* read-through, and ask yourself the following questions:

- Are you *hooking* the reader from the beginning?
- Are suspenseful scenes *drawn out* for the ultimate tension?
- Can any information be *delayed*? This creates tension in the reader, always a good thing.
- Are there enough *surprises*?
- Are character-*reaction* scenes deep and interesting?
- Read *chapter endings* for read-on prompts.
- Are there places you can replace describing how a character feels with *actions*?
- Do I use visual, *sensory-laden words*?

Now, do a *dialogue* read-through:

- Dialogue is almost always strengthened by cutting words within the lines. For example: "I do not want to go in there now because it looks too scary" becomes "I don't want to go in. Too scary."
- In dialogue, be fair to *both* sides. Don't give one character all the good lines.
- Great dialogue surprises the reader and creates tension. View it like a game, where the players are trying to outfox each other.
- Can you get more *conflict* into dialogue, even among allies?

Learn to love rewriting because it's a necessary part of the craft. You are going to be a better writer every time you go through this process. And your plots will be stronger by far.

EXERCISE 1

To get a feel for the revision process, take two or three chapters of a work in progress and print a fresh copy. Go through it and make the following marks in the margin:

- A checkmark (√) if you feel the story dragging
- Parentheses around incomprehensible sentences
- A circle in the margin where you feel material may need to be added. This may be in the form of stretching out tension or making the writing less "jerky"
- A question mark for material that may need to be cut. This could include long expository sections or places where you're "telling" rather than "showing"

EXERCISE 2

Look at the chapter beginnings and endings in your sample. Is there an immediate hook in the beginnings and a prompt to read on at the ends? Revise them accordingly. Play with several alternatives, and then select the best.

EXERCISE 3

You can increase your awareness of revision by marking up novels you read with the symbols listed in Exercise 1. If something doesn't work for you, try to figure out why. If something *does* work, try to figure out why. This is self-teaching of the craft at a high level.

chapter 12

[PLOT PATTERNS]

When you steal from one author it's plagiarism; if you steal from many, it's research.
—WILSON MIZNER

Over the years, numerous writing instructors have pointed out recurring types of plot patterns. The number of patterns varies. Is it thirty-six? Or three?

No matter what number you prefer, it is helpful to consider different patterns if only to understand what they're trying to do. Understanding plot patterns helps you gain a clearer comprehension of plot overall.

There is another benefit to studying plot patterns—they may suggest fresh plot ideas to you. While the way a story is told belongs to an author, the pattern does not. Feel free to borrow liberally from the patterns as you brainstorm your own plots.

You can even combine patterns to create a fresh plot. That's what Dean Koontz does in *Midnight*, a combination of the film *Invasion of the Body Snatchers* and H.G. Wells's *The Island of Dr. Moreau*. He set it in a contemporary location and peopled it with his own character inventions, and there you have it—an original tale that shot up the bestseller list.

Below are some of the more prevalent plot patterns. I have not attempted to make a complete list. But these patterns seem to recur frequently, suggesting their timeless value.

THE QUEST

This may be the oldest plot of all. A hero goes out into the dark world and searches for something. It might be for a sacred item, as in the story of Sir Galahad and the search for the Holy Grail. It might be the search for a person.

The quest for knowledge or inner peace can also form the basis of this plot pattern. *The Catcher in the Rye* is a quest plot—a young man searches for a reason to live in a world where most people are phonies.

Rudiments of the Quest

- The Lead is someone who is incomplete in his ordinary world.
- The thing searched for must be of vital importance.
- There must be huge obstacles preventing the Lead from gaining it.
- The quest should result in the Lead becoming a different (usually better) person at the end; a fruitless quest, however, may end in tragedy for the Lead.

Structure of the Quest

Act I introduces us to the Lead and shows us some inner lack that the quest will help to remedy. If there is no dissatisfaction in the Lead, then there's no believable motivation for him to go on the quest.

In *The Catcher in the Rye*, we see in various ways that Holden is not at home in his skin. He is moody, sensitive, and somewhat depressed.

The doorway of no return in Act I is the point at which the Lead commences the quest. In *Catcher*, it occurs after Holden has a fight with his roommate, Stradlater. This prompts Holden to leave school and go to New York. The quest has begun.

In a quest story, there is a series of encounters along the way, giving the plot an episodic feel. In most of these episodes, the character suffers a setback. That's the conflict. But as he struggles to overcome each setback, he moves another step closer to his objective, and thus the plot unfolds.

In *Catcher*, Holden gets a room at a hotel. He then begins a series of encounters with people in the city. There is an encounter with a prostitute and her pimp, and later with a couple of nuns. He has a date with a girl named Sally that ends badly. He gets drunk.

The quest is not going well for Holden.

The second doorway, the doorway that leads to the final act, is usually a major crisis or setback, or some discovery or major clue. In *Catcher*, Holden ends up in Central Park at night, freezing. He believes he is going to catch pneumonia and die. He has been afraid to go home for fear of what his parents will think of him. But now, thinking that death is near, he wants to see his little sister, Phoebe.

The encounter with his sister leads him to the central revelation of the book. She asks him what he wants to be, and he tells her he wants to be a catcher in the rye, an image of someone who saves children from falling off a cliff.

There is a final haunting image with Phoebe on a carousel, and a famous last chapter that leaves open the question of whether Holden has found what he was looking for.

The quest is a powerful pattern because it mirrors our own journey through life. As we encounter various challenges, we suffer setbacks and victories, but strive to move on. We all have a quest, whether we recognize it or not.

REVENGE

Another of the oldest plot archetypes or patterns is revenge. That is the way tribal man operated. You kill one of my brothers; I go after one of yours. Early storytellers probably inspired the tribe and trained boys with stories of heroic revenge.

Revenge is a gut-level pattern, and therefore highly emotional.

Rudiments of Revenge

- The Lead should be sympathetic since revenge is usually violent business.
- The wrong done to the Lead or to someone close to the Lead is usually not his fault; if it is, the wrong is out of proportion to the fault.
- The desire for revenge has an effect on the Lead's inner life.

Structure of Revenge

In Act I, the Lead and his ordinary world are introduced. This world is a place of comfort so that, when it is violently disturbed, the reader will easily accept a novel-long desire for revenge.

The disturbance to the world is *the wrong*.

Following the wrong is a period of suffering. This bonds readers to the Lead, and gives them a rooting interest in the plot to follow.

The Lead is someone who is wronged, or who is close to someone wronged. Charles Portis's *True Grit* is about a girl's revenge when her father is murdered.

The wrong can also occur when the Lead is betrayed (and often left for dead) by a person he believes is a friend or ally. *The Hunter*, by Donald E. Westlake (as Richard Stark), is an example and forms the basis for the movies *Point Blank*, starring Lee Marvin, and *Payback*, starring Mel Gibson.

Or the Lead might be set up to take the fall for a crime he did not commit, as in *The Count of Monte Cristo*, by Alexandre Dumas.

The first doorway of no return is usually when the Lead discovers who did the deed. Or, in the alternative, discovers a way to get at the wrongdoer.

The objective, as we have noted elsewhere, can take one of two forms, to get or to get away from something. In the revenge plot, it is to *get* revenge. The deeper motive is to *restore order*. A wrong has been committed, and by getting revenge the Lead hopes to balance the scales of justice.

The Lead will be opposed, usually by the machinations of the one on whom he hopes to exact revenge.

Or the opponent (in the case of Dumas's tale, three opponents) may not know what's going on. The Lead is hiding his intentions. The various confrontations he faces will amount to threats to his concealment.

Act II consists of a series of confrontations that keeps the Lead from gaining his objective. He has a chance to kill the opponent but is frustrated by some obstacle. The obstacle may be a circumstance or another character, perhaps an ally of the opponent.

So it goes, back and forth, as the Lead takes steps toward revenge and is set back.

Finally, he is given a prime opportunity—maybe it's a way to take away the opponent's own loved one, his business, or his position of power. This is the second doorway, the one leading to the climax.

Or maybe all the powers of the opponent and his allies create the biggest obstacle of all—the Lead is resoundingly defeated and almost dies.

But the Lead survives the major crisis and rebounds to complete his objective or gives it up, as suggested above.

Sometimes the Lead exacts his revenge, and it is satisfying to the reader.

Other times, he may give up his desire for a greater good—mercy or some higher good. This must satisfy the reader through the idea of sacrifice: By giving up his objective, the Lead gains something far worthier. Giving up a desire for raw revenge and replacing it with a desire that puts the greater good first actually restores the balance.

A revenge plot is a great way to explore human nature. The very real emotion of revenge is understood by all of us.

What is the best way to proceed? Is it better to personally seek cosmic justice through revenge or leave it to proper authorities? Is it better to show mercy or is mercy, in some contexts, a fool's game?

What does the desire for revenge do to a soul, especially if revenge is the objective over a long course of time?

Taking your readers on a revenge ride is a great way to make them turn the pages. When the setup is strong, and the wrong terrible, readers will desire revenge right along with the Lead.

A note of caution: It's tempting in a revenge plot to make the opponent a 100-percent villain. This is understandable since the writer thinks it will increase readers' outrage.

Readers, however, will feel manipulated if you do this. Give the opponent his own good reasons for doing what he did. Far from diluting the effect of the revenge motive, it will deepen the reality of your novel in the reader's mind. And that's always a good thing.

LOVE

When it comes to this one, you can have either of the lovers be the Lead character, or create parallel plots with each lover taking a Lead role.

Romeo and Juliet is a parallel love plot. Shakespeare gives us glimpses of each of the lovers apart and then together.

Getting the love of the object of one's affections is one goal.

Or the lovers may have the objective of getting together in spite of obstacles.

In a classic, one-Lead love story, the opposition can come from the other lover, who does not return the affections of the Lead. Many romantic comedies follow this pattern.

Or there can be a rival for the lover's affections, and this is the main obstacle for the Lead.

Finally, if the lovers want to be together, the opposition can come from another source: the families, as in *Romeo and Juliet*, for example.

Love stories can end happily, sadly, or tragically.

Obviously, if the lovers end up together, they're happy.

If one of the lovers ends up dead, it's sad.

If both lovers end up dead, then you've got a tragedy on your hands, like *Romeo and Juliet*.

Rudiments of Love

• Two people have to be in love.

- Something has to separate them.
- They either get back together or tragically do not.
- One or both of the lovers grows as a result of the pattern.

Structure of Love

There are numerous variables here, depending on the type of love story. In Act I, for example, the lovers might meet for the first time, and one falls in love with the other. Act II becomes the struggle to gain the love of the other person.

Or perhaps the lovers fall in love with each other in Act I, and Act II introduces something that threatens to keep them apart, as in *Romeo and Juliet*. The lovers struggle to get together as forces oppose them.

Another popular variant on love, of course, is when the destined lovers hate each other when they first meet, as in the film *The African Queen*. The challenges they face *together* draw them toward each other over the course of the story.

In a straight love story, the old formula often is best: boy meets girl, boy loses girl, boy gets girl.

In other words, the lovers get together, but then something happens to put them in opposition.

This pattern also works well as a subplot.

The classic Frank Capra film, *It Happened One Night*, is worthy of study as a perfectly structured love story. Clark Gable plays a cynical reporter, and Claudette Colbert is a runaway heiress. He meets her on a bus and they take an instant dislike to each other. But Gable strikes a deal. He won't reveal her whereabouts if she will give him exclusive rights to her story.

That gives them each an incentive to stay together. And gradually they come to love each other.

But then a huge misunderstanding takes place. Colbert mistakenly believes Gable has run out on her. She thinks he only wanted the story after all. So she returns to the fiancé she does not love. Gable thinks Colbert has run out on *him*.

This is the circumstance that has them opposed to each other near the end. In the nick of time, the misunderstanding is cleared up and the lovers are reunited.

Love stories are resonant in two ways. If they end happily, it gives us hope. Maybe we can find love in this world, too.

If they end tragically, we have a bittersweet reminder that it is better to have loved and lost than never to have loved at all.

ADVENTURE

Adventure stories are among the oldest in literature. They originally created a vicarious thrill for the audience, who were usually stuck in one physical location for life.

These stories were also used to inspire and encourage acts of discovery for the benefit of the community.

Are we any less needful of adventure stories today? While we can travel anywhere now, most of us are in predictable life patterns. That's not necessarily a bad thing; predictability and certainty help us feel secure. But every now and then, we wonder what if we just chucked it all and went looking for adventure?

In the late '60s there was a TV show called *Then Came Bronson*, starring Michael Parks. Bronson was a guy who chucked the rat race, got a motorcycle, and just hit the road.

The credits started with Bronson pulling up next to a guy in traffic. The guy looks beat and frustrated. He asks Bronson where he's going. Bronson shrugs and says, "Wherever I end up, I guess."

The guy gives a rueful smile and says, "Man, I wish I was you."

Then Bronson went on his adventure of the week.

To write an adventure story, make the readers wish they were your Lead.

Rudiments of Adventure

- The Lead sets out on a journey. Rather than a quest for some object, this is a desire for adventure alone—to experience what's "out there."
- There are various encounters along the way with interesting characters and circumstances.
- The Lead usually has some insight into himself or his life after the adventure.

Structure of Adventure

To go on an adventure, you have to *leave*. In Act I, therefore, the Lead is introduced just before he goes in search of adventure, thus showing briefly the life he's going to leave behind. There may be various forms of dissatisfaction that the Lead has with his current environment. This may arise out of a real challenge to the Lead's well-being, as in *The Adventures of Huckleberry Finn*, or a perceived need to get out into the world and do something, as in *Don Quixote*.

Let's consider *The Adventures of Huckleberry Finn* for a moment. Despite Mr. Twain's warning in the foreword that anyone attempting to find a plot in the book will be shot, his title exposes him. The adventures of Huckleberry Finn are the plot.

Huck begins his tale living with the widow Douglas. Then his Pap shows up and takes Huck to his cabin. Eventually, Huck fakes his death and gets to Jackson's Island, where he meets up with the escaped slave, Jim.

The river portion of the adventure begins, with Jim and Huck floating on a raft down the Mississippi. Then they're separated. Another adventure involves Huck with the Grangerford family, a reuniting with Jim, more raft time, meeting the Duke and the King, and so on.

What makes the adventure story work here is Huck's unique voice and the colorful characters he interacts with. In such a plot, the adventures must each stand on their own as mini-plots.

The challenge of the adventure plot is in keeping it from becoming purely episodic. That is, you shouldn't have the Lead just jump from one episode to another and come out the same at the end.

Character change, or at least reflection, is therefore crucial. As in the quest, the adventurer should come to a new understanding of life, himself, or both.

THE CHASE

Most of us have had dreams of being chased. We are trying to get away from some dark figure, but the more we try, the slower we go. It seems as if we're going to be nabbed for sure.

But then we wake up! And what a relief it is! The threat is over. We have escaped.

The same feeling drives the chase pattern. There is threat, chase, and ultimately relief. If we sympathize with the person being chased, the relief is based on our own feelings of knowing the right person escaped.

If we are on the side of the person chasing, however, our relief is based on a sense of justice that the right person has been caught.

Rudiments of the Chase

- Somebody has to be on the run for a strong reason.
- The chaser, who can be the Lead or the opposition, must have a duty or obsession (or both) with catching the person he's chasing.
- Often the chase is based on a huge misunderstanding.

Structure of the Chase

Act I usually establishes sympathy for the Lead, who is forced to run because of some terrible mistake (as in the movie *The Fugitive*); because he's getting out of a bad situation (like a prison); or simply because he's done something wrong for a good reason (*Les Misérables*).

If the Lead is running, he should be flawed so as not to stack the sympathy deck too high. The chase often brings about a change in the Lead, who learns many things about himself.

Sometimes the Lead is the chaser, as Sheriff Brody is in *Jaws*.

Usually the chase must come to an end, and we find out who wins. But an ambiguous ending can have a haunting effect. At the end of the classic Warner Bros. movie *I am a Fugitive From a Chain Gang*, we have Paul Muni fading into the shadows, after being asked how he can continue to survive. "I steal," he says, as he disappears.

ONE AGAINST

Rudyard Kipling extolled several virtues in his famous poem "If." One being, "If you can keep your head when all about you are losing theirs, and blaming it on you ..."

There are times we must stand up for what we believe, even if most people are against us. This takes a lot of inner strength, more than in most other plot patterns. We value reputation. The one-against story is powerful because the Lead carries off that moral duty, and we admire him for it.

Rudiments of One Against

- The Lead embodies the moral code of the community.
- There is a threat to the community from the opposition, who is much stronger than the Lead.
- The Lead wins by inspiring the rest of the community.
- The Lead's inspiration may come through self-sacrifice.

Structure of One Against

In Act I, the Lead is presented as someone in the hero mold. He is looked up to by those in his ordinary world. The doorway to Act II comes when the Lead's world is threatened by the opposition, or when the opposition and Lead declare they are going to fight it out.

In Ken Kesey's *One Flew Over the Cuckoo's Nest*, Act I introduces Randle Patrick McMurphy, who has arranged to have himself admitted to the psychiatric ward. The ward is dominated by Nurse Ratched. McMurphy wants the men in the ward to get out from under her domination, but they are all afraid of her.

The first doorway occurs when McMurphy gets the men to pretend to watch the World Series on television. Ratched has denied the actual pleasure to the men, so McMurphy uses the power of imagination to get the men excited and involved. The big nurse and McMurphy are now in a war over the men. That's what occupies Act II.

Act III is the resolution, where the hero's example to the community inspires a rising up against the opposition, and its ultimate defeat.

Sometimes this is done through self-sacrifice. In *One Flew Over the Cuckoo's Nest*, it is McMurphy's attack on Ratched that inspires most of the voluntary inmates to leave. And it is his lobotomy that gets to the Chief. Out of mercy, he smothers McMurphy, and then throws a control panel through a window and escapes into life.

The Western film *High Noon*, scripted by Carl Foreman and directed by Fred Zinneman, is a classic one-against plot. Will Kane is the hero of the town, and he's just retired and gotten married. But as the wedding ends he learns that the killer he put away, Frank Miller, has been pardoned by the governor and is on his way to town on the noon train. He has vowed to kill Kane and has three other gunslingers waiting to help him do it.

Kane is urged to flee with his new bride, but just outside of town he decides he can't run. He turns back. He still feels it is his duty to protect the community. Besides, he'll get enough men to join him as a posse, and it will be easy.

Act II, however, proves to be a confrontation *not* with the killers, but with the town itself. Kane is unable to get anyone to join him. In a twist on one against, it is the community that becomes the opposition. They want Kane to leave because any gunplay will hurt them with the state government, and so on. Everyone has an excuse not to help.

In Act III, there is the conflict with the killers that must be resolved. Kane, with the surprising help of his wife, manages to kill all the bad guys.

But what of his relationship to the community? In this case, the hero turns away. Kane drops his badge in the dirt and, without a word, rides away for good with his wife by his side.

Another great one-against movie is *Twelve Angry Men*, directed by Sidney Lumet and written by Reginald Rose. Henry Fonda plays the one juror who is holding out for a not guilty verdict in a murder trial. He is one against the other eleven.

Therein lies the conflict. I recommend the movie for its sense of pace and tension. It will show you that you don't need a lot of physical action in your plot to create a gripping read. All it takes is characters (in this case twelve of them) who are passionately committed to their beliefs.

ONE APART

In contrast to one against, the one-apart Lead does not seek confrontation. He is not standing up for any great principle. He is the anti-hero, who merely wants to be left alone. But events keep going against him and force his hand.

Rudiments of One Apart
- The Lead is an *anti-hero*, one who does not wish to be associated with a larger community but rather lives according to a personal moral code.
- Something happens to draw the Lead into a larger conflict.
- The Lead must decide whether to take a stand or not.
- The Lead either retreats to his own, self-enclosed world again; or he decides to join the community.

Structure of One Apart

The anti-hero is portrayed in various ways as being apart from the larger community, preferring to live by his own code. For example, Hank Stamper in Ken Kesey's *Sometimes a Great Notion* is not interested in compromise or accommodation.

The quintessential anti-hero in *Casablanca* is Rick. As he says in Act I, "I stick my neck out for nobody." He is allowed to run his saloon in

Casablanca because he is completely neutral on the war. He does have a certain code of decency that surfaces on the sly, such as when a young girl seeks his help because her husband loses their money at the gambling tables.

Act II is about forces coming against the Lead, forcing a confrontation the Lead does not desire. Rick does not want to get between the Nazis and the resistance leader, Viktor Lazlo. But when Lazlo turns up in the saloon with his wife, Ilsa, who happens to be Rick's former lover, he can't avoid the confrontation.

In Act III, either the Lead continues to live apart, reasserting his rights as an anti-hero, or he comes back into the community.

In *Sometimes a Great Notion*, Hank Stamper resists until death and even afterward, when his hand (with upraised middle finger) remains as a sign of his spirit.

Rick, on the other hand, decides to rejoin the war effort. "Welcome back to the fight," Lazlo tells him. "This time I know our side will win."

POWER

We are fascinated by power. Most of us never wield very much of it. We cannot move world financial markets, like Gordon Gekko in the movie *Wall Street*. And most of us will never oversee a vast criminal empire, like Vito and Michael Corleone in *The Godfather*.

But we love seeing what it would be like.

The power pattern is all about a rise and fall, or a rise with a moral cost. Power is not seen as something a person handles well. The Ring of Power in *The Lord of the Rings* is a dangerous item to the one who possesses it.

Rudiments of Power

- The Lead usually begins in a position of weakness.
- Through ambition and the gaining of strength, the Lead rises.
- There is a moral cost to gaining power.
- The Lead may experience a fall or be willing to sacrifice power to regain morality.

Structure of Power

The Godfather is a novel about the rise to power of Michael Corleone (see notes on the structure of the novel in chapter two).

Michael's position in Act I is to stay out the family "business." He is motivated to get involved only after his father, Don Corleone, is nearly assassinated by rivals.

As Michael rises in influence, we begin to see the moral cost he is paying for all the power he gains.

In Act III, we see that Michael lies to his own wife, Kay, about the murder of his sister's husband. He has become corrupt, and the last line has Kay saying "the necessary prayers for the soul of Michael Corleone."

Words of Wisdom

"Once you have conceived a structural template," writes Philip Gerard in *Writing a Book That Makes a Difference*, "you have much more freedom within that to relax and allow the story to surprise you—since you're not struggling so hard to make sure it has dramatic coherence."

That's why plot patterns actually free up your writing. Whenever you finish a novel that you really enjoyed, take a few minutes to analyze its pattern. It may become one that you'll want to try yourself.

ALLEGORY

This is a special sort of pattern. It can come in many plot forms, but in the end, the pattern is that the characters represent ideas, and the events of the story are meant to show the consequences of those ideas.

George Orwell's *Animal Farm* is an obvious allegory about totalitarianism. C. S. Lewis's *Narnia* novels are about Christianity.

J. R. R. Tolkien's *The Lord of the Rings* is sometimes read as an allegory about the eternal struggle of good versus evil and the temptation of power. Tolkien claimed he was creating myth, which I see as allegory on steroids.

Moby Dick is another huge allegorical novel, full of symbolism.

Jack London's *The Call of the Wild* has allegorical significance. It is a dog story on the surface, the story of a domestic dog living the civilized life, forced into survival mode when dognapped and sent to the Klondike. Upon Buck's return to nature, he overcomes great odds to become not only the Lead dog, but the legendary "Ghost Dog."

PLOT & STRUCTURE

Under the surface, however, London's philosophy of the survival of the strong is at play, showing his chief influences of the time—Darwin and Nietzsche.

Notice, however, that all of these novels follow the three-act structure. If you analyze them, you'll see they all do the tasks the three acts demand, and in the proper order. That is why they work.

In *The Call of the Wild*, Act I is in civilization, and Act II is Buck struggling between two worlds. Act III is the slide into the wild for good.

Moby Dick is three acts as well: Ishmael on land. The pursuit of Moby Dick. The battle with Moby Dick.

Allegory is difficult to do well since it may come off as merely preaching in the guise of an imaginative tale. If you choose this pattern, be sure to work hard on all the elements of plot discussed in this book. Make the characters real and not just stand-ins for your ideas.

EXERCISE 1

Analyze some of your favorite novels. Can you recognize each plot as a familiar pattern or combination of patterns?

EXERCISE 2

Analyze the structure of the novels you selected. Write down what happens in each act.

EXERCISE 3

Choose one of the above patterns and sketch out a fresh plot based on it. Don't worry about making it too original at this point. Just write a two- or three-page narrative, with characters you make up. This will give you a *feel* for structure in pattern.

EXERCISE 4

Do the above, only this time combine two of the patterns.

chapter 13

[COMMON PLOT PROBLEMS AND CURES]

> *I told my doctor I couldn't afford the surgery he*
> *recommended. So he touched up my X-ray.*
> —HENNY YOUNGMAN

The nice thing about being a writer is that we can perform surgery on our work. But to do it right, we need to make the proper diagnosis. Otherwise, our manuscript may die a premature death.

I love that sequence in the movie *The Fugitive* where Dr. Richard Kimball (Harrison Ford) is trying to sneak around Cook County Hospital as a maintenance man. An emergency room nurse tells him to wheel a kid down to surgery. The kid's in pain. Kimball, still the doctor, can't help looking at the kid's X-rays and chart.

He sees that the kid has the wrong diagnosis. So he takes him to the emergency operating room instead, where he can get immediate help.

That's what this chapter is about. The right diagnosis and immediate help. You don't even have to scrub up.

PROBLEM: SCENES FALL FLAT

Always make sure scenes have tension in them, either the tension of pure action (something bad is about to happen) or inner tension (the characters worrying about something).

Even when characters are at rest in a relatively quiet scene, there should be an undercurrent signaling that things are not as calm as they seem.

The Hot Spot

Some scenes can take a long time to "get going," interrupting the pace. For this scene problem, Raymond Obstfeld, in *Novelist's Essential Guide to Crafting Scenes*, has a helpful tip about the "hot spot."

Every scene should have that moment or exchange that is the focal point, the essential part. If your scene doesn't have a hot spot, it should probably be cut.

After you locate the hot spot on paper, Obstfeld counsels that you put a circle around it. Then read the paragraph immediately preceding the hot spot. Is it necessary? Are all the sentences necessary? Underline any that aren't.

Keep going backward until you have eliminated any nonessential fluff that comes before the real heat of the scene.

Sure, you'll want to keep some things in that offer a good lead in. But you'll be surprised at how much you can actually get rid of, and how much better your scenes start to move.

PROBLEM: MISHANDLING FLASHBACKS

There is an inherent plot problem when you use flashbacks—the forward momentum is stopped for a trip to the past. If not used properly, the reader can get frustrated or impatient (not to mention editors, who tend to distrust flashbacks altogether). Here are some tips about flashbacks so they help, rather than hinder, your plots.

Necessity

About a flashback scene (we'll get to *back flashes* in a moment), ask first if it is absolutely necessary. Be firm about this. The information we get in the flashback must come that way because that's the best way to present it. (A flashback is almost always used to explain why a character acts a certain way in the story present.)

If such information can be dropped in during a present moment scene, that's always the better choice.

Function

You've decided that a flashback scene is necessary. Then make sure it works *as a scene*—immediate, confrontational. Write it as a unit of dramatic action, not as an information dump. Not:

> Jack remembered when he was a child, and he spilled the gasoline on the ground. His father got so angry at him it scared Jack. His father hit him, and yelled at him. It was something Jack would never forget.

Instead:

> Jack couldn't help remembering the gas can. He was eight, and all he wanted to do was play with it.
>
> The garage was his theater. No one was home. He held the can aloft, like the hammer of Thor. "I am the king of gas!" he'd said. "I will set you all on fire!"
>
> Jack stared down at the imaginary humans below his feet.
>
> The gas can slipped from his hand.
>
> Unable to catch it, Jack could only watch as the can made a horrible thunking sound. Its contents poured out on the new concrete.
>
> Jack quickly righted the can, but it was too late. A big, smelly puddle was right in the middle of the garage.
>
> *Dad is going to kill me!*
>
> Desperate, Jack looked around for a rag, anything to clean up the mess.
>
> He heard the garage door open.
>
> Dad was home.

You get the idea. A well-written flashback will not detract from your story if it is essential to the narrative and works as a scene.

Navigation

How do you get in and out of a flashback, so it flows naturally? Here's one way that works every time.

In the scene you're writing, when you're about to go to flashback, put in a strong, sensory detail that triggers the flashback:

> Wendy looked at the wall and saw an ugly, black spider making its way up toward a web where a fly was caught. Legs creeping, moving slowly toward its prey. The way Lester had moved on Wendy all those years ago.
>
> She was sixteen and Lester was the big man on campus. "Hey," he called to her one day by the lockers. "You want to go see a movie?"

So now we are in the flashback. Write it out. Make it dramatic.

Now how do we get out of it?

By returning to the sensory detail (sight in the case) of the spider. The reader will remember the strong detail, and know that he's out of flashback:

> Lester made his move in the back of the car. Wendy was helpless. It was all over in five minutes.

The spider was at the web now. Wendy felt waves of nausea as she watched it. But she could not look away.

Proceed With Caution

Watch out for the word *had* in your flashback scenes. Use one or two to get in, but once in, avoid them. Instead of:

> Marvin had been good at basketball. He had tried out for the team, and the coach had said how good he was.
>
> "I think I'll make you my starting point guard," Coach had told him right after tryouts.
>
> Marvin had been thrilled by that.

Do this:

> Marvin had been good at basketball. [*Use one to get us in. Now switch to the scene.*] He tried out for the team, and the coach said how good he was.
>
> "I think I'll make you my starting point guard," Coach told him right after tryouts.
>
> Marvin was thrilled.

Flashback Scene Alternatives

An alternative to the flashback scene (which you may be tempted to turn into an information dump) are *back flashes*.

These are short bursts in which you drop information about the past within a present moment scene. The two primary methods are *dialogue* and *thoughts*.

Dialogue

In the example below, Chester's troubled background comes out in a flash of dialogue:

> "Hey, don't I know you?"
>
> "No."
>
> "Yeah, yeah. You were in the newspapers, what, ten years ago? The kid who killed his parents in that cabin."
>
> "You're wrong."
>
> "Chester A. Arthur! You were named after the president. I remember that in the story."

Thoughts

We are in Chester's head for this one, as he reflects on his past:

> "Hey, don't I know you?"
>
> "No." Did he? Did the guy recognize him? Would everybody in town find out he was Chet Arthur, killer of parents?
>
> "Yeah, yeah. You were in the newspapers, what, ten years ago?"
>
> It was twelve years ago, and this guy had him pegged. Lousy press, saying he killed his parents because he was high on drugs. They didn't care about the abuse, did they? And this guy wouldn't, either.

The skillful handling of flashback material is one mark of a good writer. Using back flashes as an alternative is usually the mark of a wise writer.

PROBLEM: THE TANGENT

You think you have everything under control. You're writing away and the story is flowing out of you like Perrier Jouet champagne. This is a common feeling in the first few chapters. Beginnings are easy.

Perhaps you are an OP, and you have the story in your iron grip. But suddenly, around 10,000 words into the novel, you come to a grinding halt. You are troubled. And you get up from your desk thinking perhaps you need a Red Bull or Mountain Dew to get you back on track.

But when you return to your screen, the trouble remains. Suddenly you are not so confident about your outline or what you planned to write.

You may be fighting a tangent.

The tangent is a side road that was not on your original map. It is a suggestion of your writer's mind.

What do you do?

You have a couple of choices. You can ignore the tangent and move on, gritting your teeth and digging ahead like Charles Bronson in *The Great Escape*, knowing what the plan is and sure that you will find daylight soon.

Or you can follow that tangent awhile because it may be leading to the very place that will mean your freedom.

What I suggest you do is open a new document on your computer—or take out a blank legal pad or a pile of napkins—and write a free-form outline of your next few scenes, as if you had no idea what was to come next.

Begin this way: Close your eyes and ask your movie projector to show you a vivid scene of its choice. You don't have to force anything. Your characters will appear of their own accord, called into service by your inner projectionist.

Watch this scene unfold for a little while. Then stop and record what happened in the scene, not in full detail but in a few lines, as if you were summarizing it.

Now take a moment and ask yourself, "If this scene took place in my novel, what consequences would follow?"

New scene ideas will suggest themselves. Write them down in summary form. You can use index cards for this exercise or another favorite way of recording ideas.

Take a break. Go for a walk. Drink that Mountain Dew.

Come back to your scene cards or notes. Think about them rationally. Does the tangent suggest a story line that is fresher and more original than the one you had in mind? If so, be ready to revise any outline you have done and go for it.

If the tangent seems a bit too radical, you may use the material you've recorded as fodder for future scenes, worked in naturally.

If you go through this exercise, it is likely that your plot block will be removed. Your mind itself will have taken a little tangent or vacation of its own, and is now ready to get back to work on the story.

A good night's sleep before making major decisions is another good idea.

PROBLEM: RESISTING THE CHARACTER FOR THE SAKE OF THE PLOT

You've heard writers who say, "My characters took over the story." They usually say this with a half smile of satisfaction.

Here is a bit of my free-form journal for a female lawyer character I had to stop and get to know better:

> I'm a thirty-two-year-old lawyer in private practice. When I bite, my jaw locks. I will not give up. I can't, because I once lost a case I should have won! I'm driven by the need not to lose another case!
>
> So how do I feel about life? I think you have to work yourself almost to death, or the shadows will destroy you. You have to keep going, stay ahead of them. My attitude about all this is stoic realization:

we're all we have, baby, and that's that. I can't suffer fools or phonies, and I'll tell you so.

It helped to put those words down and hear the voice of my character. I was able to go on with a better handle on her and continue with the novel.

And don't forget to use our old friend, the movie mind. Your inner projectionist is waiting to show you a film or a scene that could be just the ticket for you.

I can't remember who suggested the following exercise, but it's a good one for generating new plot material based on getting to know your character better.

Close your eyes and see your character vividly. Dress her up for a night on the town. Have her go to a social event where she will see a number of old friends as well as some of the most powerful people in her world. She opens the door, steps into the party, and then what happens? Watch this scene in your mind. Hear the sounds, smells the smells, make it as real as possible.

At some point have someone come over to your Lead and throw a drink in her face.

What does she do? What do the others around her do or say?

Let the scene go on of its own accord.

Then take your character back home, have her getting ready for bed. She's talking to someone she lives with, or her dog, about what happened. What is she feeling? Get into her emotions.

You can do this movie-mind exercise any time during your writing, of course. And when you're not writing. At home, just before nodding off to sleep, ask yourself what your character is doing right now.

Maybe you'll dream a scene, or more likely wake up the next morning with some thoughts to record on that pad you have on your nightstand.

You do have a pad, don't you?

PROBLEM: SLOGGING

So you're in the middle of your novel and the writing has become tough slogging. You feel like you're running a marathon in mud.

This is not uncommon, even for writers who use outlines. Sometimes even the best laid plans are not enough—we look at the immediate horizon and see just lifeless scene cards lying there.

Of course this can happen to NOPs as well, and that's fine because it is part of the process. The question is, what do you do?

There are three main strategies.

[1] **Go back.** First, you can back up. Is there some place in your earlier pages that seems dull? Or beside the point? Have you lost sight of the Lead's objective at any point? Are there long blocks of dialogue that are really about nothing more than the characters exchanging talk?

Keep going back until you find a spot where you felt good about the writing, about being on track.

Now ask yourself if you can cut any of the subsequent material. Come up with a better scene idea than the one that is already there. Perhaps your Lead can take another angle on the problem, talk to a new character, or be hit with something out of left field—like a new item of negative information.

Take some time to brainstorm possible scenes to take you from the spot you are now parked in. Maybe you'll come up with something that restarts your engine; at the very least, if you take a break you might come back to your original story line fresher.

You also might consider doing a 180. That means going in the very opposite direction.

I did this in a novel of mine, *Deadlock*, where I reached a point of dullness in the story. It just didn't feel like it was working, and the scenes I'd come up with in my planning were shouting at me not to write them.

I tried to picture something better, but no pictures worth recording came on.

Finally, a little desperate, I went back to a character who had been hospitalized, close to death, but was now miraculously recovered.

I looked at her for a moment—she was in bed and feeling good— and I decided she had to die.

A 180. I know she was probably not pleased about that, but she wasn't the author. I was. And that 180 was just what the plot needed. I went on from there without another hitch.

[2] **Jump cut.** In filmmaker terms, the jump cut is a move ahead in time, sometimes within the same scene, but always with the same characters.

Try taking the characters in the scene you just wrote and moving them forward in time. Switch them to a different location if you wish, with different people around them, but give them some sort of problem—especially your Lead.

Sometimes you can jump ahead in your story, come up with the scene, and then think about how to connect your story up to that scene. Do a scene that has a lot of conflict or otherwise grabs you. This can get the juices flowing again.

After you've done the future scene, drop back and fill in the gap. You'll find material in that future scene that you can drop in. You might also find some material in the gap that you want to incorporate into the future scene you wrote.

It's all part of the alchemy of writing.

[3] **Open a dictionary at random.** Pick a strong word from that page. Now open to another page and pick another strong word.

Write something that puts those two words together. Get the literary muscles moving again.

What does this suggest about your story?

Words of Wisdom

The craft of writing is largely about solving problems. You write, then solve. On a first draft, don't get hung up too much on all the techniques and tips you are learning. When you go back to rewrite, you'll see what works and what doesn't. When something doesn't work, the tools will help you fix it.

Keep writing down the things you learn. Put them in a computer document you can add to. Review this document periodically. That's how you'll master the craft.

PROBLEM: SHUT DOWN

So what if your imagination just shuts down? Nothing there. System crashed. Your movie mind is on strike; the projectionist is reported missing. They're just showing dull retreads.

Do not despair! This happens to every writer from time to time, and it's nothin that can't be cured. Here are a few ways out, and I guarantee one of them will work for you.

[1] Recharge your battery. Sometimes writing a novel feels about as rewarding as turning a spit in the fires of hell. Worse, you may not feel you can turn the spit even one more revolution. Or you may feel *you're* on the spit. You need a recharge.

What's stopping you may be your inner editor, yelping at you *as you write*. Shut that voice off. Give yourself permission to be bad. Write first, polish later. That's the golden rule of production.

A more insidious form of blockage is loss of confidence, the feeling that everything you're putting on paper is a foolish waste of time. It is the fear, writes Ralph Keyes in *The Courage to Write*, "of being exposed as a fraud who conned a publisher into thinking I could write a book."

It helps to know that 98 percent of professional, published writers feel this way every time they sit down to write a new book. The other 2 percent I've never seen interviewed.

Take comfort in that.

"All writers without exception are scared to death," wrote Dick Simon, founder of Simon & Schuster. "Some simply hide it better than others."

Take a day off. Follow the advice found in chapter five, and push through your wall.

[2] Relive your scenes. Not rewrite. Relive. Have you ever imagined yourself to be the characters? Tried to feel what they are feeling?

Then try it now. It's not hard. Be an actor.

Often after I've written a scene, I'll go back and try to live the emotions. I'll act out the parts I've created. Almost always what I feel "in character" will make me add to or change the scene.

You can also vividly imagine the scene, step by step, in your mind. Let it play like a movie. But instead of watching the movie from a seat in the theater, be in the scene. The other characters can't see you, but you can see and hear them.

Intensify the proceedings. Let things happen. Let the characters improvise. If you don't like what they come up with, rewind the scene and allow them do something else.

Look at the beginnings of your scenes. What do you do to grab the reader at the start? Have you spent too much time describing the setting? Often the better course is to start *in medias res* (in the middle of things) and drop in description a little later.

Examine scene endings. What have you provided that will make the reader want to read on? Some great places to stop a scene are:

- At the moment a major decision is to be made.
- Just as a terrible thing happens.
- With a portent of something bad *about to* happen.
- With a strong display of emotion.
- Raising a question that has no immediate answer.

Keep improving your scenes, and your novel will soon develop that can't-put-it-down feel.

[3] Recapture your vision. What does your novel ultimately *mean*? What is it saying about life beyond the confines of the plot? How does it illuminate your vision of life? Every story has a meaning. So does every author.

John Gardner, novelist and author of *On Moral Fiction*, said, "I think that the difference right now between good art and bad art is that the good artists are the people who are, in one way or another, creating, out of deep and honest concern, a vision of life … that is worth pursuing."

So what are you writing for? If it is only for money or fame, you'll miss the spark that makes both of those things possible. Go further.

And I don't mean you have to change the whole world. Writing so readers will be transported is also a valid goal. Good entertainment is a release, and we need that. But start by asking yourself what moves you. Put that into your novels, and the entertainment value will skyrocket.

Develop a vision for yourself as a writer. Make it something that excites you. Turn that into a mission statement—one paragraph that sums up your hopes and dreams as a writer. Read this regularly. Revise it from time to time to reflect your growth. But have something in writing that will inspire you.

Root that inspiration in the world—your observations of it, and what it does to you. "I honestly think in order to be a writer," says author Anne Lamott, "you have to learn to be reverent. If not, why are you writing? Why are you here? Let's think of reverence as awe, as presence in and openness to the world."

If you stay true to your own awe, your books cannot help being charged with meaning. That's not just a great way to write. It's a great way to live.

Make a list of the major plot problems you face. Have a friend who knows your work give you his opinion. Prioritize this list by putting the biggest problems first. Using the material in this book and others, create a plan to strengthen your craft in these areas.

Find a novel on your shelf or the library that didn't work for you. Reread it and make notes on exactly why it didn't work. How would you have done it better? If you're not sure, look to some writing books until you find an answer. This is how you grow as a writer.

chapter 14

[TIPS AND TOOLS FOR PLOT AND STRUCTURE]

Give us the tools and we will finish the job.
—WINSTON CHURCHILL TO
FRANKLIN DELANO ROOSEVELT, 1941

My neighbor John loves to work on cars. For four years, I watched him tinker away weekends under the hood of a little hot rod he hoped to race. This, I was convinced, was tedious business. But John loved it. "I just like to figure out how things work and how to make them work better," he said.

Finally, the big day came. John hitched his hot rod to a trailer and headed out to Saugus, California, for his first test run. When he came back that night, I asked him how he'd done. "The engine blew," he said.

"Oh, that's too bad."

"Not really. Now I get to figure out why."

And thus began another year of tinkering. But John knew what he was doing. He had a garage full of tools, and he knew how to use each one. When it came time to take the hot rod out on the course again, it worked beautifully. He races for a sponsor now.

Through it all, John was doing what he loved.

We love writing, don't we? So I want to give you some tools and tips that you can use to strengthen your plots. Make these your own. Start your own tool chest.

And tinker away.

SHOW AND TELL

It was probably Og the Caveman, the great storyteller of the prehistoric era, who first uttered that golden rule of compelling fiction: Show, don't tell.

At least it seems the rule has been around that long. You'll hear it at virtually every fiction workshop and see it in almost all fiction writing books. That's because Og was right. The rule works. Yet confusion about this aspect of the craft is one of the most common failings among beginning writers. If you want your fiction to take off in the reader's mind, you must grasp the difference between showing and telling.

The distinction is simply this: Showing is like watching a scene in a movie. All you have is what is on the screen before you. What the characters *do* or *say* reveals who they are and what they're feeling.

Telling, on the other hand, merely *explains* what is going on in the scene, or inside the characters. It's like you are recounting the movie to a friend.

Remember the scene in the film *Jurassic Park* where the newcomers catch their first glimpse of a dinosaur? With mouths open and eyes wide, they stand and look at this impossible creature standing in front of them before we, the audience, actually see it.

All we need to know about their emotions is written on their faces. We are not given a voice in their heads. We know just by watching what they are feeling.

In a story, you would describe it in just that fashion: "Mark's eyes widened and his jaw dropped. He tried to take a breath, but breath did not come. ..." The reader feels the emotions right along with the character.

That is so much better than telling it like this, "Mark was stunned and frightened."

Hammett Had It

One of the best "show" novels ever written is *The Maltese Falcon* by Dashiell Hammett. Hammett ushered in a whole new style called "hardboiled" with this book. The mark of Hammett's style is that everything occurs just as if it were happening before us on a movie screen (which is one reason why this book translated so well into a movie).

In one scene, the hero, Sam Spade, has to comfort the widow of his partner, Miles Archer, who was recently shot to death. She comes rushing into his office and into his arms. Spade is put off by her crying because he knows it's mostly phony.

Now Hammett could have written something like, "The woman threw herself, crying, into Spade's arms. He detested her crying. He detested her. He wanted to get out of there."

That's telling. But look at what the masterful Hammett does instead:

"Did you send for Miles's brother?" he asked.

"Yes, he came over this morning." The words were blurred by her sobbing and his coat against her mouth.

He grimaced again and bent his head for a surreptitious look at the watch on his wrist. His left arm was around her, the hand on her left shoulder. His cuff was pulled back far enough to leave the watch uncovered. It showed ten-ten.

How much more effective this is! We *see* Spade glancing at his watch, which tells us just how unsympathetic he is to this display of emotion. It reaches us much more powerfully.

Just after this little episode, the widow asks, "Oh, Sam, did you kill him?" Instead of *telling* us how Spade feels, Hammett writes:

Spade stared at her with bulging eyes. His bony jaw fell down. He took his arms from her and stepped back out of her arms. He scowled at her and cleared his throat. ... Spade laughed a harsh syllable, "Ha!" and went to the buff-curtained window. He stood there with his back to her looking through the curtain into the court until she started towards him. Then he turned quickly and went to his desk. He sat down, put his elbows on the desk, his chin between his fists, and looked at her. His yellowish eyes glittered between narrowed lids.

Avoid the Dreaded List

I'm not one to quibble with a man who sold millions of books, but sometimes I get the impression Erle Stanley Gardner was rushing a bit in some of his Perry Mason books. (Of course he was—he dictated most of them.) Here is the beginning of chapter five in *The Case of the Fiery Fingers*:

Harry Saybrook, the deputy District Attorney, seemed definitely annoyed that an ordinary petty larceny case had been turned into a jury trial, and his annoyance manifested itself in everything that he said and did.

Perry Mason, on the other hand, was urbane, fair, logical, and smilingly frank to the jury.

Do we really know, in our gut, that Mason was *urbane, fair, logical, and smilingly frank to the jury* because we are told? No way. We need more than a list. We have to see it played out on the page. And Gardner does provide this whenever Mason is engaged in his famous cross-examinations. It's just that he took the shortcut from time to time.

SOAP OPERA TECHNIQUE

Back in college, I was sick for a couple of weeks, confined pretty much to the apartment I shared with three other guys. To pass the time, I started watching a soap opera. The girls in the apartment across the way were addicted to *All My Children*, and happily filled me in on all the backstory so I could dive right in.

Which I did, and promptly got hooked.

I found myself not wanting to go back to classes. I didn't want to miss any of the story lines.

But as the weeks stretched into months, I started getting this frustrated feeling in the pit of my stomach. For even though I could not tear myself away from the tube, a growing realization hit me. Nothing is ever resolved! Stories just keep going and going and going, adding twist after disaster after revelation after confrontation! It would be like this forever! Hahahahaha!

And each show masterfully juggled several story lines at once, ending one with some big cliff-hanging look or discovery, cutting over to another story that just ended the same way, then cutting away from that one with a great big cliff-hanger just before the commercial.

And millions of people can't get enough.

So what can you do with your own plotting? A couple of things:

[1] Don't resolve anything too soon. Raising questions and delaying the answers is one way to keep readers interested in the proceedings.

[2] If your plot allows you to, cut away from one scene that leaves the reader hanging to another scene, then leave *that* scene the same way.

THE PLOT JOURNAL

This is an idea I picked up from Sue Grafton. She begins her writing day by journaling. In a free-form way, she "talks" to herself as she types.

Here is a bit of my journal for *A Greater Glory*, one in my series of books about a young lawyer, Kit Shannon, in turn-of-the-century Los Angeles. The plot involved, among others, a powerful opponent named Mahoney, a medium, and a not-too-pleasant couple, the Whitneys. Kit's client was a man named Truman Harcourt.

Okay, Jim, Kit is about to confront Mahoney. What can happen?

The house is creepy. Threatening. Mahoney looks like Charles Durning. It is 1905, and he is 55, meaning he was born in 1850. Came to America, by way of NY, in 1867, aged 17, and pawed his way up. What is new about his threats? He has Irish charm to start, then turns cold as steel. He tells of his Irish background. Kit tells of her own father.

He calls in his bodyguard. Maybe it's the Bodyguard, approached and paid by Whitneys, who goes to the medium?

What if Mahoney dies and a Medium says in a séance with Mahoney's widow that it was Truman Harcourt that did this? Turns out the Medium is working for the Whitneys, who want their son to get out of marrying Truman's daughter.

I used some of the material in my writing, but not all of it. Of course the plot grew and changed, but using the journal gave me new material almost every time.

THE RAYMOND CHANDLER GUY-WITH-A-GUN MOVE

That great master of hardboiled detective fiction, Raymond Chandler, had a technique to overcome the "plot blahs." He said if his story ever bogged down, he'd send some guy with a gun into the scene. It would be a surprise, and everyone would have to react. It added the needed stimulus to get things moving again.

This is a great idea because writers usually become stuck when they are planning too much and trying too hard to control the flow of the story. By injecting a surprise, it forces new visions and connections. You may end up throwing the guy-with-a-gun out, but at least you will have thought about your story in a fresh way.

It doesn't literally have to be a guy with a gun, of course. The technique works just as well with any surprising element: A telegram arrives. An alarm goes off. A dog bites. The hero is fired.

Whatever happens that is completely unexpected will help you break the barrier you have run into.

Next time you get stuck in your story, make a quick list of things that could happen. They must be unexpected and unplanned. Let them pop into your head. Select one that suggests imaginative possibilities to you. Begin to write again, letting the plot happen as you write. Don't explain the surprise immediately. Explain it later.

THE CHAPTER-TWO SWITCHEROO

During a fiction writing class I was teaching at a writers' conference, I read the opening of a manuscript one of the students had given me. The prose was fine, but what was happening, which was nothing more than interior character work about a rock star, was *boring*. Finally, after ten pages, we got to a gripping account of the rock star coming down off drugs, the torment and torture of it. It was action, and it was gripping.

I said, "The novel should start here." And the whole class agreed. But the student had been told by her critique group that she needed all this information to come first.

Mark this: Sometimes critique groups can be wrong.

And sometimes, as we've discussed elsewhere, it's best to start your novel with chapter two.

That's right. You drop chapter one altogether and jump in with chapter two. Later, you drop in information from chapter one only if it's essential.

In *Writing the Novel*, Lawrence Block explains an epiphany he came to when writing *Death Pulls a Doublecross*. "By beginning with chapter two, I opened the book with the action in progress. There was movement. Something was happening." Additionally, there was mystery about the full-blown characters who were there. Explanations came later.

Why does this work? Because opening chapters are usually written with too much exposition. The writer doesn't even know how the plot is going to work out, so he tends to stuff the opening with description and setup.

Chapter two, however, is usually an action chapter. It moves. It hooks the reader's interest immediately. There is not as much exposition, which lends a bit of mystery to the proceedings.

- Take a novel, any novel, and open it to chapter two. Does it get you interested?
- Switch your first two chapters.
- Make any changes you have to so the new first chapter makes sense.
- Consider scrapping your original chapter one altogether. Let the exposition come out later, naturally. You'll probably find you don't need it all anyway.

THE STEP-BACK TECHNIQUE

Your best writing will almost always emerge during the heat of passion. When you have kicked your inner critic out of the way, giving your imagination full range, you create new and exciting things.

But at some point, you need to step back and see what you've got.

The best time to do that, in my experience, is when you've got an Act I. In a screenplay, that is usually by page 30 or so. In a novel, it can be anywhere from two to ten chapters. When you sense you have moved into the main conflict of the story, you have completed Act I.

This is the place to step back because your story will be driven by the elements you set up here. If they are not strong enough, you may not have enough power fuel to get through the rest of the book. It pays, then, to spend some time getting this part right.

Keys to the Step-Back Technique

Here's a quick look at the fundamentals of this technique:
- Write Act I in the heat of passion.
- Put it away for a few days, and then come back to it.
- Step back, and read your first act to see what you've got. Read like a first-time reader.
- Conduct an analysis of what you have by asking yourself the following questions:
    - Is it enough?
    - What more do I need?
    - Can I see the possibility of conflict through the rest of the book?
    - Do I like my lead character?
    - Am I excited about writing the rest of the story?
    - If not, why not? Can I change anything to make me excited?

Make some decisions, then write the rest of the first draft without stopping.

UNANTICIPATE

Because we've had centuries of storytelling, accelerating to fever pitch in the twentieth century—with books, radio dramas, movies, and television adding to the deluge—our audience is much more attuned to plot developments. They can anticipate the hackneyed and the tired from miles away.

Your job then is to fool them.

But how?

You do the opposite of what they expect. You "unanticipate."

Here's how it works. You conceive your scene or plotline. You put down the first thing that comes to your mind. It will most likely be something that's been done because you are part of that vast audience of readers you are appealing to.

Our minds jump to clichés. That's probably what you'll come up with first.

Then you make a list of three, four, or five alternatives to your original conception. You brainstorm.

Say you're working on a scene where a husband bursts in to find his wife in the arms of his best friend. What does he do?

One answer might be this: He goes to the bedroom to get a gun and shoot the two of them.

We've seen that before. It's a cliché. Readers anticipate something like this. What can we do to throw a little *unanticipation* into the mix?

Let's brainstorm on the *reaction* part. Instead of the usual, the husband might:

- Welcome his friend. "Hey, nice to see you."
- Walk out without a word.
- Run and jump out the window.

The third alternative was one that flashed into my mind. I put it down, even thinking as I did that this was a bit too wild. Besides, what if the guy dies?

And then it started to dawn on me that this could be the very unanticipated event that throws the readers for a real loop. You have a supposed leading character suddenly die like that?

Hmm.

And is he *really* dead?

Hmm.

Train yourself to make lists of alternatives when you come to major turning points. You can do this in your outlining or as you write. In either case, you'll freshen up your plot.

HOW TO IMPROVE YOUR PLOTTING EXPONENTIALLY

Chess players who want to improve their game and their rating go through a series of drills every day for a period of time, drills designed to increase their awareness and tactics.

Dancers practice routines, hour upon hour, in order to improve their art.

Elite fighting forces drill relentlessly until everything becomes second nature to them.

Go on down the line and you'll find dozens of examples of a similar dynamic. So why should writing be any different?

There is a drill you can do on your own that will give you huge returns in plotting ability. But like any worthwhile drill it's work. Hard work.

But if you will give yourself eight to twelve weeks to do this drill, you will get a huge return on your writing investment. Guaranteed.

Here's what you do:

Step 1: Get half a dozen novels of the type you want to write. They can be novels you've already read or new ones. It doesn't matter. When I went through this drill at the beginning of my career, I went to a used bookstore and bought an armload of paperbacks in the thriller genre.

Step 2: Make a schedule for your eight- to twelve-week program, so you can stick to it. You're going to have to give yourself time to read the six books through once and then spend approximately twelve hours analyzing and making notes on the books in a way I will show you, and then another six or so hours in reflection.

Step 3: Read the first book. Read it for pleasure. Be the audience. When you finish it, spend about one day just thinking about it. Did you like it? Did it move you? Were the characters memorable? Did the plot hang together? Were there any times you felt the book dragged? And so forth. Make some notes on your answers.

Step 4: Now read the second book. Take a day to think about that one, asking the same questions as you did in the previous step.

Step 5: Read the rest of the books in the same fashion.

Step 6: Now go back to the first book. You're going to need a set of index cards for this. Go through the book scene by scene. A chapter may have more than one scene in it. Do this exercise by scenes. Mark the first index card with a "Number 1" in the upper right hand corner. If you ever drop the cards on the floor you'll be able to put them back in the right order. For each scene, write the following information on a card: the setting; point-of-view character; a two-line scene summary; and scene type (action, reaction, setup, deepening, etc.). Does the end of the scene make you want to read on? Why or why not?

Step 7: Repeat this drill for the rest of the books. You will now have six stacks of index cards completely outlining the scenes in six novels. Save these. They are gold. Over the years, you will come back to these cards and look them over as detailed in the next step.

Step 8: Beginning with any stack you choose, go through the cards quickly, reading the information, remembering the scene, and going on to the next card. You are almost forming a movie in your head in fast motion. Run through the plot of the book this way. Ingrain it in your memory.

Step 9: Do the same with the other stacks of index cards. At this point, you're going to have an incredibly powerful new sense of plot bubbling in your brain. There's still one more thing to do.

Step 10: Lay out one set of cards in order on the floor. Divide the cards into the three-act structure. Using the information in chapter three of this book, try to identify the various beats required in the beginning, middle and end. Identify the scene or scenes that compose each doorway of no return. Repeat with the other novels that your leisure.

Go celebrate. If you follow these ten steps, you will jump ahead of 99 percent of all the other aspiring writers out there, most of whom try to find out how to plot by trial and error. Not that there's anything wrong with that method if progress is being made. But you will have accomplished in twelve weeks what someone else in a similar position might take years to duplicate.

INVERTING THE "RIFLE RULE"

The Russian playwright Anton Chekhov had a famous rule that went something like this: If the curtain opens for Act I and there's a rifle on the wall, it must be used at some point in the play. This is really a rule of expectation. If you set something up, it must pay off.

I think it is more helpful for the writer to invert this rule. That is, if you are going to use a rifle later in the novel as a crucial plot device, then you'd better put it up on the wall in Act I.

This is called *planting*, and you can do that at any stage of the writing process.

Maybe as you're approaching a climax you determine that it would be a nice thing for the Lead to be able to produce a flamethrower out of his wristwatch and burn his way out of the terrible situation. If you're going to do that, you need to plant that somewhere earlier in the story.

That was the role of Q in all the James Bond movies. He would show Bond the gadgets for his next mission. Usually the audience would forget some of them until the point where Bond is hanging by his ankles over a pool of piranhas. Then he would produce the gadget that he needed to get out of trouble. The audience accepted that because they would remember the earlier scene with Q.

Of course, this planting does not have to be ham-fisted. And you can also plant something early with a plan to pay it off later.

My Kit Shannon novels take place in Los Angeles in the early 1900s. In researching the time, I discovered that jujitsu was all the rage for a while, especially as a way for women to get exercise. That seemed like a neat skill to give my Lead as a way out of some trouble. So I had her sign up for classes. No big scene. But later she used a jujitsu technique on a large boxer who was trying to intimidate her. It would not have worked without the earlier plant.

STAMPEDING-BUFFALO TECHNIQUE

You can't control a buffalo stampede. They take off and go where they darn well please. Your job is to get on your horse and ride fast and furious after them.

You can, however, influence the general direction of the thundering herd. By riding alongside, whooping and hollering, you can sway the stampede this way or that. You don't plot their steps or their exact route. You just get them going sort of toward Texas, if that's your desired end.

So when you sit down to your daily writing, let your thoughts run. Let them romp. Stay out of their way. Only now and then give a little whoop to get them going in a desired direction. But mostly, watch them go.

YOUR WRITER'S NOTEBOOK

A writer's notebook is a place to keep, in orderly sections, information about your novel in progress. The value of such a journal is that it allows you to "write when you're not writing." You can be jotting notes and placing information in it all the way through the finished product.

How you divide your notebook is up to you. Feel free to fine-tune this tool according to your individual taste. Here are the five major divisions I use:

[1] Plot ideas. In this section, I keep my notes about plot. Before beginning a novel, I'll use this section for keeping free-form notes about plot developments, twists and turns, and major scene ideas.

Ideas come to us at odd times. When they do, write them down in this section, and think about how to use them later on. This is how you can work on your book even when you're away from the keyboard (or paper).

[2] Characters. I record here a description of my main characters, with some essential information about each. I want to know what drives them, what they want in the story, what they care most about, what past events have shaped them, and so forth.

I also start compiling a list of possible names to use for my characters, both major and minor. It is important to have "real sounding" names, and it's easy to compile a list. Just take any newspaper and read through the articles looking for names. Separate the first names from the last. You'll soon have more than enough possibilities to choose from, and this will save you time later on.

When you get stuck in your writing, come back to this section and look over the major character data. Ask yourself, "What do these characters really want, and why can't they have it?" That will get you going again.

[3] Research. Authors vary in their approaches to research. Some like to wait until they have a first draft and can see what areas need more study. Others spend massive amounts of time researching before they start to write. (James A. Michener reportedly read an average of two hundred books before starting one of his novels.) Others, like yours truly, do a little of both.

Whatever method you use, you'll need a place to keep your

research. These days, with Internet sites and e-mail, you can generate a lot of research quickly. Get used to filing it all in your writer's notebook. One nice benefit of research is that it will suggest story ideas to you. Now your notebook becomes truly interactive as you go to your ideas or plot section and jot down your inspirations.

[4] **Plot summary.** The plot summary keeps track of what you have actually written. After you write a chapter, summarize what you've done in a line or two. Cut and paste the first paragraph or two underneath that, leave white space, and paste in the last couple of paragraphs. Do this with each chapter you write, and periodically print these pages and put them in your notebook.

The summary outline helps you see where you've been and think about where you're going with your daily writing. When you seem lost in your story, as will sometimes happen, you can go back and reread the whole thing in summary form. This will often focus your thinking and give you ideas for getting back on track.

When you've finally completed your first draft, the summary outline can be used for a solid overview of your story, and guide you into writing that all-important second draft.

[5] **Questions.** A good writer is constantly asking questions about the story. These questions can be about plot (what would be a surprising thing that could happen here?), character (what sort of background does Lyle need to scale a building?), research (what would a USO hostess be wearing in 1943?), or anything else that springs to mind. Write all these down, and keep them in your notebook. As you answer the questions, your story will take on a richer quality. Remember, details make for great writing. Questions help you flesh out details.

Again, the great benefit of the writer's notebook is that it allows you to "work" on your book even when you're not writing. In fact, by looking it over before you go to bed, you can even work on your book while you're sleeping. And what other job, besides politics, rewards you for that kind of work?

GENRE PLOT TIPS

Here are a few tips relating to special genres. Know your chosen genre's conventions, and always add something fresh:

Mystery

While there are a number of great mystery writers who claim not to know who their killer is until they get to the end of the first draft, I suspect there are even more who plot from the scene of the crime and work backwards.

You may be doing some preliminary work on your plot first, such as setting or character. You might just have a situation in mind that sparks your imagination.

But at some point, try this: Figure out who your killer is, what his motivation might be, and construct the elaborate murder or crime he commits. Make it vivid and complex and real. See it in your mind. Some writers even construct a small set or diagram in order to visualize the scene.

Now you're ready to figure out what clues need to be dropped in your plot and what characters will be introduced as suspects.

Or you might want to fly by the seat of your pants, believing what Lawrence Block once said, that if he didn't know who the killer was as he wrote, he was pretty sure the reader would not. (He also started and never finished a good number of novels in his life.)

Thriller

The difference between a mystery and a thriller is basically that a mystery is like a maze. The reader is going from clue to clue to try to figure out what happened.

In a thriller, the feeling is more like a vise closing on the Lead. And the events get tighter and tighter, threatening the Lead in some drastic way. The opposition character is the one who is cranking the vice.

At some point then, the Lead is going to have to defeat the opponent. Why not begin your plotting with that scene? Create a final climactic battle with the opponent, and make it as stunningly original as you can.

Then you have something to write toward. You eventually may decide to change the details of the scene when you get there, but at least you'll have a signpost.

And don't forget motivation. Give your opposition character a motive for doing what he is doing, and why he fights that final battle.

Literary

With a literary novel, the writer is mostly concerned with mood and texture. Why not think about the final impression you want to make on the reader?

Think about resonance. Perhaps a final image or line of dialogue, something that creates a feeling that you're looking for.

You might even assign some music to this feeling. Find a song or a piece of music from a film score that creates a mood in you similar to what you're trying to create in the reader. Play the music in the background as you plot. Or, if you are a NOP, play the music as you write.

Romance

Romance has as its *objective* the pairing of lovers. All the other plotting revolves around that. Romance is as much about what doesn't happen as what does. Keeping the lovers apart is the great tension and frustration.

I mean getting together in the permanent sense. If your lovers do get together in the middle, they need to be driven apart by something.

So you might want to try plotting by thinking up all the ways your hero and heroine can be frustrated in their desire to be together.

It's easy to fall into romantic clichés. So work hard to freshen things up. Characters' pasts are good places to find original material. Give people dark secrets that are unique.

Restraint is often the most romantic choice. The longer characters who want to be together are kept apart, the sweeter the romance at the end.

Graphic sex scenes are passé.

Experimental

The very nature of an experiment is to try new things. When you finish that first draft in a gust of experimental glory, put it away for a month. Come back to it, and pretend you are a starving student who has only a couple of bucks to spend on a book. Start reading and see if you would buy this book. Maybe there are some plot elements you can add that will make this stronger and more readable.

But it's your experiment. If it blows up, then at least you know one way that doesn't work. And that's how we eventually got the light bulb.

I said earlier that experimental fiction, by definition, defies plot conventions and structure. But that doesn't mean you can't approach it systematically, in a way that brings out your most original material.

If you want to write experimentally, here's a method for your madness: Each morning, says Ray Bradbury, "I get out of bed and step on a land mine. The land mine is me. I spend the rest of the day picking up the pieces."

Which is to say, your material is lodged in your brain, and at night it floats around in ways you don't control. When you first get up, the sooner you can get something down on paper, the more likely you are to capture the stuff that skitters away, like trout going upstream, when you're fully awake.

Writing for ten to twenty minutes, without stopping to think about what you're writing, is the best way to do this. Just write. Those are the pieces. You pick them up later.

Science Fiction and Fantasy

The joy of science (or speculative) fiction and fantasy is that anything can happen. And that is the danger as well. You have to work harder both to justify the "rules" of your story world and to keep them naturally woven into the narrative.

This kind of fiction can be bad when elements jump out, seemingly on a whim.

The rules of good plot apply here as well. Give us the LOCK elements, and justify them.

That is to say, it's not enough that someone has magic or access to advanced technology. That character has to be full in her own right. Give her a life beyond the speculative elements of the story.

Also, science fiction and fantasy are perhaps the best genres to write about *ideas*. You can put forth a view of the world as it exists through the creation of a world that does not exist. Because of this, it can be tempting to make the idea primary and pay less attention to the plot. A big mistake.

Don't get lost in the grandeur of your own imaginative vision. Get down and do the work of plot, and your story will be the better for it.

One of the books I read early in my attempts to learn the craft of fiction was Brenda Ueland's *If You Want to Write*. In this inspirational work, Ueland makes a startling assertion: "Everybody is talented, original and has something important to say. ... Everybody is original, if he tells the truth, if he speaks from himself. But it must be from his *true* self and not from the self he thinks he *should* be."

I believed that then, and I do now. And with the tools of plot and structure, you will be able to pour your original voice into a novel that really connects with readers.

I wish you great success. Start pouring.

EXERCISE 1

Pick two of the above tools at random, and apply them to your work immediately. Assess the results.

EXERCISE 2

Choose a genre (not one with which you are familiar). Come up with a plot summary in that genre. This will stretch your plotting muscles.

EXERCISE 3

Create your own file of tools and techniques as you learn new things. Accumulate and record as much material as you can. Every now and then, do a short outline of your material. What is a short outline? In law school, I used to create outlines for my classes, and then do short outlines based on that. When studying for finals, I'd mostly depend on the short outline, which was a quick way to go over the material.

Let's say you're reading Greg Iles's *The Quiet Game*, and you're hooked from the start. So you jot down what you've picked up. For example, you might have something like: "Capture readers by the emotion of the Lead in a first-person point-of-view novel, as Greg Iles does in the opening of *The Quiet Game*":

> Annie jerks taut in my arms and points into the crowd.
>
> "Daddy! I saw Mama! Hurry!"
>
> I do not look. I don't ask where. I don't because Annie's mother died seven months ago. I stand motionless in the line, looking just like everyone else except for the hot tears that have begun to sting my eyes.

When you've collected enough of these tools, organize them into sections: Plotting, Characters, Description, Dialogue, etc. Then you can make a short outline. The above I would classify under Plotting, with a subsection, Openings. My short outline entry would look like this:

PLOTTING

    Openings

        • In First Person, grab with EMOTION

That's enough of a reminder for me. If I forget what I meant, I can go to the main outline and remember.

appendix A

[CHECKLIST: CRITICAL POINTS]

PLOT

☐ Plot happens, and it's best if you know what the critical elements are and how to master them. If you decide, for artistic purposes, to ignore them, you'll know what you're doing.

☐ The basic plot elements are summarized by the acronym LOCK. That stands for Lead, Objective, Confrontation, and Knockout.

☐ Readers are drawn into a story primarily through a Lead.

☐ You can create a Lead readers care about via identification, sympathy, likability, and inner conflict.

☐ The objective is what gives the Lead a reason for being in the story. There are two types of objectives: to get something (information, love, etc.) or to get away from something (the law, a killer, etc.). It must be crucial to the Lead's well-being.

☐ Confrontation is the engine of the major part of your plot. It is the battle between the Lead and the opposition. The opposition should be as strong as, but preferably stronger than, the Lead.

☐ A knockout ending in a commercial novel leaves the reader satisfied that the major questions have been answered, and most often that the Lead has triumphed. In a literary novel, there is room for ambiguity at the end, but the reader must feel knocked out by the feelings created.

STRUCTURE

☐ The three-act structure is solid and will never steer you wrong. It is simply another way of saying beginning, middle, and end. When the story unfolds in this three-act fashion, readers are able to connect with it better.

☐ Beginnings are always about the who of the story. The entry point is a Lead character, and the writer should begin by connecting reader to Lead as quickly as possible.

☐ Beginnings also present the story world, establish tone, introduce the opposition, and compel readers to move on to the middle.

☐ Middles are about confrontation. It is a series of battles between the Lead and the opposition. Middles deepen character relationships, keep us caring about what happens to the Lead, and sets up the final battle to come at the end.

☐ The best endings wrap up all the strands of the story, give us the outcome of the final battle, and leave a sense of resonance.

☐ Early in Act I (the beginning), something has to disturb the status quo, to make us feel there's a threat or challenge happening to the characters. This doesn't have to be a big disturbance, just something to indicate problems to come.

☐ The Lead moves into the confrontation of the middle by going through "a doorway of no return." This transition creates the feeling that the Lead *must* go into the conflict of Act II.

☐ The transition from Act II to Act III is another doorway of no return. Usually it's some major clue or discovery, or a major crisis or setback, that sets the story heading toward the climax.

PLOT IDEAS

☐ There are dozens of ways to come up with plot ideas. The key is to have a regular creativity time and use exercises to come with lots of ideas without editing yourself. Later, you choose the best ones.

☐ Nurture your ideas by looking for ways to make characters, setting, and plot elements unique.

☐ Write your novel only if you have a passion for the story, see its potential, and are precise in your plot goals.

BEGINNINGS

☐ The first task of your beginning is to hook the reader.

☐ Use great opening lines, action, teasers, attitude, story frames, or prologues to grab the reader.

☐ Watch out for dull exposition at the beginning. Act first; explain later.

MIDDLES

☐ The strongest plots have a sense of death hovering over the lead. This can be physical death, psychological death, or professional death.

☐ Adhesive holds the Lead and opposition together. If the Lead can solve his problem simply by resigning from the action, the reader will wonder why he doesn't do so.

☐ Duty is often the adhesive. A professional duty (as in a cop solving a case) or a moral duty (as in a mother fighting to save her child). Physical location can be an adhesive, where it is impossible for the characters to leave a place.

☐ The fundamental rhythm of a novel is action, reaction, more action (ARM). You control pace by how you control these beats.

☐ Raise the stakes throughout the middle portion of the novel. Stakes can relate to plot, character, and society.

ENDINGS

☐ There are three basic types of ending: the Lead gets his objective; the Lead loses his objective; or we don't know if the Lead gets it.

☐ The Lead can gain his objective, but with a negative result attached; or he can lose his objective with some positive result.

☐ Sacrifice is a powerful element in many endings.

☐ Some endings focus on the final battle the Lead must fight. Others focus on the final choice the Lead must make.

SCENES

☐ A scene is the basic unit of fiction.

☐ A beat is a smaller unit within a scene.

☐ There are four chords in fiction: action, reaction, setup, and deepening.

☐ Action is the major chord in commercial fiction. It involves a scene objective, conflict, and some sort of outcome—usually bad—for the Lead.

☐ Reaction gives us a character's emotional response. It slows the action down for reflection. A literary novel may specialize in these types of scenes.

☐ Setup can be a short scene or beat, which is used in order to give us the essential material for later scenes.

☐ Deepening is like spice, to be used sparingly since it flavors the story.

☐ Get HIP —hook, intensity, and prompt—to your scene. The hook at the beginning gets the readers interested; there must be some sort of intensity in the scene; the end of the scene must prompt readers to read on.

COMPLEXITY

☐ Add complexity to plots by considering the theme, or meaning, or "take home value" of your story. Use subplots, symbols, and motifs to carry the theme.

☐ Break long plots into units that use a three-act structure, but don't resolve until the end.

☐ A character arc in plot, where the Lead undergoes a major change as a result, is a great way to add complexity and depth.

☐ Look for the ways the plot impacts a character's beliefs, values, dominant attitudes, and opinions.

PLOTTING SYSTEMS

☐ There are two main types of plotters: the no outline person (NOP) and the outline person (OP). But there are variations on both.

☐ The NOP has the advantage of spontaneity, but will need to do a lot of work in revision and spend a lot of time on false tangents.

☐ The OP gains security at the start, but may sacrifice some promising developments because they don't fit the outline.

☐ Play with the various systems of plotting until you find one you like. Keep experimenting throughout your writing career.

☐ There are a number of familiar patterns in plot (such as the quest, revenge, love, etc.). You can borrow these and make them your own, or combine them.

REVISION

☐ Write a first draft as quickly as you comfortably can. Then set it aside and let it cool.

- [ ] Read it through as a reader, making very few marks or revisions. Use small notations for later reference.

- [ ] Now analyze the story. Is this one I want to tell? Is there another, better story trying to get out?

- [ ] Move on to analyze structure, Lead character, opposition, adhesive, scenes, minor characters.

- [ ] Brood over what you've done, make some notes, then right your second draft. Refine that draft.

- [ ] Finish with a polish, looking particularly at scene openings and endings and dialogue.

- [ ] Continue to add to your writer's tool chest for the rest of your career. A writer's education should never stop.

appendix B

[CREATING YOUR
OWN BACK COVER COPY]

STEP 1: Fill in the Following Information About Your Novel

Name of your lead character: _____

What your Lead does for a living: _____

_____

The first doorway of no return: _____

_____

The opposition: _____

Why are they opposed? What's at stake for each? _____

_____

Where will the main conflict take place? _____

_____

What is the story question? _____

How do you want the story to "feel" to the
reader (creepy, brooding, inspirational, etc.)? _____

_____

STEP 2: Freewrite for Thirty Minutes

Don't worry so much about order or wording at this point. Just freewrite, keeping all the above elements in mind. Don't stop and edit yourself. Just pour material out onto the page.

STEP 3: Edit

Go back over your material and pick out the parts you really like. Now put them into some sort of order. Take your time with this. You may want to do more freewriting or simply refine what you've got. It's your call. But have fun with it.

Here is one simple template to use. It's by no means the only way to go, but it *will* give you three workable paragraphs for your book description:

> **Paragraph 1:** Begin the first paragraph with your lead character's name and her current situation:
>
> ———————————— is a ———————————— who ———————————— .
>
> Write one or two more sentences, describing something of the character's background and current world.
>
> **Paragraph 2:** Start this paragraph with the word *Suddenly* or *But when*. Fill in the major turning point, the doorway, that is going to thrust the Lead into Act II. Describe in two or three sentences what happens in Act II.
>
> **Paragraph 3:** Begin the last paragraph with the word *Now* and make it an action sentence (as in David Morrell's *Long Lost*: "Now Brad must struggle with a harrowing mystery."). Or begin with the word *Will* , and write a couple of questions: "Will Mollie be able to claim her inheritance? Or will she be stopped by a deadly force that she can't identify? And will these events come crashing down on the Montague family itself?"

Inspirational Kicker

Just for your own benefit, add a final kicker that is pure marketing: *The Montagues* is a stunning debut novel by one of America's bright new talents, sure to capture your heart and leave you yearning for more.

STEP 4: Polish

Now you can polish what you're left with, giving it a final sparkle. This work will prove to be invaluable to you as you begin the writing or outlining process. Aim for 250–500 words as a final product.

index

PLOT & STRUCTURE

PLOT & STRUCTURE